LACQUER

Harry N. Abrams, Inc., Publishers, New York

LACQUER

An International
History
and Illustrated
Survey

Library of Congress Cataloging in Publication Data
Main entry under title:

Lacquer: an international history and
  illustrated survey.

  Bibliography: p.
  Includes index.
  1.   Lacquer and lacquering – History.
NK9900.L28   745.7′2   82-6677
ISBN 0-8109-1279-1   AACR2

Printed and bound in Belgium

Contributors

It would be impossible to acknowledge everyone who has contributed to this book: museum staff, collectors, librarians, experts and photographers all over the world have searched their records for information and illustrations. But we would especially like to pay our respects to those earlier writers and researchers on oriental lacquer who have contributed so much to present-day knowledge – Sir Harry Garner, Beatrix von Rague and Andrew Pekarik – and to Hans Huth, whose unique work on Western lacquer substitutes inspired so much current study of this much-neglected aspect of the art.

Finally we must thank J. J. Earle of the Victoria and Albert Museum for all his help and encouragement.

CHINA   Rosemary Scott
KOREA and THE RYUKYU ISLANDS   Craig Clunas
JAPAN   Julia Hutt; Oliver Impey (Japanese export lacquer)
SOUTH EAST ASIA   Anthony Christie
THE NEAR EAST, THE MIDDLE EAST AND
   INDIA   Geza Fehervari
EUROPE and RUSSIA
Italy   Jonathan Bourne
England and Scotland, France   Carolyn Eardley
*Germany, The Netherlands, Belgium, Scandinavia, Spain and
   Portugal, Russia*   Teresa Sackville-West
THE UNITED STATES   Patricia Lyons
THE TWENTIETH CENTURY   Melanie Kenton

Contents

Introduction

The history of lacquer in the decorative arts spans more than a thousand years, from its origins in China through its great period of development in the fifteenth to nineteenth centuries, to modern times when the art was kept alive in Paris by craft workers who rediscovered past techniques. Even during the 1930s, technologically advanced lacquer paints and coatings were used for the plain, undecorated surfaces that were fashionable. In Japan today, contemporary artists are using traditional tools and ingredients to create magnificent examples of the art at its finest level.

The renewed interest in decoration in the home has sparked off new appreciation of our heritage of lacquer objects from every part of the world. Furniture, screens, panels, bowls, trays, religious objects, even armour, have all played a part in the history of lacquer, a diversity that has been reflected in exhibitions from the East and from Islamic museum collections that have drawn hundreds of thousands of visitors to discover for themselves this versatile art form.

We hope that the many strands of history in this book will surprise and delight our readers. The lacquers of China and Japan are relatively well known, but the knowledge of the art in other parts of the world such as the Near and Middle East, Europe and the United States has not been easily available to the general public. This volume is intended to fill that gap.

The book opens with a basic definition of the three kinds of lacquer. The chapters that follow are arranged chronologically, by country, although most of the periods overlap. They start with Chinese lacquer, the oldest known form of the art, and end with the international work of the twentieth century.

An illustrated glossary gives precise definitions of specialized terms, with detailed pictures, and is followed by a chapter on restoring lacquer with recipes for traditional finishes and information on caring for fine pieces.

There is a list of suppliers and workshops, and museums with lacquer pieces on exhibition are also included, together with a detailed bibliography for further reading.

PHOEBE PHILLIPS EDITIONS

Illustrations on previous pages:
First page: Cabinet on elaborate carved base; 1688. The lacquer is gold on a black background.
Title page: Coromandel screen in soft golds, silvers and pinks; *c.* 1672.
Contributors page: Persian pen-box with single figure, and a bird and flower panel on the reverse; *c.* 1860.

Opposite: Document-box, of Japanese lacquer over plaited bamboo; late 17th century.

A Definition of Lacquer

The word 'lacquer' is used in so many different ways that it can be both confusing and misleading to the general reader and the collector, as well as to professional crafts people.

It should be recognized that there are three main categories: 'true' lacquer; 'resin' lacquer (also known as *lac*); and finishes which can be grouped under japanning or Japan work, and which include the various European substitutes for lacquer such as *vernis Martin*. Modern lacquer paints form a sub-category of this last group; enamel in type, they are usually sprayed on to furniture, domestic and industrial cabinets, etc, and dried to achieve a resistant, high-gloss finish.

Above: Persian casket; *c.* 1880. Painted in traditional style, it has a central cartouche of a huntsman.

Opposite: Detail of Palermo lacquer in a private theatre, Paris. See also pages 174 and 177.

True lacquer

True lacquer is the easiest to define. It is made from the sap of various species of *Rhus* tree – originally *R. succedanea* and later *R. verniciflua* – and, in South East Asia, of *Melanorrhoea laccifera* and *M. usitata*. The trees are carefully cultivated and at various times in history their planting and replacement has been a matter of law.

The sap is tapped in the same way as the sap of the rubber tree: notches are cut in the bark, and the sap or latex drips into containers hung around the trunk. The latex is greyish, and gradually darkens to browny-black; thick and viscous, it is strained before being stored, sometimes for years, in air-tight containers.

The quality of lacquer depends on soil and weather conditions, and on the time of year the tapping is done (spring is considered best). Pure raw lacquer is used for the finest work, but it can be stretched by adding various oils and saps for more commercial work. Poorer quality lacquer can be obtained from chopping up smaller branches and boiling them to extract a sappy liquid which is then strained.

Raw lacquer is poisonous and highly toxic; handling it can cause severe dermatitis, and buying and treating the raw material is usually left to assistants in lacquer workshops; artists and decorators are far too important to risk harm.

The sap must be processed before it can be used. The traditional treatment is complex and is intended to make sure the lacquer will dry to the required hard finish; pigment for coloured decoration is also added at this stage.

Lacquer has a curious capacity to resist drying in very dry conditions; it seems that the sap must absorb oxygen from the air, and, if the atmosphere is damp, the oxygen is absorbed more quickly and evenly. This is why lacquer is applied in very thin layers, each of which is dried for three days or more. If the layers are too thick, the surface dries but liquid remains underneath. Even modern lacquer finishes require great skill and patience.

A wooden base, usually as thin as possible, is smoothed down and a thin coat of natural, uncoloured lacquer is painted on. After it has dried, a mixture of lacquer and fine clay is painted on top to give a completely smooth surface. A thin layer of muslin is sometimes added to cushion the surface from the wear and tear of daily use. Another ten coats of lacquer mixed with clay are painted on, each of which is dried for three or four days and rubbed with a pumice stone to smooth out any flaws that may have appeared as the lacquer sets. A layer of pure lacquer, still uncoloured, is added and dried. These preliminary layers form a lacquer base.

Four more coats of lacquer and fine earth or ash are added to cushion the surface once more.

Finally, pigment is added, and four or five coats of coloured lacquer are carefully painted on, each of which is rubbed smooth when it has dried. Inlays or applied decoration are put on at this stage, followed by another three or four layers of pigmented lacquer. A protective top coat of natural transparent lacquer is normally added. However, this depends on the type of decoration and, with Japanese work in particular, which decorative technique is being used.

During the fourteenth and fifteenth centuries in China – the great period of carved lacquer – when a certain depth was needed for the artist's use, between a hundred and two hundred layers of lacquer could be applied to a single piece. A quicker way to achieve depth was to add quantities of ash to the raw lacquer which could then be applied in thicker coats. However, the texture was not as fine as with pure lacquer, and it is rather contemptuously described in various texts as 'piled-up red'. Some varieties of lacquer sap respond better to the addition of ash than others; the sap of *M. usitata* is said to produce a good-quality finish even when mixed with relatively large quantities of vegetable ash. However, this is not really suitable for carving, and these lacquers are normally painted or gilded.

Five basic pigments are added to lacquer: red, green, yellow, gold and brown. These blend well into the liquid and form the palette used by lacquer-painters since the first periods of manufacture in China and, later, Japan. Other pigments are not suitable for adding to lacquer, and are normally used as oil-paints on top of the lacquer ground, along with inlays and different-coloured metal flakes and dusts.

The various techniques used on Eastern lacquerwork are detailed in the appropriate sections. Much information on Japanese lacquer was codified in a report by Her Majesty's Acting Consul at Hakodate on the Lacquer Industry of Japan, published in the *Foreign and Consular Reports for Japan and Siam, 1879–83*. The text was illustrated with various tools and samples of techniques then in current use, and provides a sound basis for study. (See pages 78 and 79.)

Resin lacquer (*lac*)

Resin lacquer or *lac* was the first product to be called 'lacquer' by Europeans. It is known throughout India and Indo-China, and used extensively in Persia. It had been imported into China from at least the Tang dynasty (618–906 AD), where it was used for dyeing silk and for cosmetics, and as a gum for setting jewellery.

Lac is a dark red, transparent resinous deposit produced by the females of many species of insect, especially *Tachardia lacca* or *Coccus lacca*; native to India and South East Asia, they are related to the cochineal insect. The insects feed on sap, and the

Opposite page: Pages from a notebook with designs for various lacquer projects. Many families of lacquer-workers collected designs and sketches for decorators to use when they were working on new ideas. These pages show how many patterns could be developed from the simple shapes of pine needles and cones.

resin gradually hardens around the females and their young, providing protection from the elements as well as from birds and larger insects.

The resin can be collected in two ways. If the trees are scarce, the insects are scraped off twigs and branches and collected in a sticky mass called 'stick *lac*'. This is crushed and heated gradually until it liquefies, when the fragments of bark and insect remains are sieved out to produce a residue

For a purer material the seed *lac* is melted and filtered once more, and the top and clearest layer left to dry in thin sheets. When the sheets have cooled, the *lac* is flaked and stored. This is the basis of all shellacs.

Finally, the flakes are dissolved in alcohol (originally spirits of wine) and stored in air-tight containers to prevent evaporation.

Darker shellacs are kept for ordinary lacquer

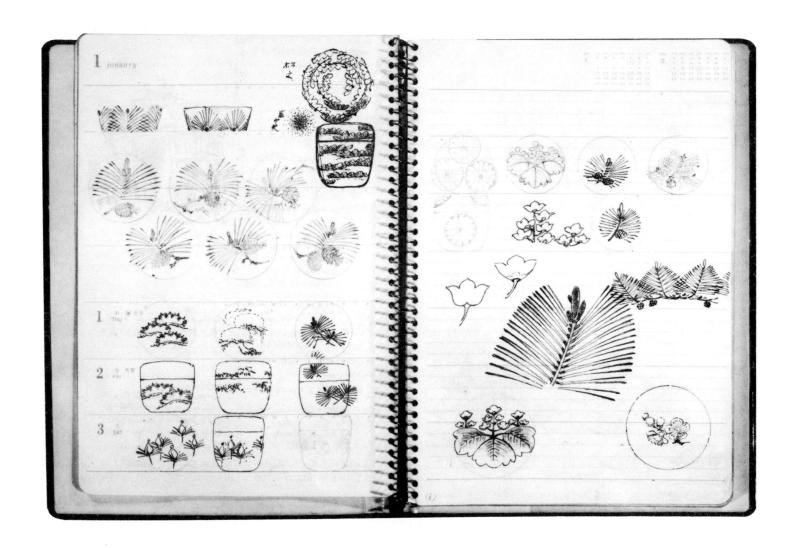

called 'seed *lac*'. When the trees are plentiful, the insect-covered twigs are collected, and are broken up and heated until the pure resin can be filtered out. In both cases the reddish tone is reduced when the insect remains are removed, but some colour is usually left.

Seed *lac* can be used as it is for coarser forms of lacquer, especially where large areas such as walls, timber frames and so on have to be covered. It can also be used on fabrics as a form of dry lacquer, in order to provide a base for finer layers of decorative painting.

decoration, or the bottom layers of wooden or leather objects.

Lighter shellacs are purified and bleached to make transparent varnishes.

When the shellac is applied to wood, metal, leather or even plaster, the alcohol gradually evaporates and the residue forms a hard, protective coating. This is normally almost colourless, but even white shellac will impart a reddish, almost golden, glow when used in many layers. This has given a distinctive tone to much Indian and Islamic lacquer.

Lac plays an important part in Islamic architecture, where whole rooms are varnished to protect the wood from heat and rot. It dries relatively quickly compared to the necessarily longer time required for true lacquer.

Smaller objects are coated with a thin layer of gesso or plaster, which is smoothed into the wood to make a glossy surface which is painted with the first layers of shellac. Decoration, usually with oil-paints or tempera, is added, and coated with one or two layers of the finest white shellac.

cut through the black coating. Undoubtedly, other similar resins are used by peoples in other communities, probably more for protecting objects against wear and tear than for decoration.

Japanning, Japan work

As the terms 'japanning' and 'Japan work' suggest, japanned finishes are European substitutes for the oriental lacquers that were fashionable during the seventeenth and eighteenth centuries, when the craze for lacquer was at its height.

This process gives a particularly rich and luminous appearance, unlike any other form of lacquer art – or indeed any other art. However, resin *lac* is not strong enough to be carved in the same way as true lacquer.

Many different insects carry resin substances in their bodies; *Coccus nige*, a native of South and Central America, also deposits its resin on trees. This is scraped off and boiled down by the Indians to make a black, waxy substance which is rubbed down to give a high gloss finish. Craftsmen decorate gourds and pots with incised drawings

Many workshops developed their own formulae to create the required oriental black and gold. The best-known source of these early mixtures is *A Treatise on Japaning and Varnishing* by John Stalker and George Parker, published in London in 1688 and still used by artists.

Most recipes are based on varying proportions of ingredients, including shellac or varnish, which dry to a hard, shiny surface, and 'japanning' is used to describe the techniques that use them to decorate furniture, metal and *papier mâché* wares.

The varnish is prepared according to individual

requirements, and pigments, usually black but sometimes green, red, yellow or white, are added to the mixture. Layers of varnish are then applied to the base, usually smoothed wood or metal which has been coated with a mixture of size and whiting to make a completely non-porous surface. Each layer is allowed to dry in a constant, warm atmosphere. The base must be absolutely dry or the finish will not amalgamate: the evaporating alcohol creates the bond between each layer. Up to twenty or thirty coats are used

substitute for oriental lacquer, and *chinoiserie* decoration was the norm. However, the finish became fashionable in its own right, and the combination of a black, glossy background and bright-coloured paintings has proved to be more durable than the exotica of the early period. Various workshops produced coloured finishes which were a long way from true lacquer. Mother-of-pearl decoration on *papier mâché* is European in appearance as well as substance.

Modern commercial 'lacquer' finishes, based on

Above left, above: Thirty-five stages in the making of a lacquer *sake*-cup. The trays hold powders, paints, bamboo tubes used to blow metal powders on to the wet lacquer, and tools for polishing. The sequence begins top left, and ends bottom right with the finished cup.

on the finest pieces. The final surface is burnished with fine powder made from quartz or bone.

Like Islamic resin lacquers, japan paints or coatings are not thick enough to be used for relief or carved pieces. To create these effects, the design can be built up from the start, with the gesso mixture; or shapes or individual areas can be applied as slips which are then painted over.

Gilding and gold leaf decoration is added to the surface. Far less durable than the finish itself, they often flake off as a result of ordinary use.

Japan work was originally intended to be a

pigment and a plasticized liquid usually containing nitrocellulose (pyroxlin), are used on metal and wood for furniture, cabinets, automobiles, etc. The formula can be changed when necessary to emphasize the required element: durability, hardness, gloss or resistance to water.

The finishes are sprayed on and dried in a dust-free atmosphere and, especially on wood, look remarkably like traditional lacquer surfaces. However, they cannot be carved, or even incised, with any degree of accuracy as the coating tends to chip and flake as soon as it is broken.

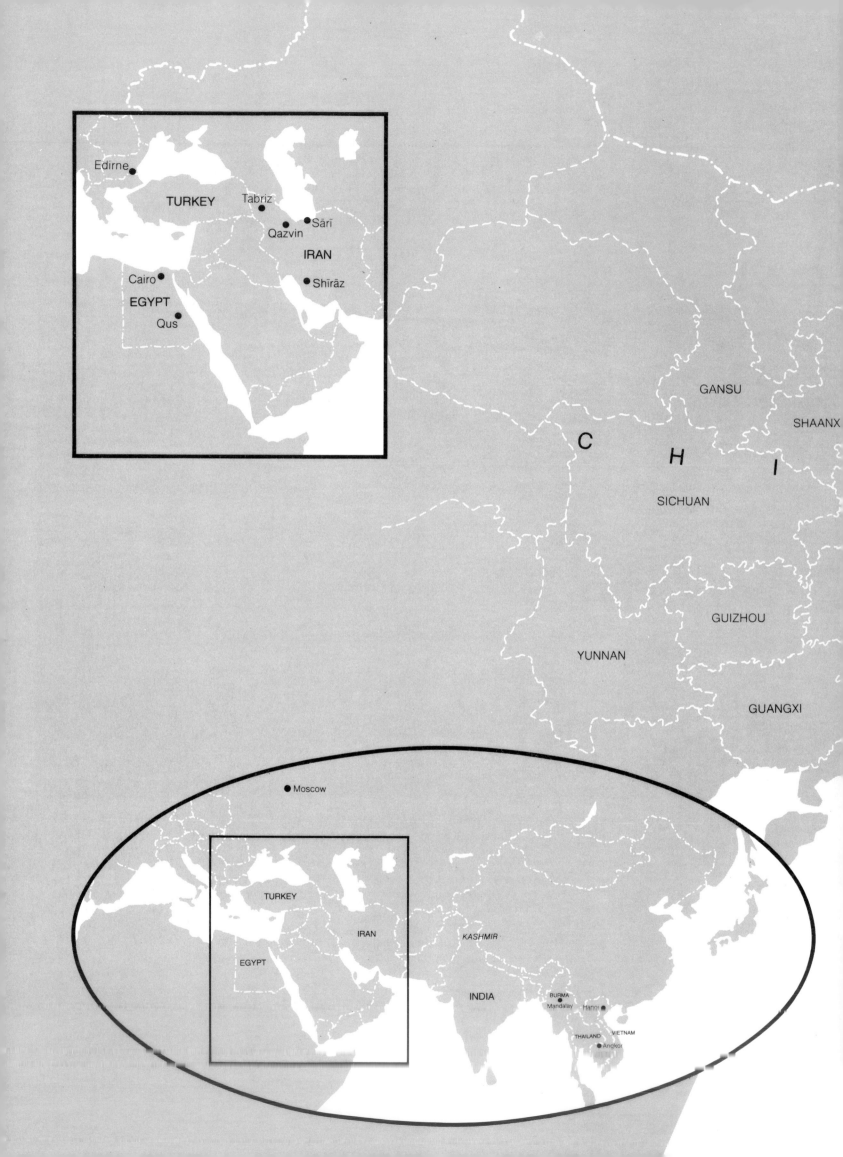

Lacquer in the East

The oval section clearly shows where lacquer was produced, from the Near East across India and South East Asia to the islands of Japan.

The square section (*above left*) is an enlargement of the Near and Middle Eastern countries and shows the main centres of lacquer manufacture mentioned in the text.

The main map is of the Far East – China, Korea, the Ryukyu Islands and Japan – and shows the major lacquer producing centres in these areas.

It is clear that lacquer-masters and their schools of artists and craftsmen were clustered in three areas: eastern China, Korea, the Ryukyu Islands and Japan; South East Asia and India; and Persia (now Iran). All were reasonably accessible to each other, and a good deal of cross-fertilization of techniques and methods of manufacture would have taken place.

1

China

China may be regarded as the cradle of lacquer art, and her products influenced and stimulated lacquer manufacture in Japan, Korea, the Ryukyu Islands and South East Asia. The effects of importing Chinese lacquer to Europe can be seen in almost all the decorative arts.

With lacquer, nature provided the Chinese with an almost perfect raw material and art provided the vision and genius to develop and perfect it. The lacquer tree is indigenous to China and has flourished over wide areas of the country since prehistoric times; indeed, Chinese literature tells us that at one time the lacquer tree could be found in all but the most northerly regions. Certainly its growth was widespread south of the Yellow river, from the coast in the east to the borders in the west.

Above: Small bottle; Qing dynasty (1644–1912).
The matching stopper is in the shape of a
chrysanthemum.

Opposite: Detail of Coromandel screen; *c.* 1619.

The mainstream of Chinese lacquer art discussed in this chapter made use of the sap of *Rhus verniciflua*, but it is possible that the sap from another lacquer tree, *Rhus succedanea*, was used in the extreme south of the country.

Excavated material shows that Chinese craftsmen have used this natural resource for at least three thousand years, and it is probable that future excavations will support even earlier claims.

Early Chinese lacquer

A study of Chinese literature suggests that lacquer was used as a decorative medium in prehistoric times. One story from the *Han Fei Zi*, a text dated to the third century BC, concerns the legendary Emperor Shun (whose successor Yu is supposed to have founded the first Chinese dynasty, the Xia). Shun apparently used vessels that were painted in black lacquer on the outside and red lacquer on the inside – the traditional arrangement – but his ministers urged him to give up this practice since the extravagance was unseemly. As well as indicating an early use of lacquer, the anecdote tells us that it was even then regarded as a luxury, and several other comments from Han dynasty texts reinforce that point. For instance, the *Hou Han Shu* (History of the Later Han) includes a passage commending the Empress Deng's frugality, because she renounced the use of Sichuan lacquerware with its gilt bronze rims. The *Yan Tie Lun* (Discourses on Salt and Iron) gives details of lacquer tributes from the states of Yan and Yu, and in the process of decrying the extravagance of the upper and middle classes particularly condemns their use of lacquer vessels when 'a decorated lacquer dish costs ten times as much as a bronze one and yet it is of no more use'. The same text tells us that 'a lacquer cup and bowl engage the efforts of a hundred men, a screen the efforts of a thousand': even allowing for considerable exaggeration, this indicates a highly labour-intensive industry.

The Shang dynasty (c. 1500–1027 BC)

The earliest known examples of the Chinese lacquerer's art are from the Shang dynasty; the early Chinese bronze age. Although lacquer itself is resistant to water, acids, heat and termites the same cannot be said for the materials to which it was applied, such as wood, bamboo and leather. These usually disintegrate during centuries of burial, and so there is generally very little hope of successful excavation of the remaining lacquer fragments. With the Shang dynasty, however, came the construction of substantial tombs where the ruling classes were buried surrounded by precious objects, and it is from such archaeological sites that the earliest lacquer has been unearthed.

Some of the ritual bronze vessels which have been discovered are in a remarkably good condition, and have a black substance used as infill between the raised lines of their relief decoration. It has been suggested that this might contain lacquer, in this instance used as an adhesive for the quartz and carbon fragments that make up the bulk of the infill. Scientific tests were unfortunately inconclusive, and all that could be said was that the infill contained an organic material, the composition of which did not preclude its being lacquer! A similarly cautious attitude was adopted when archaeologists at the site of the Shang capital at Anyang uncovered traces of red pigment clinging to the soil 'ghosts' of what had been elaborately decorated timber structures. The timber, carved with complex relief designs, had disintegrated over time leaving impressions in its place, and the red pigment was tentatively identified as lacquer. The Japanese archaeologist who studied the site, before the war with Japan in 1937 halted his excavations, noticed that the pigment had also been used as an adhesive for shell inlays within the wooden design.

It was not until 1973 that another Shang dynasty excavation site at Taixicun, in Hebei province, provided conclusive evidence for the use of lacquer as a decorative medium as early as the twelfth century BC. The fragments of a wooden dish with a deep band of relief carving were coated with lacquer: the inside of the dish was lacquered red, while the raised relief lines had been picked out in black lacquer. This accords with all the other examples so far unearthed from Shang dynasty sites, where lacquer was used to enhance carved decoration rather than to produce independent decorative schemes. Judging from the decoration on the soil 'ghosts' and the Taixicun fragments, the designs are very similar to those seen on contemporary bronze vessels, based on stylized animal forms, and repeating geometric motifs.

Very little lacquer material has been unearthed from the Western Zhou (1027–771 BC) or the Spring and Autumn Annals (770–481 BC) periods, but what there is indicates that the low relief carving of the Shang dynasty continued. Excavations at Shangcunling in Henan province can be dated through the inscription on a weapon, which links the site with the State of Guo, annexed in 655 BC. Some of the soil 'ghost' vessels found there were originally lacquered, and one seems to have had inlaid shell roundels for which lacquer was presumably the adhesive. It is, however, in the next two periods – those of the Warring States (475–221 BC) and the Han dynasty (206 BC–221 AD) – that great developments in lacquerware can be seen, and in recent years excavations in the People's Republic of China have uncovered a wealth of lacquer material in extremely good condition from this time.

Opposite page: Sword with lacquered wooden fittings; 3rd–2nd century BC. The details (*below*) show the pommel and, on the right, the hilt which is carved in interlaced openwork with a design of dragons, reflecting the influence of the Warring States.

The Warring States

The Warring States period was exactly what its name implies, for although the individual states all nominally owed allegiance to the King of Zhou, they fought each other continually to achieve a dominant position. Two states eventually proved most powerful – the States of Chu and Qin – and the victory of Qin over Chu in 222 BC heralded the unification of China under a single emperor, Qin Shi Huangdi. After so long a period of upheaval this shortlived dynasty brought a period of effective, if harsh, consolidation, and laid the foundations on which the succeeding Han dynasty could build a united and prosperous empire.

Many excavations have taken place in the region around Changsha in Hunan. This area came under the influence of the State of Chu, and despite the conquest by Qin in 222 BC that influence can be seen in the art of the region as late as the first century BC. Some of the most striking Warring States finds from this area are leather shields, stretched on a frame with bronze mounts and strengthened with layers of lacquer. They were not only light, strong and durable but also beautifully decorated, with their surfaces painted in lacquer of several colours including black,

yellow, brown and two shades of red. The designs of complex interlaced and articulated forms are based on dragons and clouds, or waves similar to those seen on inlaid bronze designs and cast-bronze mirrors, and some art historians see these as the foundation from which Chinese landscape painting developed. The designs were certainly well suited to the lacquer-painter's brush, and were used most effectively in several colours on a number of objects of this period. One of the most charming is the 'laughing dragon' box, where the lid is decorated with three concentric bands – one of articulated clouds and two of geometric motifs – surrounding a central creature which is part dragon and part cloud, and which looks for all the world as if it were enjoying a good joke!

Further examples of the use of lacquered leather for military purposes can be seen in the armour excavated in 1978 from a Warring States period site in Hubei province. This armour, for soldiers and their horses, is mainly leather scales coated with several layers of red or black lacquer to strengthen them, and in some cases painted decoration has been added in lacquer of a contrasting colour. The scales were then fastened together in an overlapping arrangement to give maximum protection. A few pieces, such as the horses' head-plates, appear to have been partly moulded to shape, and this has produced a certain amount of relief decoration under the lacquer coating. This discovery is highlighted by a fourth century BC document, the *Zuo Zhuan*, which recounts the story of a general who lost a battle against the State of Zheng in 606 BC. He also lost a great deal of equipment in the process, but when rebuked for this he replied that it could be replaced. However, when asked to specify where the replacements would come from, he was forced to admit that the lacquer for the armour would be difficult to get. (Another reference to the shortage of lacquer appears in the Han dynasty, when attempts were made to re-establish lacquer trees in Henan province.)

The fifth or fourth century BC chariots excavated from a tomb at Huixian in Henan appear to have been given a protective coating, and a small amount of this was recovered from the driver's box of one of the chariots, and identified as lacquer. In addition to providing such protection, lacquer was still used to enhance and protect carved wooden designs, such as the carved and lacquered coffin boards excavated in Changsha. These are carved with pierced and interlaced designs, and are covered with a plain coating of lacquer that served to preserve the board as well as to bring out the carved design. Sword fittings of the period display similar decorative use on a smaller scale, and an excellent example is a chape, hilt and slide with a pierced, interlaced dragon

Opposite page: Bronze mirror with lacquered back; Han dynasty (206 BC–221 AD). The lacquer-painting shows mythological creatures and figures including Xi Wang Mu, Queen Mother of the West.

Below: Toilet-box; Han dynasty. Red and black lacquer in geometric designs combines with mythical creatures inlaid in silver among waves and clouds, painted in a free-flowing linear style. There is a silver inlaid quatrefoil in the centre of the lid.

motif, well preserved by its lacquer coating. The most exciting find of lacquer material from this period was the fifth century BC tomb of Marquis Yi of the State of Zeng, excavated at Suixian in Hubei province in 1979. Two of the coffins are coated with lacquer with painted designs in contrasting lacquer; that on the inner coffin includes figures from the spirit world. Many of the other tomb objects are also lacquered, including a variety of musical instruments. A *se* (zither) is carved in relief at one end and painted with plain lacquer, while the rest of the instrument has decorative motifs in lacquer of contrasting colours. Musical pipes and a drum were also found, and the large stands for a set of sixty-four bronze bells were lacquered as well. A *dou* (lidded bowl) with unusually elaborate relief-carved handles is painted with geometric motifs, while a box in the shape of a mandarin duck includes an archer and a *fu-shang* tree along with more abstract designs. An interesting piece of evidence of Chinese astronomy is provided by the lid of a trunk, lacquered in black with the names of twenty-eight constellations painted in red lacquer between a tiger (the white tiger of the west) and a dragon (the green dragon of the east) also in red lacquer: the earliest known appearance of this motif.

Painted lacquer representations of the inhabitants of the spirit world like those on the Marquis of Yi's coffin can also be seen on a zither excavated from a tomb at Xinyang in Henan province, although here they are painted in a different style and in several colours. Similar figures also appear – this time among clouds – on a coffin from another excavation which belongs to the Han dynasty.

The Han dynasty (206 BC–221 AD)

The tomb, at Changsha in Hunan province, belonged to Li Cang, the consort of the Marquis of Dai, and dates to the second century BC. Its special construction has preserved the lacquer-ware, silks and the body of the deceased in almost perfect condition. The large number of lacquer objects display a wide variety of construction and decorative techniques, and careful study of these provide us with considerable insight into their manufacture in the Han dynasty. There were various methods used to prepare a wooden base for lacquer: some of the boxes, vases and dishes were made by turning the outside shape on a lathe and then gouging out the inside, while oval shapes like winged cups and their containers, as well as water pitchers and spoons, were simply carved. Cylindrical vessels such as single-handled cups and *lien* (toilet-boxes) were made by rolling a very thin strip of wood into a tube and then adding a planed base; linen was usually pasted over this and layers of lacquer applied and polished. Spoons and ladles were sometimes made from bamboo, a thick cross-section being used for the bowl and a carved strip for the handle. Other Han sites show that boxes and trunks were sometimes made of basketwork, while lacquered leather shoes have also been found in Korea.

The most sophisticated method for making the base of lacquer objects can be seen on the cylindrical cups and boxes, often those with the most exquisite decoration, and the technique is known as 'dry lacquer'. A form of the correct size and shape for the internal dimensions of the vessel was first made in wood or clay. Layers of cloth (usually hemp or ramie) and lacquer were applied over this, and when they dried the wood or clay form was removed. More layers of lacquer could then be applied and polished. The resulting object was thin and light, but strong and less liable to warp than those using a wooden base. Such wares appear to have been especially prized and often have inlays of precious metals with gilded bronze rims or handles.

Lacquerware with silver inlays, or the remains of silver inlays, has been found in many Han dynasty excavation sites. Some of the finest come from the area of Haizhou in Jiangsu province, and most are boxes – either large toilet-boxes, or the smaller cosmetic ones, with comb- and pin-boxes found inside them. Quatrefoil or trefoil inlay is used on the top of the lid while inlays in animal forms decorate the sides of the lid. One particularly attractive example displaying this technique is a horseshoe-shaped comb-box. Lacquer was also applied to metal, as the Shang dynasty ritual vessels showed. In this period it was used on the back of bronze mirrors, and one example has a black background painted with red dragons, and figures highlighted in white.

Precious metal inlays were one of several new techniques introduced during the Han dynasty; another was the combination of painting in lacquer with painting in an oil-based pigment. Here, colouring materials such as malachite or cinnabar were mixed with an oil that was probably *tong* oil (made from the seeds of *Aleurites cordata*). The use of this oil-based paint probably originated from attempts to expand the number of colours available, since lacquer itself successfully combines with only a limited number of colorants. Oil-based paints were also combined with another new technique, that of applied gold leaf. (The gold leaf had quantities of silver powder added to it, but was nevertheless referred to as 'gold leaf'.) This was stuck to the black lacquer ground and decorated with oil-based paint in colours that included red, yellow, grey, green and white: blue has also been found, but it appears to be the result of oxidation of the bronze powder used to produce gold paint. The oil paint was unfortunately far less stable than the lacquer, and had a tendency to peel off.

Incised decoration also appears during the Han dynasty. A sharply pointed instrument was used to incise a very fine solid or dotted line into the lacquer, and this was emphasized either by taking the incision down to the contrasting layer of preparation material beneath the lacquer, or by filling the incised lines with pigment of a contrasting colour. The lines were executed in a controlled but flowing style, and were used not only for the geometric and scrolled decorative motifs that comprised the major part of the repertoire of early craftsman, but also – and with remarkable skill – by the middle of the period to portray birds and animals. The inclusion of animals among the motifs occurred not only on incised wares, but also on the painted ones. The flat painting style seen on the earlier wares continued, but to a large extent it was restricted to scrolls and geometric motifs. Two new painting styles emerged, however: fine-line and ribbon-line. The first used a fine delicate line that stood in very slight relief against the lacquer background. This encompassed all the motifs of the flat-painted and incised-line lacquerwares, but its style was more closely akin to the latter. One innovation that these two fine-line decorative techniques have in common is the depiction of animals and mythical

Below: Wine cup with crescent-shaped handles, made of lacquered cloth; Han dynasty (206 BC–221 AD). The thick raised lines of the painted design are reminiscent of embroidery. The mounts are gilt bronze. An inscription on the base gives details of manufacture.

beings in a landscape derived from cloud and wave scrolls: a design often seen on boxes with quatrefoil inlays.

Ribbon-line painted lacquer decoration is seen on wares excavated from tombs belonging to a Han Commandary at Lolang, near modern P'yong-yang in Korea. On these the lacquer design was applied in wide, thick ribbon-like lines, usually rather formal in style, and producing an effect reminiscent of embroidered textiles. Examples of this technique with signs of wear show that the heavy lines were built up in the same colour as the background colour, and only painted with a contrasting colour for the final coat. Often the same motifs are to be seen on both the fine-line and the ribbon-line painted wares.

The production of moulded lacquer in this early period has created considerable interest. A combination of lacquer and ash was applied to a wooden base, moulded to the shape required, and then polished with an abrasive tool and finished with a coat of lacquer. This moulded or 'built-up' lacquer is described in the *Ge gu yao lun* (Essential Studies of Antiquities), where it is called *dui hong*. It was used to imitate carved lacquer, and occurs later with the Yuan dynasty, but it has also been suggested for the construction of some small black figures said to originate in the Changsha area around 200 BC. It is also the most probable method of construction for a small roundel (probably a sword pommel) which has relief decoration, and which was once thought to be an early example of carved lacquer.

Much of the lacquerware from the Lolang tombs incorporates another feature of particular interest in the study of Chinese lacquer: they are inscribed. Inscriptions on Han lacquers are not uncommon, and they may be incised through, painted on, or stamped under the lacquer. They commonly give such information as the object's owner, its capacity or use, or convey auspicious messages. Many of the inscriptions incised on the bottom of vessels excavated both from Lolang and from other Han sites provide even more interesting information, and the inscription found on the bottom of one winged cup is an excellent example.

A British Museum publication gives the following translation:

4th year of Yüan Shih (AD 4). Shu Commandary, West Factory. Imperial cup of wood, lacquered, engraved, and painted, with gilded handles. Capacity one sheng, sixteen yüeh. Initial work, I. Application of lacquer, Li. Top work, Teng. Gilding of bronze handles, Ku. Painting, Ting. Engraving, Feng. Finishing, P'ing. Production, Tsung Tsao [?]. Official in charge of the soldiers of the factory guard, Chang. Manager, Liang. Deputy, Feng. Assistant, Lung. Head clerk, Pao Chu.

Not only does this inscription tell us when and where the cup was made and that it was intended for the Imperial court, but it also gives considerable insight into the organization of the official lacquer factories of the Han period. It seems clear that lacquer objects were made in considerable numbers both in privately run workshops and in official factories, and some of the latter from the Western Han period (206 BC to 8 AD) are mentioned by Li Qi in his commentary on a chapter of the *Qian Han Shu* (History of the Former Han). Another commentator, Ru Shun, tells that three official factories produced lacquer goods: one was in the Henei Commandary (located in Yewangxian, near modern Huaiqing in northern Henan); another was in the Guanghan Commandary (near the modern Guanghan in Sichuan), and the last in the Shu Commandary (also in Sichuan, near Chengdu). Our inscribed cup was obviously made at this last factory, but lacquerware has been found with inscriptions which involve both the Sichuan factories – fine-line painting coming from the Guanghan Commandary and ribbon-line from the Shu – and there seems no reason to doubt the existence of the third factory in Henan.

Han dynasty workshop products have been found at a considerable distance from the metropolitan centres. I have already mentioned the lacquer excavated from the Han Commandary in Korea, and it seems likely that such wares were presented by the court to officials in the far-flung Han Commandaries. Lacquerware was also sent as gifts to foreign rulers and traded with (and plundered by) the Xiungnu. Examples have been found as far north as Noin-Ula in northern Mongolia, and they were certainly traded on the Silk Route across Central Asia. Lacquer is of course an ideal item for trade, being a luxury product for which high prices could be obtained per unit volume, but the wares were also durable and lightweight, and lent themselves to large-scale manufacture and quality standardization.

One final example of the Han lacquerer's art must be mentioned; it is unique among excavated material, but too impressive to ignore. One of the Han tombs at Lolang in Korea is known as the 'Tomb of the Painted Basket', and it is the basket from which the tomb derives its name that provides one of the few and splendid examples of the human figure portrayed in painted lacquer. The sides and lid of the basket are bordered with wide decorative bands, and in these bands are seated ninety-four grouped figures apparently in conversation. Each has been individually treated by the lacquer-artist, both in facial expression and detail of dress, and many figures have their names written beside them. These can be identified as coming from the Han repertory of ancient sages, paragons of filial piety, and princes. Many areas of

Chinese decorative art do not use the human figure until the relevant technique has reached a sophisticated stage, and the Lolang basket shows this to be true of painted lacquer as well.

Despite developments during the early and middle years of the Han dynasty, the later Han period saw a decline in the popularity of lacquer. Chinese literature mentions a craftsman of the second century AD called Shen Tupan, who worked for ten years on an important group of lacquerwares, and a recent excavation at Datong, Shanxi province, has produced evidence of some continuation of lacquer painting in the tradition of the painted basket of Lolang, in the form of panels which date to the Northern Wei period (386–585 AD). These carry high-quality lacquer-paintings depicting court women and their attendants engaged in a variety of activities. Chinese texts also tell of a Prince Xiao Pozhuan (484–502 AD) of the Northern Wei, who is said to have had his palace decorated in red and green lacquer, but no substantiating evidence has yet been found. Apart from these, however, there is very little indication of interest in lacquer until its dramatic re-emergence in the Tang dynasty, some four hundred years after the end of the Han. But these early periods had laid the foundations for all but one of the techniques that were to be applied to lacquer in the succeeding dynasties, the exception being carved lacquer.

The Tang dynasty (618–906)

Under the Tang dynasty China once again reached the peak of achievement attained under the Han. The economy prospered, the military power of the empire aided both internal and foreign relations, and the court achieved a level of culture and sophistication reflected in all branches of the arts. The capital of the Tang empire, Chang-an (the modern Xian in Shaanxi province) was the largest and most cosmopolitan city in the world, welcoming traders, travellers and diplomats from all nations and religions, and the influence of these foreign cultures can frequently be seen in the art of the period. Ironically, this cosmopolitanism means that certain types of Tang lacquerwork are better represented in Japan than they are in China itself. One of the most magnificent collections of Tang wares in Japan is to be found in the Shōsōin Imperial repository in the grounds of the Tōddaiji Monastery at Nara, where the widow of the Emperor Shomu had them locked away after his death in 756 AD. Art historians disagree about the origins of some of the collection, which may have been made by Chinese craftsmen or by imitative Japanese or Korean craftsmen. A Japanese provenance for these items is considered most unlikely by the Japanese themselves, and while it is not impossible that the items are the product of Chinese-influenced Korean workmen, it seems more likely that they were made by the Chinese. Some of the loveliest lacquer items among the Shōsōin treasures are mirrors and musical instruments, decorated with lacquer and inlaid with mother-of-pearl and ivory.

Problems arise with the terminology used to describe lacquer inlaid with mother-of-pearl. The two most usual terms are lo-tian to describe the type seen on Tang dynasty wares; and laque burgauté to describe a later type of mother-of-pearl inlay, but Sir Harry Garner rightly decries the use and misuse of the term laque burgauté, which was coined as recently as 1862. The Chinese adopted the term lo-tian in the Tang dynasty to describe the type of inlay that is supposed to have originated in Lulingxian, Jianfu, Jiangxi province, but the term has since been used in such a way as not to differentiate either the type of shell or the way it was used. The Japanese have various terms applied to different types of shell and method, but even these are not used as precisely as one could wish. Like Garner, therefore, I will abandon all those and keep to the term 'mother-of-pearl', used since the sixteenth century to describe the iridescent layers found in various sea and freshwater shells, and will detail each technique individually.

Mother-of-pearl was used on Tang dynasty lacquerware to produce decorative patterns, often based on flower motifs and sometimes showing Sasanian influence. A very rare example of figures in a landscape can be seen on a mirror discovered at Luoyang in Henan in 1956. This shows two figures, one of whom is playing a lute, and a crane in front of them. The shell is the creamy inner surface, of either the nautilus from the Ryukyu Islands, or a Yangtze freshwater shellfish. It was used in fairly large, thick pieces with incised details. The colour variations and the brilliance of later wares is missing, but they are extremely fine pieces of craftsmanship. Mirrors decorated in this way are bronze, with the mother-of-pearl designs inlaid into lacquer on the back. The adhesion between the bronze and the lacquer tended to be rather poor and so a large number have not survived burial very well. The musical instruments, such as the lutes in the Shōsōin, are predictably wooden-based but they are decorated in a similar manner. These inlaid mother-of-pearl lacquers are important not only as the forebears of later variants of the technique in China, but also as the inspiration for Japanese and Korean work. Lacquer itself was probably introduced into both countries in the sixth century, but the Tang dynasty introduction of mother-of-pearl inlay into Korea and Japan laid the foundation for the wares of the Korean Koryŏ dynasty, and for the wares that were to be produced in Japan.

Another inlay technique revived and adapted in

the Tang period was that using precious metals – either gold or silver foil. The use of metal foil existed in the Han dynasty, the inlay on these pieces being simply a basic cut-out shape, while the Tang examples have finely incised details and exquisitely complex shapes. Phoenixes, other birds, butterflies and all kinds of flowers, plants and plant scrolls are depicted in delightful detail, mirroring the designs on *repoussé* silverwares of the same period. The Chinese name for this inlaid metal foil decoration is *ping-tuo*, a term that first appears in the Tang dynasty. A unique example of such metal foil work is an eight-lobed mirror case inlaid with phoenixes and floral scrolls in silver, and another is one of the few surviving examples of the technique applied to a curved surface: a basketwork ewer lacquered and decorated with inlaid silver foil. A further instance of a curved surface is a small begging-bowl made on a fabric base and decorated with lotus flowers, but most other examples are mirrors, which have frequently suffered in the same way as their mother-of-

Below: Bronze mirror; Tang dynasty (618–906). The lacquered back is inlaid with phoenixes, birds, butterflies and plants in gold and silver, and delicate scrollwork.

pearl counterparts from inadequate adhesion be-tween the bronze and the lacquer. In some cases only the gold and silver survives without its bronze body, and a number of such fragments can be seen in Western collections.

Buddhism developed between the Han and Tang dynasties, and its effect was not only seen in painting and in decorative motifs, but also in the emergence of an art hitherto somewhat neglected in China: sculpture. From about the fourth cen-tury Chinese Buddhist sculpture in stone, bronze and wood developed through a number of phases until, by the Tang period, it reached an extremely sophisticated and subtle level. Lacquer craftsmen applied their skills here as well, though once again more of their work survives in Japan than has so far been discovered in China. The figures prob-ably began to be made as early as the sixth century, and Japanese texts certainly refer to such Chinese figures dating from the seventh century, while eighth century figures survive in a number of Japanese temples.

The sculptures were made by the 'dry lacquer' technique used for boxes in the Han period. Layers of lacquer-impregnated fabric were applied to a clay base to build up the figure, and when sufficient strength had been achieved the surface was given a final lacquer coating. In some cases a layer of gesso was applied before the lacquer, to give the statue finer details. The finished figure could then be painted or gilded if required, and the clay core removed. Figures made in this way were very light and easy to transport (even if, as in some cases, they were life size), and they were not susceptible to damage by termites, unlike their wooden counterparts. This technique continued to be used for Buddhist statuary into the thir-teenth century.

An example of moulded lacquer and ash like the earlier examples but dating to the seventh century has survived in Japan. It consists of a circular panel surmounting a rectangular pillar; the moulded lacquer decoration is applied to the panel's wooden base. The roundel design of a phoenix among clouds and flowers, and the floral scroll on the pillar itself, are reminiscent of Tang bronze mirror and silverware designs.

In 1964 a Chinese archaeological journal re-ported the excavation of four undecorated (mono-chrome) lacquer boxes from a Tang dynasty tomb at Jia-zhuang in Caixian, Henan province: three boxes had a six-lobed shape while the fourth was round. Lacquerware of this kind is rare in Tang dynasty sites, but closer consideration of them will be possible with the lacquers of the Song period.

One last aspect of Tang lacquer may not in itself seem very exciting, but it introduces carved techniques to the existing range. The Warring States period saw lacquer applied to leather scales in armour, and this practice continued into and beyond the Tang dynasty. But the lacquer armour excavated at Fort Miran in East Turkestan does not only have lacquered or painted scales; it has

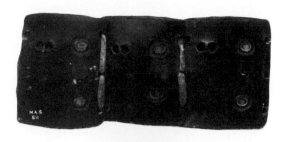

also been carved on a slant with circles, S-shapes, commas and semi-circles which reveal layers of reddish-brown and black lacquer. Fort Miran was the site of a Buddhist temple built around the third century AD, but later abandoned. The fort was taken over in the mid-eighth century as a Tibetan military post when the Tibetans occupied Gansu province. There is no doubt that the armour found at the fort by Sir Aurel Stein in 1906 is Chinese and not Tibetan, and it must have been captured from the Chinese during raids in Gansu during the eighth century. The curved pieces of untanned leather have been lacquered on both sides; on the convex side there are up to thirty layers. Each band of colour revealed by the carving is made up of a number of layers, and on some pieces additional layers have been added to produce a central spine. The pieces themselves may look rather insignificant – rectangles with a curved lateral profile, mostly about 7 centimetres (3 inches) long – but they are the first step in the production of the marbled and carved lacquers that were to achieve such beauty.

The Song dynasty (960–1279)

The decline and fall of the Tang dynasty and its aftermath caused considerable fragmentation in the tenth century. In northern China the Five Dynasties (907–960 AD) each rose to power and fell in quick succession, while in central and southern China the powerful 'Ten Kingdoms' defied the northern rulers and set up independent states, enjoying reasonable peace and prosperity while waiting for a political resolution. The Song dynasty was founded almost by accident when the army of the Later Zhou (the last of the Five Dynasties) staged a coup and placed one of their generals, Zhao Kuang-yin, on the throne. In the

Above: Lacquered
wooden cup; Song
dynasty (960–1279).
A refined subtle beauty
of form and colour was
characteristic of Song
monochrome wares in
both lacquer and pottery.

campaigns that followed Zhao (posthumous title
Tai-Zu) brought all but one of the southern states
back into the empire, but the dynasty was constantly threatened by its neighbours to the north
and west. The Khitan state of Liao harried the
Chinese in the north and north-east and gained
control of part of north China, but in 1127 the
whole of north China fell to the Jurchen Tartar
state of Jin and the Song court fled south, setting
up a capital at Nanjing. Despite this disruption
there were periods of considerable prosperity
under the Song, and two significant changes
occurred. The power of the feudal aristocracy was
crushed and control fell into the hands of the
scholar-official class who (at least in theory) held
their positions entirely on merit, and the economic centre of China shifted from the north to the
south, with a resulting shift of emphasis from land
to maritime trade. The decorative arts moved

away from the colourful, highly decorative Tang
wares towards a more refined style which relied
for its effect on beauty of form and subtlety of
colour. This is particularly noticeable in the
ceramic wares of the period, but it can also be seen
in the best known of the Song lacquerwares, the
monochrome wares.

The Chinese custom of inscriptions provides a
lot of information about these monochrome lacquerwares, just as it did with the Han dynasty
painted wares. In a number of cases such excavated pieces give the cyclical date, the place of
manufacture and the name of the craftsman. Most
of the dates fall in the eleventh and twelfth
centuries, and five centres of manufacture have
been identified. In the early days of uncontrolled
excavations, many examples from excavations at
Zhuluxian in Hebei province found their way into
Western collections, and the inscribed ones date

from the early eleventh century and give Tanzhou (near Changsha in Hunan, famous for Warring States and Han lacquer) as the place of manufacture. Three different places of origin are identified from inscribed lacquer excavated from tombs at Yangmiao Zhu (near Huai-an in Jiangsu), dating from the second half of the eleventh century; Wenzhou in the south of Zhejiang province, Hangzhou in the north of Zhejiang province, and Jiangning Fu (present-day Nanjing) in Jiangsu province. Wenzhou occurs in a description of Kaifeng, the Northern Song capital, written in 1147. This street-by-street account of the city includes reference to a shop selling lacquerware from Wenzhou, some 600 miles away. And a

tomb near Wuhan in Hubei, with coins dating as late as the first decade of the twelfth century, has yielded six inscribed lacquer vessels, of which two name Xiangzhou, in Hubei, as the place of manufacture. The official histories of both the Tang and Song dynasties mention Xiangzhou lacquerware, and contemporary Song references extol its virtues.

Hangzhou is cited again on Song lacquer from tombs at Wuxi in Jiangsu province, and from four tombs at Laohoshan near Hangzhou. The latter finds are probably slightly later, since they use the name Lin-an for Hangzhou and this was not adopted until 1129. Hin-Cheung Lovell has pointed out that all these lacquer factories lie

Below: Hexagonal table with Ta-li stone top; Song dynasty. The smooth, warm red lacquer is set off by the marble. Ta-li is known for its fine marble, still being produced.

between the latitudes 28° and 32° north in central China, and suggests that the climate for the growth of lacquer trees was most favourable in this area during the Song. The colours used on these monochrome wares are limited to black, dull red, various brown tones, and a red-tinged black achieved by applying a layer of black over a layer of red. Sometimes the base and the inside of the footring are in a contrasting colour, and the inscriptions are frequently painted in a contrasting colour. One Chinese text tells us that green lacquer was first made in the Song, but so far there is no supporting evidence for this.

Nearly all the monochrome lacquers are bowls, dishes, cupstands or boxes. Their shapes, inspired by flower forms and especially the lotus, closely match those of Ding ceramics, but the related theory which suggests the existence of lacquer factories at Dingzhou in Hebei is not supported by any evidence. And while the eleventh and twelfth century examples follow the Ding ceramics in merely hinting at a flower form by subtle foliations and shallow lobing, the thirteenth and fourteenth century examples tend to follow Qing-bai ceramics on which these aspects are more exaggerated. The base for the lacquer is usually wood covered with cloth, or just cloth. One fourteenth century text, the *Ge gu yao lun*, tells us that plain lacquers were made on gold and silver bodies, but no examples of Song date have yet been positively identified, although the tomb of Wang Jian (847–918), who founded the State of Qian Shu in Sichuan, yielded a five-lobed bowl that could answer this description. It has a double body – silver on the inside and lead on the outside. The outside lead surface was originally lacquered, but very little of this has survived. The inner silver surface is decorated with a gold foil design. The same text assures us that carved red lacquer was made in the Song, and another sixteenth century text confirms that, adding that some were made on gold and silver bases. As yet, however, no Song carved lacquer has been identified.

Mother-of-pearl inlay in the Tang style used large, fairly thick pieces of shell in ornate floral-based patterns with incised details, and this continued during the Song dynasty. An example found in 1978 at the Ruiguang monastery pagoda in Suzhou, Jiangsu province, is a box with a wood base covered in black lacquer into which a mother-of-pearl floral design has been inlaid. (The *Ge gu yao lun* records this style's being made for the court, with some of the best examples incorporating copper wire.) The same site has yielded examples of other lacquer techniques dating to the Five Dynasties and Northern Song periods, including a tall square-sectioned wooden-based box. This is decorated on all four sides with lively and skilful depictions of the four 'Heavenly Kings' in painted lacquer. The figures are very dramatic, and their slightly caricatured faces and swirling garments are reminiscent of a Tang style.

Several boxes excavated in 1973 from Ruian in Zhejiang, and dated before 1042, display another lacquer variant. These wooden-based boxes have been covered in lacquer and then gold-painted with diapers, scrolls and figures in a rather linear style. Moulded lacquer has also been used as an *appliqué*, framing the panels of painted decoration and supplying a background of floral scrolls: it has also been gilded, and in some cases highlighted with pearls. But the most exciting Song decorated lacquers were unearthed in 1977 from a Southern Song (1128–1279) site at Wujin, in Jiangsu. These included boxes decorated in the *qiangjin* technique and a *tixi* (carved marble lacquer) mirror-case.

Qiangjin literally means etched or incised gold, and happily it is a Chinese term which may be adopted without fear of confusion. The technique is described in the fourteenth century *Zhuogeng lu*, which explains that an adhesive made of lacquer and orpiment (yellow arsenic trisulphide) is applied over the incised design and gold leaf is pressed into the incision, with any spare gold being carefully collected for future use. The author of the *Zhuogeng lu*, Tao Congyi, also describes *qiangyin*, where silver rather than gold is used and the adhesive is made of lacquer and lead carbonate powder, but the silver tarnished too quickly and this variant did not enjoy the popularity of *qiangjin*. Until recently the latter technique was thought to have begun in the Yuan dynasty, but the Wujin discoveries have now established an earlier date. *Qiangjin* is not only important in its own right; its influence on *tianqi* lacquer in China, and on the *qiangjin* lacquers of the Ryukyu Islands which followed the introduction of Chinese versions in the fifteenth century, is also significant. Fourteenth century Chinese sutra boxes with *qiangjin* decoration have been carefully preserved in Japan, where they have consistently been more admired than in their homeland.

Two of the rectangular boxes from Wujin have *qiangjin* decoration, but in very different styles. On one a single floral spray is centrally placed on each face of the box and its lid, but the top of the lid shows a figure in a rather summarily drawn landscape. On the other rectangular box, however, all sides of the box and lid are covered with a complex, skilfully executed floral scroll incorporating a number of different types of flower and leaf, and set against a background of tiny dots which throws the design into relief, and is reminiscent both of metalwork and the use of pearl-matting backgrounds on some Cizhou ceramics. The lid-top of this second box shows a very accomplished landscape with a willow tree on a rocky promontory in the foreground, and the tiny dots are again used to good effect to denote the water of the lake and the sky. A tiered toilet-box with a six-lobed bracketed shape familiar from monochrome lacquers of this period is also decorated in *qiangjin* technique, with floral motifs around the sides. On the lid-top two women appear in a garden, attended by a servant who holds a bottle in her outstretched hand.

The *tixi* lacquer mirror-case from Wujin was made to hold a bronze mirror, and it is a particularly important find for the use of yellow confirms claims made in the *Ge gu yao lun*. Descriptive terminology for this lacquer is difficult, and there is a long history of the use and misuse of various Chinese names. Chinese archaeologists seem to have reverted to *tixi*, the term used in the *Ge gu yao lun*, which translates as 'carved rhinoceros'; a more usual phrase is *xipi* but – depending on which characters are used – this can mean 'rhinoceros skin', 'rhinoceros navel', or even 'western skin'! The Japanese term *guri*, which refers to the spirals of the decoration, has found favour among some Western art historians and collectors but the safest course is to call these wares 'carved marble lacquer', and their allied smooth-surface wares 'flat marbled lacquer'.

Carved marbled wares are produced – like the Tang dynasty lacquer armour – by the application of a number of layers of lacquer in contrasting colours. The top layer is usually black with thinner red layers beneath it: a red top layer is rare in China, although quite common among the late eighteenth and early nineteenth century carved marbled wares from Japan. Colours in the early Chinese periods seem to have been confined to red, black and yellow, although a different red and green were added to the repertoire in the Ming dynasty. The design is cut into the lacquer with a sharp instrument, producing broad grooves either of a V-shape through five or six red and black layers to a final yellow layer, or of an open U-shape exposing two or three layers of red and black and ending with a black layer. The decorative motifs are virtually unchanging, and consist of spiral scrolls and cloud-like shapes based on *ru-yi* heads. A similar design appears in slip decorations on Yuan dynasty ceramics from the Jizhou kilns, and on Song dynasty silver. The designs on the Wujin mirror-case are skilfully cut with broad V-shape incisions, and their arrangement is perfectly adapted to the object's shape. This is not a crude early attempt but an accomplished execution of a tested formula, and suggests that the technique was well established in the Southern Song period.

Lacquer continued to be used as a medium for Buddhist statues in the Song dynasty, though as before very few survive in China today. Small figures made in 'dry lacquer' (in the same way as the Tang period examples) continued to be made in southern China: one particularly pleasing example is a seated *lohan* (disciple) figure dated by an inscription on the base to 1099. The figure has the plump face and the carefully executed details of dress which are associated with wooden Buddhist sculpture of this date. A set of life-size *lohan* heads in 'dry lacquer' comes from northern China, but the dating of these is difficult, and precision greater than between the tenth and thirteenth centuries has not been achieved. The well-defined individual characteristics suggest the heads may be portraits. They survive in several Western collections, and probably came from a Buddhist temple south of Beijing (previously Peking).

The Yuan dynasty (1280–1368)

The Mongols, who had already conquered all of inner Eurasia and made incursions into Central Europe, overran northern China in the 1250s. In 1260 Kubilai Khan declared himself the first Mongol emperor of China and took the dynastic name Yuan seven years later. The foreigners who visited China during this period include the Venetian Marco Polo, who travelled as one of Kubilai Khan's aides from 1275 to 1292 and astounded a rather sceptical European public on his return with tales of 'black rocks' (coal) used as fuel, paper money, and the tremendous wealth and size of Chinese cities. Until comparatively recently the Yuan dynasty, during which the Chinese were ruled by a foreign and to their minds barbarian people, was regarded as uninteresting in the decorative arts, and was ignored in favour of the preceding Song and succeeding Ming dynasties. Artistic recognition was reserved for the scholar-painters; men who would normally have been employed in government service but who either refused or were not invited to serve under the Mongol conquerors. They used their excess leisure time for cultural pursuits, and were sometimes able to express subtle opposition through their paintings. An exhibition on Chinese art under the Mongols in 1968, and the publication of a number of articles and a book on Yüan porcelain and stoneware by Margaret Medley, however, changed our view of the Yuan period and revealed it as an era when craftsmen experimented with techniques and designs.

Monochrome lacquer continued to be made in the Yuan dynasty. Most of the examples that can safely be dated to this period are dishes, cosmetic-boxes or sweetmeat-boxes. A three-tiered cosmetic-box (with small inner boxes like the Han dynasty examples) was excavated from the tomb of Qian Yu (1247–1320) at Wuxi, Jiangsu province. It is lobed, and a good example of an intermediate style between Song and developed Yuan. The lobes are well defined with a bow-shaped profile, unlike those on a four-tiered box from the Yuan dynasty tombs of the painter Ren Renfa and his family. The tombs, dated 1327–51,

are at Beimiaocun, near Shanghai, in Jiangsu. The four-tiered box has a greater number of lobes and they are bracket-shaped, giving a double-S profile that results in sharp vertical ridges on the box's sides. The same profile change is on monochrome lacquer dishes, where the gently curving Song outlines are replaced by the pointed bracket-lobes of the Yuan. The same outline appears on a silver box from a hoard at Hefei in Anhui, which probably dates to the first half of the fourteenth century, and on a porcelain dish with *shu fu* ('official' white ware) glaze. Hin-Cheung Lovell believes that the silver and porcelain pieces derived their shapes from lacquerware.

Two more developments are characteristic of Yuan monochrome lacquers: the lack of a footring, and the decorative use of wire. While Song wares usually have a definite footring Yuan wares frequently do not, although this is not always immediately apparent, for they often appear to have a foot which mirrors the lobes of the rest of the vessel. Only close examination reveals that the foot is really part of the vessel's body, with a circular hole recessed into the base. This is the case with a bracket-lobed box which also shows the decorative use of wire. Wire had been set into the edges of lacquerware to give it added strength, but on this box pewter wire follows the foliations on the side of the box to make nine petals on both the lid and base. More wire on the lid creates four concentric rings which surround an inset, incised and pierced mother-of-pearl roundel.

Mother-of-pearl inlaid lacquer was greatly prized in the Yuan dynasty. It seems still to have been manufactured at Lulingxian, although the *Ge gu yao lun* mentions Jiangxi, where it seems lime, pig's blood, *tong* oil and even the rhizomes of lotus root were mixed in, which made it very weak. From the same source, however, we learn that mother-of-pearl lacquerware, carefully made with delicate designs which included figures, was produced for rich families throughout the Yuan dynasty, including large items such as chairs, tables, benches, beds and screens as well as smaller objects. The great change in mother-of-pearl lacquers was, however, in the designs and techniques used to achieve them. Instead of the earlier floral designs which could be produced with large thick pieces of shell, lacquer-artists turned their attention to pictorial designs based on the 'figures in a landscape' paintings of the Song and Yuan dynasties. For these a great number of very tiny pieces of iridescent *haliotis* shell were needed, and while some details were provided by incising most were achieved by the minute pieces of shell themselves. A writing-set shows a variety of delicate patterns on its tiers, and illustrates what could be produced with this new technique.

Qiangjin (incised gold) lacquer of the Yuan period is mentioned in a number of texts; these

Right: Detail from plate on page 37; 14th century. The incised black decoration in low relief shows birds among peony flowers and reveals the underlying red layer.

include the *Ge gu yao lun* and the *Zhuogeng lu* of the fourteenth century. The latter specifically mentions a *qiangjin* artist at the beginning of the Yuan period (and possibly the end of the Song) called Peng Zhunbao from Xitang in Zhejiang province. He was particularly famous for his designs of figures, landscapes, pavilions, flowers and birds. Excavated evidence of Yuan *qiangjin* is not forthcoming; indeed, examples of any kind appear to be scarce in China. Seven Chinese sutra boxes of this technique and date are now in Japan, and an eighth was formerly in a Berlin museum, but disappeared in 1946 during the Russian occupation. Five of the sutra boxes, all of which are owned by Japanese temples, are the same size and have very similar decoration. The boxes, which are rectangular, are made of wood with a lacquer-impregnated ramie (fabric) covering. This has been covered with grey primer and several layers of black lacquer, and the main decoration on the sides consists of an ogival panel containing a pair of birds (phoenixes, parrots or peacocks) among clouds against a background of peony scrolls.

Three of the boxes have inscriptions in black lacquer stamped inside the lids. One gives a date equivalent to 1315 and adds 'made by the Jin family of Yuzhu jiao, Hangzhou'. Another has a similar inscription which reads 'made by the Song family in front of the Ming-jing temple'. An inscription painted in red lacquer on the bottom of this box states that it was intended for a particular sutra in the Jôdo-ji temple and gives a date of 1358, by which time it was probably owned by that temple and already in Japan. The fourth and fifth boxes have no inscriptions, and one differs in its decoration from the others in showing a seated Buddha under a canopy, flanked by two disciples. The sixth sutra box has the bird motif larger in size, while the seventh is much restored, with Buddhist decorations. In all cases the peony scrolls are drawn in fine detail and very closely packed, and great care has been taken to reproduce the texture of the birds' feathers. They are all decorated in a similarly ornate and flowing style (except the seventh, where the style is rather stiff). The box with the seated Buddha differs slightly in having the area around the panelled birds filled with cloud forms; on the others there are only a few clouds, and fine lines fill the rest of the space.

The carved marbled wares from the Song continued in the Yuan dynasty, and we are told that those on a yellow base were admired but tended to come apart. The designs remained similar to those on the Song examples, and the technique was apparently used on dishes, cup-stands and bowls. The most exciting development of the Yuan dynasty was red carved lacquer. Chinese texts claim that this was made in earlier dynasties but the Yuan is the first for which we can positively identify carved red lacquer (as opposed to carved marbled lacquer) and for which there is excavated evidence.

It may seem strange that the Chinese took so long to develop lacquer carving, but a considerable thickness of lacquer needs to be built up to provide a suitable carving medium, and its very properties make this both difficult and time-consuming. The process of changing lacquer from a liquid to a solid involves the polymerization of two of its main components, urushiol and an enzyme laccase. The polymerization will take place only in the presence of air and a certain degree of humidity, and so if too much lacquer is applied at once a thin top layer will set but the lacquer below will remain liquid. The coats must therefore be applied in very thin layers and these must be allowed plenty of time to set properly before the next is applied. Each coat is between .03 and .05 millimetres thick and must be polished before the next one is added. On some Ming dynasty pieces up to two hundred layers are used and so clearly this was a highly labour-intensive technique! When properly built up, however, it becomes an excellent carving medium. A moulded lacquer and ash mixture was sometimes used as a substitute, but this *dui hong* or *zhao hong* (red-coated) could be shaped only by moulding and abrading, not by carving. It is obviously regarded with little favour by the author of the *Ge gu yao lun*, who describes it in derisive terms.

Real carved red lacquer (called *ti hong*, carved red, by the *Ge gu yao lun*) has been linked to the Yuan dynasty both by Chinese and Japanese literature and by recently excavated material. A round incense-box with a key-fret design round the sides of both box and lid, and with a scene of two figures in a landscape on the flat top, has been excavated from a tomb dated not later than 1351 at Qingpuxian in Jiangsu province. The box has neither the precision of carving nor the balance of design that will be seen on later wares, but it does make use of two different diaper forms to differentiate between land and water: a forerunner of the three diapers for land, water and air. A second excavated example represents a minor miracle of survival, for this small carved lacquer jar lay under almost 70 feet (22 metres) of sea water for more than six hundred years. It formed part of the cargo of a boat that was wrecked on its way from China to Japan in the 1330s, and sank off the Sinan coast of south-west Korea. The wreck was discovered in 1975, and has been dated from coins minted around 1310, and from the inscription on a black lacquer bowl giving a cyclical date (*xin wei* year) of 1331. The ship carried monochrome red and black lacquers, but the little carved red jar is of particular interest. It is decorated with peonies which have been cut into the lacquer with considerable depth and precision. The flowers have incised details and the leaves are full and rounded, showing an accomplished use of a complex motif on a small awkwardly shaped object and suggesting a technique well past its infancy.

Some idea of fourteenth century carved lacquer comes from records of the wares that were sent to Japan. A catalogue of the more important objects belonging to the Zen temple Enkaku-ji in Kamakura was compiled by a priest of the Butsu-nichi-an sub-temple, and this lists a considerable number of Chinese carved lacquers in both red and black including plates, bowls, trays, tiered and other boxes, and incense containers. Lists of gifts sent to Japan in the years 1403, 1406 and 1407 also mention carved lacquers. The 1403 list includes fifty-eight pieces and provides considerable detail, while the 1407 list mentions thirty incense-boxes and twenty round boxes, and gives the diameter of some of the latter. The 1406 list simply says that there were forty dishes of eight different kinds. While these dates are early fifteenth century ones, the lists nevertheless indicate that carved lacquer must have been produced in considerable quantities during the fourteenth century too, especially since the objects themselves probably took at least two years to make.

The 1403 list gives measurements as well as details of decoration; the latter will be interesting to compare with information on fifteenth century official wares, and so it is worth including them now. The dishes, apparently, carried landscape and floral motifs or showed birds against a floral background. One dish had a landscape devoid of figures. The small boxes were decorated with landscapes on top and a key-fret or lotus-petal border. Chinese texts mention two types of landscape combined with floral motifs: one shows a landscape with figures (and usually buildings); the other has no human figures. No excavated examples are known, but one small lobed dish which shows two figures in a pavilion and a third outside may be fourteenth century.

I have already mentioned the excavated box with a landscape on the top of the lid and key-fret border on the sides. The decoration with birds and a floral background is not surprising considering the decoration on the *qiangjin* sutra boxes in Japan, and it is quite possible that some of the boxes in Western collections which show two birds among flowers could also be from the fourteenth century.

The *Ge gu yao lun* and the *Zun sheng ba jian* both mention two lacquer-artists who made carved lacquer at the end of the Yuan dynasty. These men, Zhang Cheng and Yang Mao, are said by both sources to have produced thin and cracked lacquer, but the *Ge gu yao lun* adds that their work was very good, and much admired by the Japanese and the people of the Liuchiu islands. It also says that both men worked at Xitang, Yang hui,

Above: Plate; 14th century. The raised edge is in black. See page 34 for detail.

in Zhejiang, but that imitations were made in Yunnan. A new factory was apparently set up at Xitang in Jiaxingfu and made great numbers of carved lacquers, but only a few were hard and the ones with a yellow ground chipped easily. Many lacquer items in collections all over the world have inscriptions claiming Zhang Cheng as their maker but a number of these are patently false: the Japanese produced lots of imitations. But some of the inscriptions may be genuine, and one which is thought to be so by the Chinese themselves is a round box in the Palace Museum in Beijing. It is decorated with a single peony spray carved right through the lacquer to the base. This is a well-executed piece with only slight cracking, and its decoration has much the same feel as that on the jar recovered from the Sinan wreck.

The Ming dynasty (1368–1644)

The Yuan dynasty ended in a series of peasant uprisings and a new native dynasty was established in 1368: the Ming, or bright, dynasty with its capital at Nanjing. Its founder was Zhu Yuanzhang, a commoner, and while he lacked heroic flair, peace and economic stability were nevertheless re-established. His reign (posthumously called the Hongwu period) was a time of social levelling through the abolition of slavery, changes in taxation and the reallocation of land; the civil service examination system was also re-introduced, and a hereditary standing army established. In foreign affairs China regained her predominant position in Asia, and Europeans began to establish themselves in significant numbers, despite a certain amount of court discouragement. The Portuguese at Guangdong pressed for diplomatic and trading relations as early as 1514, and by 1557 there was a Portuguese settlement at Macao. Matteo Ricci established Catholic missionary headquarters at Beijing under imperial patronage in 1601, and by the end of the dynasty many other Europeans were also entering China.

The fifteenth century

In the fifteenth century carved lacquer reached a peak of unequalled excellence. Work of this period, particularly that attributed to the reigns of Yongle and Xuande (1403–24 and 1426–35 respectively), has always been especially prized by Chinese connoisseurs, and as early as the sixteenth century there is evidence of the favour it found at court. The Qianlong Emperor (1736–95), an inveterate collector and patron of the arts, not only mentions thirty-six items of lacquer from these periods in his poems, but also added inscriptions to several items in the imperial collection, as he did to particularly fine paintings. The inscriptions were incised into the lacquer and then filled with gold: one such device bears the date of 1781. The period has also been much admired by

Above: Lacquer dish; reign of Yongle (1403–24). The three diaper conventions are used: squares for land, wave lines for water, and elongated, horizontal lines for air. Two sages are shown in front of a pavilion.

but there is no evidence for this and it is almost certain that Zhejiang and Jiangsu remained the centres of high-quality lacquer production for the court at least until the sixteenth century. (The centre in Yunnan was an exception which produced carved lacquerware in its own particular style.) Literary tradition tells us that lacquer-workers were sent from Sichuan in the Tang dynasty to set up a new factory in Yunnan.

I have already mentioned the description of lacquer production given in the *Zhuogeng lu*, and this was confirmed by Sir Harry Garner in 1963. His investigation disclosed a wooden base covered by a thick layer of black lacquer mixed with a considerable quantity of ash. A layer of cloth had then been added, followed by seven thin layers of yellow lacquer. On top of the yellow layers a hundred red layers were identified, interrupted by four black layers about a quarter of the way up the red section: the lacquer's total thickness was about 3 millimetres (⅛ inch). The *Zhuogeng lu* tells us that several months elapsed between the preparation of the base coats and the first layer of lacquer, and if we estimate four or five days for each layer to dry and be polished before the next was added, each item must have taken about two years to prepare before it was passed to the carver.

The four black layers provided a thin guideline in the red lacquer, and were used by the carver as a warning device when he was approaching the yellow layer below the red, and should stop cutting away the background to his design. It has also been suggested that the lacquer was applied so that it broke away more readily at the bottom of the black layer. Early in the fifteenth century the carving appears to have been done with a single-edged knife. Long thin incisions were made with two cuts of the knife, and a fine needle was used for very delicately incised details. During the Xuande period a needle was increasingly used, and small chisels with different edges were introduced which cut down the labour involved. By the Jiajing and Wanli periods (1522–66 and 1573–1619) the knife was very rarely used; the effect on the carving was increased freedom at the expense of crisp precision.

The three most frequent types of decoration on these 'official' wares were figures in a landscape, flowers and trees, and dragons or phoenixes in clouds or flowers. Pattern-books were obviously much used, as we can see from the diaper backgrounds and the repetition of even large sections of the landscape scenes. It is also noticeable that when a top and bottom floral border is used the pattern is reversed, indicating the use of an inverted template. The wares decorated with figures in a landscape use a distinct convention for diapers to indicate air, water and land. The air and water diapers are cut to just above the yellow layer; the land diaper just a little higher. These

Western collectors and examples from it were imported to Europe in considerable numbers in the late nineteenth and early twentieth centuries. We have already seen that early fifteenth century carved lacquerwares were sent as gifts to the Japanese shōguns, and examples survive in Japan to the present day.

The description 'Imperial wares' is often used to describe a group of particularly high-quality wares from the early fifteenth century, but the term is inaccurate: 'official wares' is preferable, although still not absolutely correct. The wares were made in official factories in Zhejiang and Jiangsu under the supervision of the *Yu yongjian*, a department of the Imperial Household set up to control the supply and maintenance of items made for the court. A sub-department, the *Tian shifang* (department of sweetmeats) is also sometimes mentioned on these early wares. The only wares that can properly be described as 'Imperial' are those which were presumably made for the Emperor, and are thus decorated with the Imperial dragon. The factories, however, did not work for the court on a full-time basis: the artisans worked part of the time for the court or their feudal lord, and part of the time on their own behalf – although the privately made items were not always made to such a high standard as the 'official' wares. Like the factories of the Han dynasty, these official workshops operated a production line system with people specializing in particular aspects of lacquer manufacture, rather than each craftsman working alone and seeing the processes through.

It has been suggested that a palace factory (the *Guo yuan*) was set up in Beijing in 1421 when the Yongle Emperor moved his capital from Nanjing,

Right: Bowl lid; 15th century. In cinnabar red carved lacquer, the bowl is on a stand of later date. Work of this period found favour at court, and examples were also exported to Europe.

Below: Box; early 15th century. Floral scrolls decorate the sides, with figures in a landscape on top, motifs often found in work from the factories of the Imperial Household.

diapers are carved with minute precision on the fifteenth century 'official' wares: the land diaper is usually composed of squares running on the diagonal, each enclosing a tiny eight-pointed star, with the water diaper in regular off-set wave shapes produced by concentric inverted C-forms. The air diaper is a combination of a complex laterally elongated S-form with horizontal lines, possibly derived from the key-fret border. The landscapes themselves incorporate figures, animals, buildings, fences, ornamental rocks and various trees – the last with carefully detailed leaves and bark.

The most popular box and dish shapes which are decorated with landscapes usually carry a

Opposite page: Dish
carved in red, green and
yellow lacquer; 1489. An
inscription on the base
refers to the Orchid
Pavilion, shown in the
detail (below).

border of the four seasons' flowers, rather than the key-fret or spiral scroll favoured in the fourteenth century. These flowers are always in order: peony – spring; pomegranate – summer; chrysanthemum – autumn; and camellia – winter. If more than four flowers are required then other seasonal varieties are added, and the floral borders are carved right down to the yellow layer, which provides a plain background. When flowers are the main motif this, too, is carved down to the yellow layer, and is usually restricted to a single species. One exception is a particularly beautiful box with a design composed of the 'three friends of winter': pine, prunus and bamboo. (The box is also unusual among those with floral motifs in that the plants are carved at different levels: prunus underneath, then bamboo and lastly pine.) This is a favourite motif in the Chinese decorative arts, and each plant represents the attribute of a gentleman – bamboo is seen to bend in the wind of adversity or change but not to break; pine symbolizes endurance and constancy even in adversity, surviving as it does in even the most rocky soil; and prunus blossoms when other plants do not, and represents beauty and independence. Together, the three also symbolize the three religions of China: Confucianism, Taoism and Buddhism. The objects with a main flower motif have borders of the four seasons' flowers like those with landscape designs. A border of clouds is usually seen when the main motif is dragons, while the flower or lotus scrolls provide the border for phoenixes. Dragons are shown amongst clouds, waves and flowers against a diaper background of the type used for land, although one exception can be seen on what is probably the most remarkable item of fifteenth century Imperial carved lacquer: a table decorated with dragons, phoenixes and floral borders. The workmanship is remarkable even by fifteenth century standards, and every millimetre is exquisitely carved.

Round boxes were made with matching borders on the top and bottom, but in some cases the lids have been mismatched with the bases, and so for example a floral top is paired with a cloud base, which should really have a dragon motif on top. The objects were made in great numbers and in standard sizes (a feature of ceramics and cloisonné enamels as well), and it would have been very easy for the lids to get mixed up in the palace storerooms.

A feature of these items as well as those of other techniques – and which is even more common in the Jiajing and Wanli periods – is the removal of the fifth claw of the Imperial dragons. Only the Emperor was entitled to the five-clawed dragons, and so if the piece was to go to anyone else the fifth claw had to be removed. In some cases it was entirely removed; in others a small dot was left.

The removal might have occurred if the object was presented by the Emperor, but the most likely cause for most of the mutilation that took place is described by Shen Defu in the sixteenth century, when lacquer objects were smuggled out of the palace in Beijing and sold in the market which was held once a month near the City God's Temple.

A small group of wares dating to the fifteenth century have Buddhist motifs. One box is decorated with the eight Buddhist emblems: the Chakra or wheel, the conch shell, the umbrella, the canopy, the lotus, the vase, the paired fish, and the entrails or endless knot, while others show two Buddhist lions chasing a brocade ball.

A number of pieces bear an inscription dating the object to either Yongle or Xuande. Many of these are spurious, but while very few can claim to have been put on at the time of manufacture, some appear on fifteenth century pieces. If an inscription was put on at the time of manufacture the mark will be smooth, because it has been cut into the lacquer when it was not quite set: marks added later have slightly rough edges. (Re-lacquered bases with smooth marks can, however, be deceptive.) The inscriptions on fifteenth century pieces usually appear on the left-hand edge of the base, and some reign marks are superimposed on another, or even as with one example have a Yongle and a Xuande mark side by side on the same piece. In Chinese ceramics and in lacquer from other periods the worst interpretation can be attached to reign marks, but with these fifteenth century pieces it is unlikely that deceit was intended. The marks were probably added during palace inventories, and simply reflect the change of view regarding the date of an object: Yongle marks even appear on fourteenth century items.

The non-official wares of the period have, as yet, been less thoroughly studied, but their decoration is similar to that seen on the 'official' wares. Details such as the position of the guideline are sometimes slightly different, and a wider range of shapes is seen including tiered boxes, which although they appear on the 1403 list of gifts sent to Japan have not been found among the 'official' wares. The 'official' style must have continued after the end of the Xuande period but there are very few pieces that can be dated with certainty between then and 1522, the beginning of the Jiajing period, although a small group of objects can with reasonable certainty be dated to the reign of Hongzhi (1488–1505). All the pieces are extremely fragile, and the depth of lacquer is in some cases only about half that on the early fifteenth century 'official' wares. The carving is fine and delicate, shallower but much freer than that on the earlier pieces. The main question this group poses is where they were made: it seems likely that they all came from the same workshop since they resemble one another but no other known pieces. The most important among them is a dish decorated with a scene identified by a 56-character inscription in raised black lacquer on the bottom of the dish as the Orchid Pavilion of Prince Tang. Further inscriptions are incised as part of the front decoration on the lintel and vertical posts of the pavilion; these give a date equivalent to 1489, the name of the artisan Wang Ming, and a place name – Pingliang – in Gansu, a western province. Did Wang Ming inscribe his birthplace, or was the dish actually made in Gansu? The dish is so different from the wares of the eastern provinces that a Gansu provenance seems by no means impossible. It has a much

thinner layer of lacquer, it is polychrome in that the yellow layer forms part of the design, and on this dish – though not on the others in the group – dark green has been used. The diapers are also irregular and undulating, indicating work that does not originate from an officially controlled workshop. Another box, carved in much the same style and with some of the diapers cut through to the yellow, has no inscribed date but it does bear the name Wang Ming and the place name Pingliang. Two more pieces in similar style but without inscriptions have also survived.

From the records of gifts sent to Japan, and particularly those for the years 1406 and 1433, we know that furniture decorated in the *qiangjin* (incised gold) technique was sent there in the fifteenth century. In fact a considerable amount of Chinese *qiangjin* lacquer seems to have been sent during the fourteenth and fifteenth centuries, especially during the Yongle and Xuande periods, despite the fact that the Chinese themselves do not appear to have held it in high regard. The introduction of this technique to the Ryukyuan Islands in the first half of the fifteenth century encouraged the development of *qiangjin* lacquers there, but also led to considerable confusion among art historians, who until quite recently attributed the fine works of these islands to a Chinese provenance. Excavated material from China is in short supply for these wares but one important and recent discovery was a robe-box, excavated from the tomb of Prince Zhu Tan in Jiuxian, Shandong province. This box and the small boxes found within it are made of wood covered in red lacquer, and they are decorated with *qiangjin* designs of a completely different kind to those on the Yuan dynasty sutra boxes. The main decorative motif is a roundel containing

an Imperial dragon among clouds. The rest of the motifs are based either on clouds or the 'classic' scroll, and large areas are left undecorated. Instead of the long fine lines of the sutra boxes the decoration is produced by the use of lots of short thick lines that give a solid, heavy and rather formal appearance.

Three small foliated *qiangjin* boxes can be dated to the first half of the fifteenth century, and again they are different from the Zhu Tan robe-box. Two of these are a pair; the third was excavated at Jiangyang in Jaingsu province. Chinese archaeologists date this last box to the fifteenth century, and indeed its base is inscribed with a cyclical date corresponding to 1345, 1405, 1465 and so on. Of these the most probable date seems to be 1405. All three boxes have bracket foliations producing a sharp vertical ridge, similar to the Yuan monochromes. Another similarity is found with the application of black lacquer over red lacquer to produce purple, which is the colour description applied by the Chinese archaeologists to the excavated box, while the other two show the red lacquer where the black has worn. These boxes are decorated on top with a pair of phoenixes among flowers, the fluted sides have peony scrolls, and the vertical sides have the key-fret design which also reappears on carved wares. The Jiangyang box has an official audience scene on the top, a lotus scroll on the fluted sides and a version of the classic scroll on the vertical sides. None of the foliated boxes have the formality of decoration of the robe-box, and their designs cover the whole surface but lack the rich, solid effect of the gold decoration on the Zhu Tan box. The gold, of course, shows up more brightly when incised through to red than against black, and while the earlier *qiangjin* examples are black the later ones tend to be red.

The fifteenth century saw the development of another decorative lacquer technique – the *tianqi* or filled-in lacquer technique, which is also sometimes known by the Japanese term *zonsei*. (The latter term tends to be used rather loosely and should be avoided, while the Chinese and English terms are both descriptive and precise.) A difficulty arises in distinguishing so-called 'wet' and 'dry' *tianqi*, although the 'dry' technique is the more common. This involved allowing the background lacquer to set hard, and then cutting away a design which was filled with lacquer of contrasting colours, and then polished. The outlines of the design, once smooth, were incised and gilded, a process which not only made the design stand out but also neatened any imperfections in the coloured inlay. The result was a brilliant design that withstood a great deal of wear, since the coloured lacquer was generally inlaid to a depth of about half a millimetre. The technique was sometimes combined with painted decoration. The 'wet'

technique, far less common, inlaid the contrasting lacquer into the top layer of base lacquer while the latter was still wet. Lacquer can only be applied in very thin coats, and so an inlay into just one layer produces a very shallow colour which does not wear well. According to Chinese descriptions of the technique the 'wet' version was not polished – presumably so as not to render the design thinner than it already was. Unsurprisingly, it is very often difficult to distinguish 'wet' *tianqi* from painted wares.

There are two written references to what appears to be *tianqi* lacquer being made in the reign of Xuande (1426–35). One occurs in the details of the life of a lacquerer named Yang Xuan, who is supposed to have been sent to Japan to acquire the gold dust lacquer technique so admired by the Chinese, and imported by them in considerable quantities. However, according to the story, he not only learned the Japanese techniques but invented what sounds like *tianqi*, with which the Japanese were reportedly most impressed. The most magnificent fifteenth century example of *tianqi* lacquer is an Imperial cabinet, on which the design of dragons and phoenixes ties in closely with that on the carved red lacquer table mentioned earlier. On the front of the cabinet each of the ten variously sized drawers is decorated with a dragon and a phoenix flanking the handle. The back of the cabinet features a dragon and phoenix in clouds inside an ogival panel, and four more phoenixes appear against floral scrolls in each of the four corners of the rectangle. Although the box has faded slightly in places, the range of colours is still extraordinary. In addition to black and gold, there is yellow, orange, brown, two different greens and three different reds. There are, however, very few other examples of *tianqi* lacquer which may safely be attributed to the fifteenth century.

The technique of inlaying small thin pieces of iridescent shell taken from the inner layer of the *haliotis* started in the Yuan dynasty, but the technique was further refined in the Ming and Qing dynasties and some of the wares are of a superb quality, and increasingly resemble paintings. Exact dating is a problem because very few of the mother-of-pearl wares are inscribed with a date. One of the earliest Ming examples is a foliated round box dated to the late fourteenth or early fifteenth century, decorated on the lid with an audience scene showing gifts being presented and a border of floral scrolls. Incising the small pieces used in the pictorial wares must have been difficult and was probably done *in situ*, but this box provides detail of textile decoration on the robes, as well as detail on the rocks, trees, and fungi. The box also has a feature seen on earlier monochrome wares, the use of twisted wires – in this case around the main decorative panel.

The fragment of a mother-of-pearl box was recently excavated from the site of the old Yuan capital Dadu, just north of Beijing. It was not found in a tomb, but rather in a building that was being demolished, which did not help dating. It has, however, been placed with reasonable certainty in the early fifteenth century. A landscape is depicted on the fragment and this has been identified as a representation of the Moon Palace, from the legend of the Moon Fairy. The pieces of mother-of-pearl have been selected for their colour, and even the most minute of them has been carefully shaped for roof-tiles, window lattice, clouds, smoke and the individual leaves of trees. Another early fifteenth century dish is interesting on two counts, for on one hand it combines painting in gold lacquer in the centre with mother-of-pearl designs as subsidiary decoration, and on the other it has a bracket-lobed rim of a type frequently seen on fourteenth century porcelain. A spray of cape jasmine in gold is used as a main motif, while a minutely detailed brocade-like scroll in mother-of-pearl covers the fluted well and rim.

The sixteenth and seventeenth centuries

Sixteenth century carved lacquerware shows a decline from the previous period's outstanding quality. Attempts were obviously made to cut down the time involved in carving, particularly by replacing the knife with a gouge as a carving instrument. The few floral borders to be seen in this century lack precision and are less well arranged than earlier examples, and the range of decorative motifs is comparatively reduced, with fewer landscapes. Imperial wares of the Jiajing period (1522–66) are often polychrome (red, green and yellow), but they have very little variety of design and are almost entirely restricted to dragons and phoenixes, the symbols of the Emperor and Empress. But the incorporation of auspicious characters gained in popularity, and the same three that occasionally appear on earlier pieces – *shou* (longevity), *fu* (happiness) and *lu* (wealth) – are used on one box. The *shou* character, filled with flying birds, is set against a diaper background providing the main motif, while the *fu* and *lu* characters are inscribed in two different scripts. The sides of the box are decorated with five-clawed dragons, and the base has a six character Jiajing mark incised and filled with gold.

Some furniture in the form of chairs and cabinets is of a very high quality, and must have been made for the court: one folding chair with a footstool which incorporates five-clawed dragons in the design would certainly have been intended for the Emperor. The chair cannot be dated with certainty either to the Jiajing period or to the early sixteenth century, for the very high standard of carving, the tightness of the design, and the form

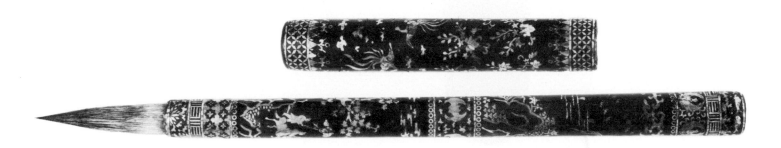

45 China

Above: Travel coffer; Wanli period (1573–1619). Metal handles and mounts set off the contrasting dragons, reversed on the top and bottom. The central motif contains the character for *shou* (long life).

Below: Dish; 1595. The decoration is in the *tianqi* technique with a five-clawed dragon and flaming pearl. The detail (*above*) shows the date of manufacture.

of the peony scrolls on the footstool all suggest an early date, while the form of the dragon adds contradictory evidence.

Few objects survive that can be dated to the short reign of Longqing (1567–72), and towards the end of the next reign, that of Wanli (1573–1619), we see a decline in the popularity of carved lacquer. The 'official' wares of the Wanli period, however, tend to be of a more reliable quality than those of Jiajing. A particularly good example with a design typical of the period is a polychrome dish decorated with a dragon and a phoenix chasing a flaming pearl. The border is divided into four cartouches of flowering plants with birds, between which single flowers are set against a diaper background. The dish is dated 1593. Inscribed dates of the Wanli period are usually very precise, because of the introduction of an eight-character mark which included the cyclical date. Most such dated pieces fall within the last decade of the sixteenth century. Many pieces of both the

Jiajing and the Wanli period suffer, as did earlier pieces, from the removal of the fifth claw of the Imperial dragon, but it is interesting to note that in a number of cases this has been replaced later. Very little lacquer survives from the seventeenth century, either from the end of the Wanli period or from the succeeding reigns of Tianqi (1621–27) and Chongzhen (1628–43), and what there is is characterized by rather shallow carving and poor quality.

Non-official wares of the sixteenth century considerably outnumber the 'official' pieces, and as with seventeenth century examples they are generally of a higher quality. The largest such group is of small round or cylindrical boxes with decoration carved all over the outside including the base – a feature not seen on 'official' boxes during the Ming dynasty. Most of the boxes are red, but a few have a black design carved down to a red background. The decoration is usually of flowers, fruits, birds and flowers, and birds and clouds, with an occasional landscape. The treatment of most subjects is quite different from that in the fifteenth century, for the designs are given far more open space, and instead of being carved to a plain yellow ground they have red diaper grounds. The diapers used are usually those for land and water, rarely air, and only one diaper is used on the background of each piece. Diapers of various kinds – several on one box – are also used on some of the individual fruit, while other fruit on the same box may have a more naturalistic treatment. Occasionally peaches or pomegranates are used but the fruit are usually lichees, although the earlier care to differentiate between species is not seen. Bird and flower motifs are also shown against various diaper backgrounds, and in one case this has been combined with gold lacquer-painting on the inside of the box.

A similar range of designs is also seen on a number of rectangular boxes, made in a singularly impractical form with the two halves of the box kept together by a loose tray inside the box. These boxes, which appear to have been made from the early sixteenth century to the beginning of the seventeenth century, are carved on the top and sides, but unlike the round boxes they have a flat uncarved base devoid of even a footrim. The base, however, is usually decorated – often with a swirling open petal form – and one group of bowls and stem cups have the same type of carved designs as the small boxes. These sixteenth century wares are interesting because they are grooved inside to take a metal lining. The key-fret border often reappears on metal-lined bowls and cups, and this can be seen on a number of carved lacquerwares of both the sixteenth and seventeenth centuries.

The fifteenth century saw the emergence of a group of lacquerwares probably coming from

49 China

Above: Incised lacquer panel; 16th or 17th century. *Tianqi* decoration shows the four-clawed dragon with a flaming pearl.

Above: Dish from Yunnan; 16th century. The main decorative motif consists of bamboo, pine and prunus, the 'three friends of winter'. The unusual border imitates bamboo.

Gansu, and in the sixteenth century there is evidence of another provincial centre many miles from court producing carved lacquer in a distinctive style – this time in Yunnan. The second edition of the *Ge gu yao lun* published in 1462 and the *Ye huobian* published during the reign of Wanli (1573–1619) both refer to Yunnan lacquer. We are told that lacquer workshops were established there as early as the Tang dynasty, but undoubtedly they must have existed by the fifteenth century, and sixteenth century examples can be identified with reasonable certainty. The author of the *Ye huobian* describes Yunnan lacquers as being dull coloured and badly carved, but with other redeeming features. The sixteenth century examples we have are dull red carved to a plain buff background, and their carving has unpolished edges with an occasional 'dragged' look, as if the carving had been done before the lacquer was completely set. The designs are arranged quite differently from the previously mentioned non-official wares, for the decoration is carved very close together, often with quite a lot of small overlapping elements that give the designs a 'busy' and highly textured appearance. Landscapes are rarely used, and the designs more usually show flowers or the 'three friends of winter'. One example of the latter is unique in incorporating various mammals, reptiles and insects, and is also interesting in that it clearly shows the use of concentric ridges in the depiction of

clouds and rocks which is characteristic of these Yunnan wares.

Carved marbled pieces appear to confine their colours to black, red and yellow, but green appears occasionally on pieces dated within the Ming dynasty, as in the case of a cup-stand dated to the fifteenth century. The use of both V- and U-shaped grooves continued until the seventeenth century, but towards the end of the sixteenth century the V-shaped grooves became more popular. The decoration was still restricted almost entirely to designs based on the 'classic' scroll or on cloud scrolls, but the skill of the craftsmen in adapting these to fit particular vessel shapes is remarkable. Many of the objects to which this technique was applied are round, lobed, hexagonal or octagonal, and so the designs tended to be arranged in concentric bands with adjustments in number and size of the individual motifs as the bands moved outwards. A rare example of characters being carved as part of the design can be seen on one box, where the lid's central medallion comprises the longevity character, surrounded by four other characters which can be translated as 'May there be perfect peace throughout the world.'

In the late sixteenth and early seventeenth centuries carved marbled lacquer was combined with other techniques such as mother-of-pearl inlay. One square, slightly lobed box has broad borders of carved marbled technique using 'classic' scroll design surrounding a mother-of-pearl landscape, which is enclosed in a mother-of-pearl decorative border. Another seventeenth century box and a similarly dated dish combine carved marbled lacquer with a landscape painted in gold. Carved marbled lacquer scrolls are also combined with ordinary carved lacquer designs of landscapes, birds and flowers, with the carved lacquer on top and the carved marbled lacquer underneath. Two beautiful trays, one round and one square, are particularly well-carved examples of this combination, but their date has yet to be agreed. And, while the technique of carved marble lacquer probably continued into the early part of the Qing dynasty, its popularity had waned by the end of the seventeenth century.

Akin to the carved marbled wares is another but less common type of lacquer – flat marbled ware. Despite various interpretations of Chinese texts that seem to claim an early date for them, there is as yet no evidence that they were made before the sixteenth century. The technique involved building up a design in relief-moulded lacquer and ash, and then applying layers of different coloured lacquer over this raised design, in the way used with carved marble. When this was completed the whole surface of the vessel was ground down to a smooth finish producing a coloured pattern rather than a relief: the most common designs are those

Above: Stem cup; 16th century. The V-shaped grooves are carved through layers of red and black lacquer to a buff ground. These succeeded U-shaped grooves in popularity.

incorporating spiral scrolls. There are some very rare examples of pictorial decoration, and a few early seventeenth century examples of flowers and birds, but such specific designs did not work very well in this technique.

There is very little evidence of *qiangjin* (incised gold) lacquer until the second half of the sixteenth century, which has been attributed to the rise in popularity of *tianqi* (filled-in) lacquer. But the *Xiu Shi lu* (Records of Decoration of Lacquer, preface

dated 1625), which describes lacquer techniques in the late sixteenth century, records the use of *qiangjin* on both black and red backgrounds, with close gold lines to make the design more prominent. There are several examples in Japan of late sixteenth century *qiangjin* technique which are decorated with bird and flower designs, but the lacquer on these is very thin and they are extremely fragile. One seal-box relates quite well to the Zhu Tan box, but its quality is not as good and the decoration is spaced differently. They are similar in shape and in their bronze mounts, and both have a roundel of dragon in clouds as their main motif, but the border designs are rather different and the decoration on the seal-box is much looser. The most impressive of the sixteenth century *qiangjin* lacquers is a box which carries a well-executed example of figures in a landscape on its lid, of a type seen in other techniques. The gold lines are close together and give a richness to the decoration. The brocade effect on the borders, and the enclosing of the side decorations within cartouches, are also seen on the carved wares.

In contrast to the very few pieces of *tianqi* lacquer remaining from the earlier periods a considerable number of items have survived from the reign of Jiajing (1522–66), and several are inscribed with a reign mark. A typical example of these is a five-lobed box which uses characters as its main motif. The central medallion on the lid contains the *shou* (longevity) character, and the flat top of each of the five lobes is decorated with another auspicious character set against a diaper background. The vertical sides of the box are decorated with floral designs, while each curved section of the lobes shows a dragon in clouds. This is one of many pieces where the fifth claw of the dragon has been obliterated – in this case by the addition of a small cloud. Another example of surreptitious tampering with the evidence can be seen on a cabinet which, like the box, makes use of versions of the *shou* character in its decoration; here, along the sides of the lid. The cabinet originally had a six character Jiajing reign mark, reading *da Ming Jiajing nian zhi* (great Ming made this in the reign of Jiajing). The two middle characters giving the name of the reign period have been removed and those of Xuande (1426–35) added. The four original characters are in the style popular in the Jiajing period, and so the deception is not convincing. The box is nevertheless very attractive, carrying a floral scroll round the base and a variety of flowers, fruit and fungi.

A significant number of *tianqi* lacquers have also been preserved from the Wanli period (1573–1619). Many of these are inscribed with a reign mark, and in the majority of cases this includes a cyclical date. One very high-quality piece is a cylindrical brush-pot, with an inscribed Wanli mark giving a cyclical date equivalent to 1601. The brush-pot is decorated with four ogival panels containing two five-clawed dragons in clouds above mountains and waves (dragons are shown in this way on court robes). The dragons face each other across a *shou* character and two flaming pearls, under two clouded swastikas, while the background outside the panels is a diaper composed of swastikas inside squares: a typical ground in the Wanli period. (The swastika

sign is merely a shortened version of the character *wan* implying long life or blessing; it has none of the connotations associated with it in Europe.) Dragons are also the main motif on a wardrobe in the *tianqi* technique. After the end of the reign of Wanli there was a decline in the standard of *tianqi* pieces which included a lot of overpainting, but they continued to be made until the end of the Ming dynasty, although the technique did not regain a high standard until the reign of Qianglong, in the Qing dynasty.

A manuscript from the late sixteenth century describes various types of gold painting on lacquer, as well as raised designs imitating Japanese lacquers and decoration with gold foil. But although the Chinese were familiar with Japanese lacquers as early as the fifteenth century and were most impressed by them, there is very little evidence of the Chinese imitating the Japanese use of sprinkled gold and different shades of gold, and the majority of the surface gold decoration of this period is simply painted. The earlier examples of gold-painted decoration on the Song dynasty boxes from the Ruian Pagoda appear to be followed by a gap until the sixteenth century, and there are no references to gold-painted wares among those sent to Japan in the fourteenth and fifteenth centuries, and none in the Imperial Palace collection before the Wanli period (1573–1619). A pair of very impressive drug cabinets, however, dated to the reign of Wanli with a six character mark on the back, is in Beijing. They are lacquered in black, and the outsides of each of the doors and sides is decorated with two cartouches containing a pair of five-clawed dragons in clouds chasing a flaming pearl. There are also fruiting sprays against a diaper background. The fronts of all the drawers (there are about sixty) are also decorated with gold-painted dragons flanking each handle. Inside the doors two panels depict flowers growing from ornamental rocks with birds and butterflies, and the same decoration is used on the back with the reign mark.

There are some magnificent Ming and Qing wardrobes, and several fall within the sixteenth century. Characteristically these have cupboards above for hat-boxes, and one example was known to have two square hat-boxes which unfortunately have now disappeared. Five-clawed Imperial dragons appear in gold-painted decoration on the front of this wardrobe, set above mountains and waves and against very regular lotus scrolls, while the sides and the back have landscapes. The linear design has been painted in red over which the gold has been applied, the normal practice on these wares. If the background is black the linear design is painted in red and then gilded; a red background has a black design. This enables the designs to stand out better.

Gold-painted lacquer designs are commonly

found combined with basketwork, sometimes with the addition of painted decoration in colour or mother-of-pearl. A bowl which has been in Europe since the sixteenth century is of a type probably made in considerable numbers for the Chinese domestic market, and would not have been specially preserved in that country. The outside is basketry, and the inside is black lacquer decorated with a floral spray, fish and water-weeds, and edged with a band of flowers in on porcelain in the sixteenth century, and it is also found on lacquerware. This is the so-called *kinrande* technique (a Japanese term meaning gold brocade), and in porcelain was applied to either blue and white or enamelled pieces. The gold foil was stuck on with an adhesive like egg white, and trimmed and incised to create a floral design. A few lacquer examples remain, usually red – as with one large dish in Japan, which is possibly the best known piece decorated in this style. The flat

Above: Twelve-sided dish; 16th century. The panels of *kinrande* (gold brocade) decoration contain birds, animals and plants. The dish stands on a separate pedestal.

cartouches. These have been painted in gold with the addition of a little painted red lacquer.

Gold-painted decoration was also combined in the seventeenth century with carved marbled decoration. Typically this is seen on dishes with carved marbled scrolls on the outside and gold-painted designs – frequently landscapes – on the red or black lacquer inside. Another decorative technique requiring surface gold was developed

central area has a beautiful pastoral scene with trees and flowering plants, among which birds fly and animals play. The well of the dish is decorated with floral designs, while the flat rim has a key-fret border. Another very simple version of the technique appears on a bowl decorated with flying birds and leaf sprays. While these wares were much admired in Japan and in the West very few have been preserved in China, and the technique

Above: Detail of cabinet; 18th century.

Above right: Stem cup; 17th century. Gold designs on a sprinkled gold background provide a rare example of a Chinese imitation of the Japanese *hiramaki-e* technique.

Opposite page, left: Pair of ewers, possibly used for sweet syrups; 18th century. The spouts emerge from fiercely grimacing masks and the central section is flat for easy handling.

Opposite page, right: Box; late 16th or early 17th century. At least ten different kinds of leaf are depicted in the mother-of-pearl inlay.

appears to be peculiar to the mid-sixteenth century. One of the very few attempts by the Chinese to imitate Japanese gold lacquerware – with sprinkled gold and different shades of gold – can be seen on a small stem cup dated to the seventeenth century and decorated with emblems taken from the 'eight precious things' and the eight Buddhist emblems: butterflies and flowers in a slightly raised decoration. The background is uneven gold and the decorative motifs are in different shades of gold.

Landscapes continued to be the favourite motif on mother-of-pearl lacquer in the late Ming. The Moon Palace appears again on a sixteenth century octagonal box, and the detail provided by the tiny pieces of shell is once again enhanced by careful incisions. The borders are cloud-shaped half cartouches with floral decoration, and in typical period style these are surrounded by a diaper background. One of the few precisely dated pieces is a round box with a main motif of figures in landscape, and landscape side panels with a diaper ground between them. The date, equivalent to 1537, is incised on a pillar of one of the pavilions in the main motif. Some examples use the same bird and flower designs seen in paintings, and a few rare examples show a Korean influence. This is seen in the floral scrolling device used in the centre of one sixteenth century octagonal dish, the sides of which are decorated with charming panels of animals in a landscape. Few examples seem to

have been made for the court, but an octagonal box is decorated with a five-clawed dragon. Here the pieces of shell are rather thicker and the piece is of less high quality than the landscape examples, but it has a Longqing mark (1567–72) and is also inscribed *Yuyongjian* in the same way as used with carved lacquer. A seventeenth century group of objects makes particular use of larger, thicker pieces of shell with incised details. The effect is formal but effective, and the items, often boxes, are well made.

The earliest polychrome designs on lacquer were painted in lacquer, but again the technique seems to have lapsed between the sixth and sixteenth centuries. It seems unlikely that such an obvious decorative technique would have been abandoned completely, and examples from the intervening centuries may well yet be discovered. The sixteenth century examples are difficult to distinguish from 'wet' *tianqi* items, but a considerable number of very attractive examples of painted lacquer appear combined with finely plaited bamboo. Some of these basketry examples have the added bonus of either precise or cyclical dates. One of these is a large rectangular box dated 1600, with a red panel of decoration inside painted with rocks, flowers and several pairs of birds including phoenixes, cranes and ducks. The outside of the lid has three landscape scenes, the central one showing an archery contest that can be identified from the 'Biographies of Empresses and

A considerable amount of high-quality painted lacquerware was produced throughout the seventeenth century including some large items of furniture, but one of the most interesting is a terrestrial globe dated 1623. The names of the countries are given phonetically in Chinese characters, and a long inscription includes geographical and philosophical notes which have been 'carefully noted by the ministers Yang mano (Emmanual Diaz) and Ling Huamin (Nicholas Longobardi) from the West'.

The Qing dynasty (1644–1912)

With the Qing dynasty, power in China once again fell into alien hands, this time those of the Manchus. But the transition between the Ming and Qing dynasties was not particularly disruptive and the Manchus declared themselves the preservers of Ming heritage; they even dealt leniently with Ming loyalist factions. China was returned to a state of internal peace and economic prosperity, while her influence over neighbouring states was once again extended. The eighteenth century and the reign of Qianlong (1735–96) was the last 'golden age' of Chinese imperial tradition – indeed, the virtues of Chinese government and society were extolled by Voltaire! Many Europeans developed a taste for Chinese objects, especially during the reigns of Kangxi (1661–1722) and Qianlong, and examples of Chinese art

Royal Concubines of the Tang dynasty'. There are two seals inside the lid; one gives the date and the other claims to be 'the seal of Jin Chenshan', who must have been the painter rather than the maker of the box. Jin Chenshan's seal appears on another box painted in a similar style. Many of the basketry pieces include ornamental borders painted in gold: one example is dated 1600 and shows on its lid a horseman riding towards a pavilion. Other examples have gold diaper grounds included in the design. Gold is also used for outlines on a charming red tray decorated with birds and flowers, and inscribed with a cyclical date equivalent to 1606.

Above: Qianlong panel; 18th century. The decoration in four colours shows the Sichuan campaigns led by General Agui. Panels of this type were hung in the Imperial palaces.

Opposite page, left: Tray decorated in *tianqi;* late 18th century. The detail (*below*) shows the inscription on the base, 'eight-sided lucky tray'.

Opposite page, right: Box; 18th century. The shape was inspired by chrysanthemum petals. The base (*below*) shows a poem by the Qianlong Emperor, dated 1777, incised and gilded.

exported to Europe had a lasting effect on European decorative arts.

After the decline in Ming carved lacquer there is none that can be attributed to the first reign of the Qing dynasty, that of Shunzhi (1644–61), even though thirty factories were set up in the palace in 1680 to make metalwork and carve jade, lacquer and ivory for the court. Nor is it possible to identify carved lacquer from the reign of Kangxi (1662–1722) or that of Yongzheng (1723–35). But the reign of the Qianlong Emperor (1736–95) saw a resurgence of interest in carved lacquer, and many examples have survived both in the Imperial Palace collection and in Europe. The colour of the red carved lacquer has been described as strong but dull compared with the purple-tinged red of early Ming lacquers; the edges of the carving are sharp and unpolished, and the designs tend to be very detailed and highly decorative. The most splendid example is a throne which is said to have come from the Imperial Hunting Palace at Nan haizi. The carving is a *tour de force,* with amazingly complex decoration including dragons, landscapes, clouds, birds, bats, peaches, floral scrolls, emblems and characters, all deeply carved (mainly in red lacquer) down to layers of light green, dark green, yellow and brown. Other items of furniture survive but these are on a

smaller scale, and the majority of items are round covered boxes and bowls.

The addition of all kinds of characters is a feature of the period, and the carved lacquers sometimes include descriptions of the piece itself. Characters are also a feature of the decoration of a bowl and cover which incorporates the characters *wan shou wu jiang* (ten thousand years without end), an inscription also seen on *famille verte* plates apparently made for the sixtieth birthday of the Emperor Kangxi in 1713. The carved lacquer bowl may also have been made to commemorate a birthday. The official Imperial workshops were not destroyed until 1869 (during the Taiping uprisings) and a good deal of carved lacquer was produced in the late eighteenth and the nineteenth centuries, but the artistic flair had gone, and one eminent art historian admirably summed up the later Qing period by remarking that, 'like Sèvres porcelain, these lacquers fulfil very well the task of looking expensive, but they must not be mistaken for art'.

Two types of Qianlong lacquerware may be seen as imitating carved lacquer. The first is moulded lacquer, to which has been added *appliqué* designs like those on real carved lacquer. The second is a group of 'official' lacquerware in the shape of covered bowls, dishes and boxes made

on a very thin, light base (their walls are only one millimetre thick), and covered in vermilion lacquer. The pieces are undecorated except for their fluted form, which resembles a chrysanthemum. A number of these have reached Western collections, and bear inscriptions of poems by the Qianlong Emperor together with precise dates. Translations of some inscriptions have been made, and one reads:

> It is made in the shape of a fragrant chrysanthemum
> But compared with the chrysanthemum it is more delicate
> As I sip tea I am pleased to compare it
> With taking dew from this freshly picked flower
> Imperial brush of Qianlong in *bingshen* [1776] year

Flat marbled lacquer continued to be made in the Qing dynasty and has been found on boxes of the period, but the most impressive examples are seen in furniture. One seventeenth century chair has a seemingly random design in the *xipi* (rhinoceros skin) technique already mentioned.

Tianqi lacquerware re-emerged in the Qianglong period (1736–95), often of a very good quality and many with reign marks, but it is noticeable that the minute decoration details are often painted in. An octagonal tray is typical of the style, with a very precisely drawn and positioned design giving a highly decorative yet formal effect. Once again the *shou* (longevity) character – this time in its roundel form – plays an important part in the decoration of the tray, combined with phoenixes and bats. Bats are a favourite period motif; the character for 'bat' is a homophone for the happiness character and so its symbolic effect is important. To the Qianlong reign mark a further inscription describing the piece as a 'lucky eight-sided tray' has been added. Similarly stylized decoration can be seen on an ingot-shaped three-tiered box which has a finely carved red lacquer stand: the decoration there is equally stylized but quite different in concept from that on the box.

Various developments in mother-of-pearl inlaid lacquer occurred during the Qing dynasty. The seventeenth century saw the introduction of sprinkled mother-of-pearl grounds, more precise colour selection of pieces, the addition of colour tints to the back of the shell fragments, and the use of sprinkled and foil gold and silver. Some of the most impressive items are thrones and screens, and a number of these were sent to Europe. A particularly magnificent screen comes from the

Left: Table with elaborate mother-of-pearl inlay of landscape scenes, diapers and plant designs.

Below: Cabinet; Ming dynasty (1368–1644). The doors and the drawers inside are decorated with mother-of-pearl floral motifs, some of which have probably been tinted.

reign of the Kangxi Emperor (1662–1722). It is almost 3 metres (9 feet) high and was made in three panels, with very dramatic mounts decorated in geometric designs with silver foil. The panels all have mother-of-pearl landscapes, with the mother-of-pearl set in black lacquer; the background is red overpainted with gold. The central panel is the most spectacular and depicts a landscape with beautiful pavilions: to one side is the figure of Xi Wangmu, the Queen Mother of the West. Tiny sprinkled fragments of mother-of-pearl can be seen on the steps, grounds and clouds, while the rest of the picture is composed with small carefully shaped pieces, even for such details as the minute end-tiles of the roof and the individual needles on a pine tree.

Sprinkled silver as well as gold and silver foil is seen on some seventeenth century mother-of-pearl inlaid dishes, with formal floral borders and landscape scenes in the central panel. Some small eighteenth century cups use mother-of-pearl which has been tinted, and then applied to a white base to show up the colour: the designs are rather formal and they may have been made in an 'official' factory. Although they do not have reign marks, some of the cups in this style do carry

inscribed poems or the seal mark of the maker. One is decorated with a stylized petal design using various diapers within the petals, a device also seen on a hexagonal box of the period and which may have been influenced by Japanese wares.

Silver linings also appear on Qing mother-of-pearl wares, and one, a cup in gold lacquer, is peach-shaped. Its mother-of-pearl decoration shows bats among clouds. But much freer designs can be seen on some pieces which combine mother-of-pearl and gold-painted details: five such early eighteenth century boxes belong to a cabinet which is decorated in painted lacquer and inlaid with gold and silver. The boxes themselves have mother-of-pearl, gold and inlay, with fish and lotus leaf designs. Mother-of-pearl also appears with lacquer decoration on to metal, rather than pieces lined with metal. A Kangxi period pewter teapot is decorated with lacquer applied directly on to the metal, and the mother-of-pearl inlay shows women in a garden. The decoration also includes the use of sprinkled mother-of-pearl. Allied to such work is that which includes inlays of bone, hardstones and ivory, where the pieces are often carved in high relief, and combined with painted lacquer decoration.

The last lacquer technique of any importance was that known as 'Coromandel' or 'Bantam' work, introduced in the seventeenth century. Lacquered, as opposed to hardwood, furniture in China had normally been used in palaces, temples, and places of entertainment rather than the home, but the European export trade now opened a new market. A lot of lacquerware was exported to Europe by the East India Company: lacquered trunks are mentioned in records as early as 1683. By 1690 the Company issued instructions that only the highest quality wares should be purchased, and records from the cargo sales of three ships at East India House at the turn of the century show the popularity of vast numbers of items such as screens, cabinets and beds.

By the eighteenth century the markets for Fujian lacquer included Java, Japan, India, Mecca and Russia. Beijing and Suzhou were the centres from which carved lacquers were obtained, while painted wares came from Guangdong and Fuzhou. The quality of the Guangdong lacquers was by all accounts variable, for apparently lacquerers waited until the boats docked to see what the latest European fashion was, and then rushed off to produce goods to accommodate it: the result was hastily made and poor-quality lacquer. Chinese lacquer-artists certainly accommodated European tastes. Cabinet patterns were sent to China in Charles II's reign, and the author of *A Discourse of Trade Coyn and Paper Credit*, published in 1697, noted that 'artisans were sent out to introduce patterns suitable for sale at home'. Models were also sent in the reigns of Queen Anne and George I, resulting in Chinese versions of European desks, dressing-tables and chairs. The process worked in reverse as well, and both Japanese and Chinese lacquers were copied in England, France and Holland: Chippendale was one successful cabinet-maker who was known to use Chinese models.

Many of the exported items were made in Bantam work, named from the Javanese port from which the Dutch East India Company shipped them to Europe, but it is now usually called Coromandel, from the Coromandel coast of south-east India, another area used in transshipment from China. Such lacquer combines a number of techniques. It is usually produced on a wooden base to which a coat of white base material is applied, mixed with lacquer to a thickness of about one centimetre (⅜ inch). This white layer is rubbed down and given a few layers of brown or black lacquer, and the design is then cut into the white base material. Pigments of various colours – usually oil-based – are added to the design. The decoration is often carved so as to leave outlines in relief but the pigment is not built up to the level of the relief lines. The wares produced were quite vulnerable to damage and

the pigment was inclined to loosen, but cabinet interiors, and other pieces that did not suffer wear and tear, have often survived well.

Some of the finest examples of Coromandel lacquer are large folding six- or twelve-panel screens. Some of the best were made for home market presentations, and have inscriptions giving the date and the occasion of the gift. One of these is dated 1690 and was a birthday present; another is dated 1672 and was a retirement present for the Governor of Yunnan. The latter depicts a festival in the women's quarter of the palace, and shows 162 female figures; the same subject is shown on another screen in Beijing. All the dated pieces were made in the seventeenth century, but those made for export are undated.

Some screen panels were made into mirror-frames, cabinets and table-tops, while chests and trunks were popular as blanket chests in English country houses. Among the most popular items, however, were cabinets with brass handles, locking-plates and corner-mounts, often set on stands that were carved in Europe. A well-preserved Coromandel cabinet of this design, dated to the reign of Kangxi, is decorated in a number of colours including white, blue, green, red and brown. A landscape appears across the front doors, and a pair of mandarin ducks are shown on a pond with aquatic plants on the sides.

Coromandel lacquers continued to be made and exported throughout the eighteenth and nineteenth centuries, although their quality declined.

Modern China

Lacquer craftsmanship continues today in the People's Republic of China, and while some of the artistic styles may have changed, many aspects can be traced back through the centuries.

The main centres of lacquer production are the same as those of the dynastic periods: Beijing, Sichuan, Fujian and Jiangsu, although lacquer workshops are also found in Shanghai and in the provinces of Shansi, Gansu, Guangdong, Jiangsi and Guizhou. With the exception of some furniture, screens and large pictures, most items are

bottles, trays, bowls, boxes, tea sets, cups, jewellery and imitations of early lacquer.

The Beijing workshops are particularly well known for their carved lacquer, and the Beijing Carved Lacquerware Studio specializes in traditional carved red ware. The lacquer is applied to a base of either wood or bronze, and the decoration is often highlighted with *appliqués* in jade or ivory. The number of layers of lacquer on these pieces is not so great as those on the finest Ming dynasty examples and the carving does not have the same precision and polish, but the pieces frequently have great charm. This is particularly true of the boxes made in bird or animal shapes which display the Chinese genius for combining realistic animal forms with abstract decoration.

The two main lacquerware centres in Sichuan are Chongqing and Chengdu. The Chengdu workshops specialize in objects decorated with incised designs filled with gold powder and finally polished, while Chongqing produces designs painted on the surface of the lacquer, and others in inlaid shell fragments. Shansi units, like the Qishan County Handicraft Studio, have developed an interesting archaism, producing figures which seek to imitate, in lacquer and inlaid shell, the bronze figures with gold and silver inlays of earlier periods. Several studios in Fuzhou, in the province of Fujian, make beautiful, light, 'baseless' lacquer items. These have painted decorations, some composed of traditional formal bird and flower designs and using gold on the surface of the lacquer. In contrast, other designs are more naturalistic and emerge from the shadows of layers of translucent varnish.

It is, however, the Yangzhou craftsmen in Jiangsu who produce lacquerware most ideologically in tune with modern China, such as screens and pictures showing modern Chinese life. These use carefully prepared jade, ivory and shell inlays in a heroic style that can also be seen in some modern Chinese paintings. Most of the items are made for export, for the Chinese are mindful of the example of their forebears, who realized that lacquer – precious, strong and light in weight – was an ideal item of trade.

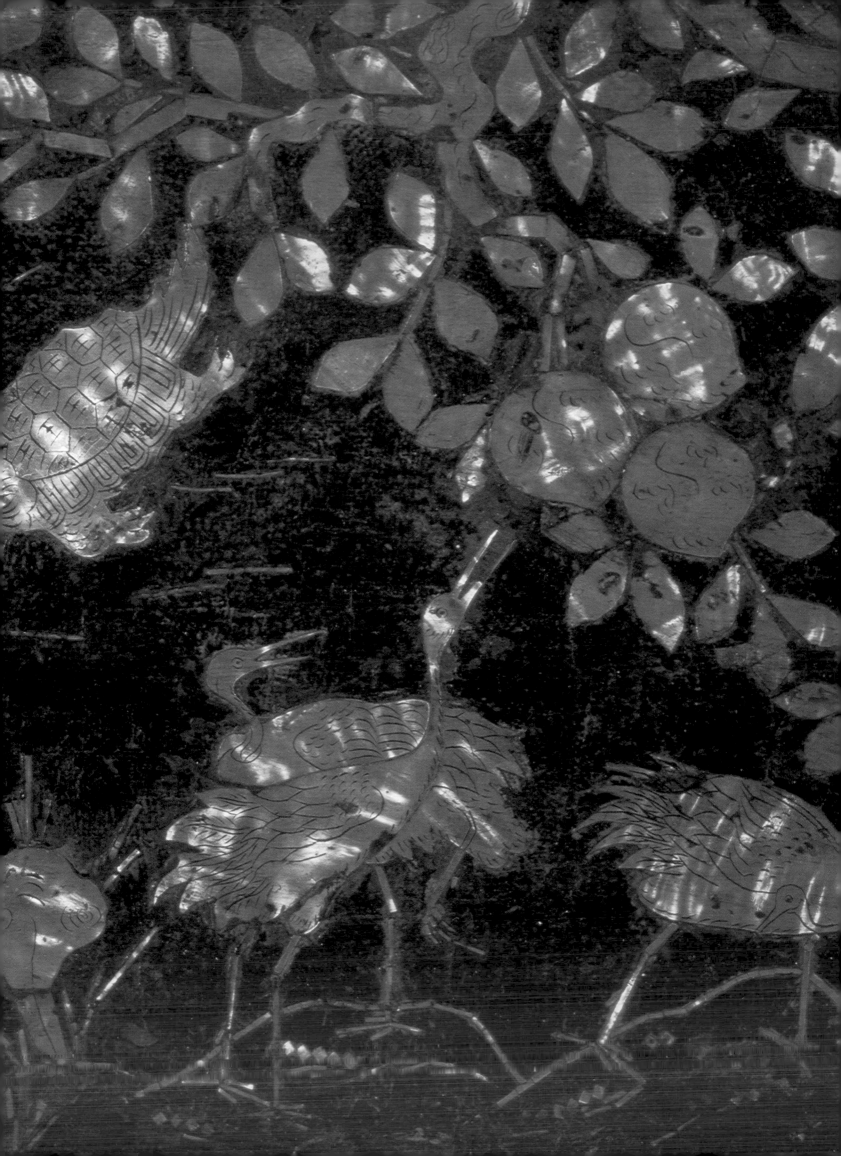

2

Korea

Though relatively little known in the West, the culture and art of Korea are considerably more than appendices to those of China and Japan. The Korean peninsula has frequently played a crucial role in the transmission of cultural influences from continental Asia to Japan, but its own arts have adapted and modified Chinese styles and techniques to distinctively Korean ends.

Chinese political control was established over northern Korea after 108 BC, and the earliest lacquers to have been found, such as a famous basket decorated with paragons of filial piety, belong properly to the history of Chinese lacquer; but such items, luxury imports from a prestigious culture, must have inspired a native tradition of painted lacquer which flourished in the early centuries AD under local Korean dynasties.

Above: Lobed tray with mother-of-pearl inlay.

Opposite: Detail of table-top; 18th century. The landscape scene is in mother-of-pearl.

A variety of lacquer-producing tree, *Rhus trichocarpa*, seems to be indigenous to Korea, but tradition suggests that the major source of lacquer for craft production, *Rhus verniciflua*, was transplanted from China, presumably together with the technology to exploit it. This must have taken place during the Han dynasty (206 BC–221 AD), particularly after 108 BC. The Chinese administration centred on Lelang (Nangnang in Korean), and it was the excavation of this site by Japanese archaeologists in 1931 that yielded the earliest examples discovered in Korea.

A turbulent history and a harsh climate have not furthered the preservation of fragile artefacts; consequently, surviving early Korean lacquerwork is extremely rare and fragmentary. Broken pieces of what may have been vessels are known, but more impressive are excavated panels and lacquered wood coffins. The latter, associated with the tombs of the kings of Koguryŏ who ruled over northern Korea from the fourth to the seventh centuries, are decorated with red and white floral motifs on a black ground. White is unobtainable as a true lacquer colour, and entails some form of oil-based painting. That a wide palette was in fact used at this time is suggested by contemporary murals in Koguryŏ tombs, where powerful abstract and floral scrolling, beasts, plants and human figures are vividly portrayed in art which develops the Han Chinese love of motion.

Southern Korea, divided between the kingdoms of Paekche and Silla, was also capable of producing sophisticated painted lacquers in the first centuries of independence. They were the means whereby the technique was transmitted to Japan. Japan obtained a first acquaintance with Buddhism from Korea, and with it the religious art necessary to adorn great temples and monasteries. The models for many of these places of worship were Korean; Korean craftsmen built and adorned them, and it is in Japan that the finest early Korean lacquer is preserved. The Hōryū-ji in Nara holds two such pieces, the lacquered wood sculpture of the Boddhisattva Avalokitesvara known as Kudara Kannon, and the mid-seventh century painted lacquer shrine known as the Tamamushi shrine (illustrated in the chapter on Japanese lacquer, on page 72). The name derives from the beetle *Chrysocroa elegans* (*tamamushi* in Japanese), the iridescent wing-cases of which are held by the shrine's open-work metal fittings in a technique restricted to Korea. The painted panels depicting scenes from the life of the Buddha are executed in the true lacquer colours of red, green and yellow on a black ground, in a style which again is rich in movement and action. Probably made by Koreans in Japan, the Tamamushi shrine is a telling monument to the quality of Korean art of the period. No such

object survives in Korea itself. Nor do any examples survive in Korea of religious sculpture in the 'dry lacquer' technique of moulding lacquer-soaked cloth.

Still less do any traces survive in lacquer of Korea's artistic intercourse with Tang dynasty China (618–906 AD). No Korean equivalent of the Shōsōin storehouse in Japan exists to preserve the luxury lacquers imported from China, or the native imitations which doubtless existed. It is possible that pieces inlaid with mother-of-pearl in the Shōsōin itself may actually be Korean. Certainly, at this period, the technique known in Chinese as *ping-tuo* must have been transmitted to Korea, and it was a style which was totally to dominate Korean lacquering down to the present century. Known in Korean as *najŏn*, the technique entails inlaying fragments of various shells and other materials in a lacquer ground to form a design; the lacquer itself has no decorative role other than that of being a lustrous background. The plastic or textural qualities of the material so ably exploited in China and Japan were ignored in Korea in favour of a full exploration of the possibilities of this Tang Chinese technique, which continued long after its abandonment in China.

The Koryŏ period (936–1392 AD)

The oldest surviving masterpieces of the *najŏn* technique of inlaid lacquer date from the Koryŏ period, when Korea was unified by kings of the Wang family ruling from a capital at Kaesŏng. Many crafts flourished under royal patronage, and the ceramics of the period are in collections all over the world. Only a handful of lacquer pieces survive, however, but they are enough to suggest what has been lost.

It seems likely that a continuous tradition of decorative inlaying existed in Korea from its introduction in the seventh century. The *Koryŏ-sa*, 'History of Koryŏ', published in 1423 contains references to such work in the eleventh century, but there is more powerful evidence from the early twelfth century in the account of a Chinese envoy to Korea. Xu Jing wrote his *Illustrated Account of an Embassy to Koryŏ in the Xuanhe Period* in 1124, when with typical Sinocentric condescension he admitted that, though the quality of Korean lacquer was rather poor, the Koreans did do fine mother-of-pearl inlay work; and he singles out for praise the production of saddles decorated in this way. Chinese lacquer of the period was dominated by severe and elegant undecorated pieces, with no inlay.

Xu's mention of saddles – secular and practical objects – is interesting in that a majority of existing Koryŏ inlaid lacquers have specifically religious functions, as containers for Buddhist texts or for paraphernalia such as rosaries associ-

ated with Buddhist worship. Partly this may be because of better conditions for preservation, over the centuries, in monasteries; but there does seem to have been a close association between inlaid lacquers and the Buddhist faith, of which the Koryŏ royal family were pious patrons. Again according to the *Koryŏ-sa*, a special workshop called the *Chŏnham Tŏgam* was established in 1272 by King Wŏnjong to manufacture accoutrements (including caskets for Buddhist sutras) to be used in worship by the queen and court ladies.

The decoration of *najŏn* lacquers in the Koryŏ period draws on a restricted repertoire of motifs. Typically, the surface of the sutra boxes, which are of high rectangular shape with a coffered lid, is completely covered with bands of the formal floral scroll known in Chinese as *xiang cao*, 'fragrant grasses', and in Japanese as *hōsōge*, 'precious emblem flower'. The scrolling is executed, usually on a dark brown ground, in an unnaturalistic, geometrically precise manner which breaks with the traditions of decoration assimilated from Tang China and is distinctively Korean. Other decorative elements are all subordinated to this floral scrolling. Some sutra boxes carry the names of the texts for which they were designed, or carry characters used as a way of keeping a large number of boxes in order. These may be in inlaid mother-of-pearl or else are done in open-work cut metal. One very fine circular rosary box now in the Taima-dera temple in

Nara, Japan, is boldly inlaid with large Sanskrit letters representing the abbreviation of the name Akṣobhya, a Buddha particularly revered by the Chinon (Chinese, *Zhenyan*) sect.

Just as Chinese decorative motifs were modified in Korea, so techniques of manufacture were developed which were to become characteristic of Korean lacquerwork. Though inlay was mainly in mother-of-pearl, tortoiseshell was used in conjunction with it. Objects with wooden cores were given a coating of lacquer-soaked hemp before inlay was applied, glued in place and lacquered over until it was totally concealed. Only when the lacquer was polished down, probably with charcoal among other abrasives, did the design reappear perfectly flush with the surrounding lustrous lacquer. The semi-transparent tortoiseshell was sometimes applied over red or green pigments in an originally Chinese technique called *fu hong*, 'covered red', or *fu cai*, 'covered colours' in Chinese. Some pieces show traces of gold lacquer applied as a final stage.

A unique feature of these lacquers, and one which has no Chinese precedent, is the use of metal wires inlaid in the decoration. The wires are generally finely twisted and may be either of a very pure silver, when they are usually confined to decorative use, or of a whitish copper alloy, more usual where support for exposed sections such as corners and edges was required.

Although objects with a religious function

Left: Vase; 15th century. The brown and black mottled lacquer is decorated with three bands of lotus scrolls and birds in flight inlaid in mother-of-pearl. Although decorative motifs became larger, there was no dramatic departure from Koryŏ period work.

predominate among surviving Koryŏ lacquers, secular items also exist. These seem chiefly associated with cosmetics. An example is a small flattened bottle probably used to contain some type of unguent oil. Boxes are less rare. They include one six-lobed example, and more than one crescent-shaped specimen. Four crescents would fit round a circular central box to form a set of five containers. Exactly such a set, with a matching tray, was in the collection of the last monarch of Korea during the early part of this century, but it has since disappeared and is today known only from photographs.

Koryŏ lacquered cosmetic-boxes raise more forcibly than do the Buddhist objects the difficult question of the relationship between ceramics, metalwork and lacquer at this period. In all three media inlaying was an important (almost the major) decorative technique, and scholarly opinion has varied over the years as to which of the three came first. It is the ceramics which have been most fully investigated, elegant high-fired stonewares glazed in a variety of shades of light green (often called 'celadon') and inlaid with geometric and pictorial motifs in contrasting clays. The designs are often the same as those found on lacquerware, while the widespread use of clay inlay of two colours is reminiscent of the contrast in lacquer between mother-of-pearl and tortoiseshell.

Despite the survival in relatively large numbers of Koryŏ ceramics, there are grounds for arguing that it was lacquer which influenced the ceramics and stimulated the development of clay inlay, a technique little practised in China. We have seen that the Chinese ambassador Xu Jing made specific mention of lacquer inlaid with mother-of-pearl, but his writings contain no reference to the inlaid ceramics which would have appeared equally exotic to his eyes. He does, however, mention the production of green-glazed ceramics *without* inlay. This would suggest that inlaid lacquers were being produced before the inlaid ceramics. Furthermore, where exact parallels of form exist between lacquer and ceramic objects such forms are far more natural to the worker in wood than to the potter. For example, sets of five cosmetic-boxes – a central lobed one and four others curving round it – are known in inlaid ceramics, but the shape would be awkward to make in clay and it seems highly likely that the prototype existed in some other medium.

A definitive resolution of the problem is made very difficult by the extreme rarity of Koryŏ lacquers. Tantalizingly, the only substantial example of an object decorated with a pictorial design (rather than a geometric one) has now disintegrated to the degree that it offers little information. This is a box similar in proportion to a sutra box but decorated with the sort of

landscape with willow trees and wildfowl commonly seen on ceramics or inlaid metalwork. The open design, a vivid contrast to the totally covered surfaces of most Koryŏ lacquerware, clearly has connections with ceramics, with bronze vessels inlaid in silver wire, and possibly even with recently excavated Chinese lacquer pieces from Wujin, which date from the thirteenth century and are done in the *qiangjin* or 'incised gold' technique. Further archaeological finds in Korea may help to build up a more accurate picture of the interplay between the arts of this fruitful period. Certainly more types of Koryŏ lacquer once existed than now survive. The existence of much pierced open-work in the ceramics fuels speculation about the possible existence of pierced and carved woodwork with a coating of lacquer for both decoration and protection.

The Yi dynasty (1392–1910 AD) and the twentieth century

From 1392 to its extinction by the Japanese in 1910 the Korean kingdom was called Chosŏn, but the period is better known as the Yi dynasty after the name of the ruling family. Confucian influences from China displaced among the élite the Buddhism which had once commanded such devotion, but court patronage of the arts, centred on the new capital at Seoul, remained important. Yi society was far more rigidly stratified than that of pre-modern China, with hereditary status groups which almost amounted to castes. In this situation, strict sumptuary laws were much easier to promulgate and enforce than was the case in the more fluid society of China. Decorated luxury lacquer goods were among the craft products limited by edict to the hereditary governing and land-owning class known as *yangban*. In addition to royal workshops in the capital, government workshops in the provinces existed to cater for this élite. A census of 1469 gives 311 craftsmen in paints and lacquer employed in this manner.

Lacquerwork of the early Yi period shows no dramatic break with that of Koryŏ. The surviving repertoire of shapes is larger, including an important vase, as well as a variety of boxes for secular and religious storage use. Formal scrolling in inlaid mother-of-pearl was still the dominant motif, but the use of metal wire as a decorative feature seems to have been abandoned. The designs themselves are bolder and larger. More of the lacquer ground is left exposed as one or two large flowers take the place of geometrically precise rows. Bigger, thicker and fewer pieces of shell were used.

In 1488 Dong Yue, a Chinese ambassador to Korea, wrote a poem, the *Chaoxian fu*, 'Rhapsody on Chosŏn', in which he says of the royal palace at Seoul: 'The three ceremonial gateways

Right: Brown lacquer box; late 18th century. The Japanese-influenced design of poppies and grasses contains tortoiseshell inlay. The sides are decorated with a geometric swastika pattern.

lack mother-of-pearl decoration'. His point may well be that such decoration was so associated in the Chinese mind with Korean lacquer that he was surprised not to find it in architectural use.

By the sixteenth century a wider decorative repertoire was current in Korean lacquering, with the use of powerful asymmetric designs. These included more naturalistic subjects such as birds, flowering trees and grape-vines. Also distinctive is the way that external metal fittings such as hinges and corner plates are emphasized in a manner not practised in China or Japan.

Lacquer suffered along with the other arts from the devastation of Korea attendant on Japanese

invasions in the 1590s. Craftsmen were carried off to Japan as prisoners of war, where their influence on the lacquer of that country was considerable. As well as a national disaster the invasions were a watershed in many areas of Yi culture.

Late Yi lacquer shows, on the technical side, a return to the use of wire inlay in association with mother-of-pearl. Tortoiseshell also came back into fashion, but without the underlaying of any pigments. Fully pictorial scenes appear for the first time. Landscapes with figures and animals are depicted, some of these scenes have roots in a debased form of the landscape painting practised by the *yangban* élite, while others take their

Above: Black lacquer
box; 18th century. Lotus
scroll decoration
continued to be used,
but the petals became
more naturalistic.

designs from printed illustrated books, a highly
developed Korean art form. Pieces of lacquered
furniture have been identified as carrying scenes
taken from *Illustrations of Actions in Accordance with
the Five Relationships* of 1588, a book containing
stories of paragons of correct Confucian social
conduct. No inlaid lacquer furniture has yet been
claimed as being earlier than the eighteenth century, but from the last 150 years or so of the Yi
dynasty there survive a considerable number of
impressively decorated pieces, usually tall chests
used for storing clothes and bedding. Pictorial
scenes are formed by the mosaic use of very large
numbers of rectangular chips of mother-of-pearl,
though figures and animals may be cut out of one
piece of shell with incised details. The background
lacquer may be red or black, and the result is
exuberant rather than elegant.

The centres of production of such lacquered
furniture, which continued into this century,
seem to have been in southern Korea. Northern
Korea, the source of the best raw lacquer, preferred furniture (mainly chests and low tables) and
utensils of plain red lacquer over a black undercoat. These pieces often have the rubbed look of
Japanese *Negoro* lacquer but they do not share its
aesthetic pretensions.

Though not strictly speaking a lacquer technique, the Korean manufacture of decorated horn-
work (*hwagak*) should be mentioned. Brightly
coloured small chests and caskets were produced
at least from the eighteenth century by painting
on plates of transparent ox-horn, which were then
glued to a wooden core with the decorated side
inwards. These wares may be a folk survival of
the once flourishing painted lacquerwares of
Koguryŏ.

In this century, Korea's unhappy history has
not been conducive to the preservation of craft
traditions. However, strenuous efforts have been
made in recent years to revive the inlaying of
lacquer among other arts, by the designation of
working artists as Living Cultural Assets. One of
these artists is Kim Pong-yong, whose *najŏn* inlay
is executed with a sparseness and a restraint which
display the absorption of certain Japanese influences, but is yet entirely within the native
Korean tradition.

3

Japan

Many of the arts and crafts of East Asia are traditionally seen to have had their invention and perfection in China: indeed, the people of that long-enduring civilization had viewed themselves as the natural cultural and political centre of the world. To cite but one well-documented example, practical skills in the firing of porcelain, including the control of glazes and the development of decorative techniques, were achieved through Chinese perseverance and ingenuity; the very word used in English to cover the whole range of high-fired pottery when it was eventually imported to the West was, and still is, 'china'.

With lacquerware, however, the Japanese took what were already highly developed techniques and models from the Chinese and nurtured a tradition of lacquerwork which became unmistakably and uniquely Japanese. By the time that Europeans had become acquainted with lacquer techniques of the Far East, the term adopted – *'japanning'* – referred directly to the one-time pupils and not to the inventors and original masters of the art of lacquerware.

Above: Modern bowl carved in the form of flower petals, by Suzuki Hyosaku II.

Opposite: Inrō; 19th century. A servant kneels in front of a samurai. Signed Jitokusai Gyokuzan.

From the protohistoric era to the Nara period (645–749 AD)

According to Japanese tradition, Prince Yamato Takeru no Mikoto is credited with initiating lacquerwork in Japan when, in the middle of the third century AD, he discovered a clump of lacquer trees in Akiyama, Yamato (present-day Nara prefecture). In fact, archaeological evidence has firmly established the origins of Japanese lacquerwork at an even earlier date, that is sometime from the third century BC onwards. Early finds of lacquer in Japan are scattered throughout several provinces, the most important being those from the village of Korekawa near Hachinohe in the present-day Aomori prefecture. Unlike the wealth of highly sophisticated lacquerware unearthed in contemporary China, Japanese examples represent tentative experimentation in a medium whose techniques were in their infancy. Initially lacquer was employed for its inherent durability as a protective layer over wood, pottery and basketwork in the form of such articles as bows, bowls and articles of personal adornment. In time, however, the decorative potential of this medium was exploited and certain lacquerwares from the prehistoric period reveal designs of a simple nature, or rely on a contrast between a red and black lacquer surface.

With the establishment of the Yamato clan as rulers of Japan during the Kofun period (third to sixth century AD) the use of lacquer became more widespread and was subject to more formal organization. Guilds of skilled craftsmen were set up at court in order to control their work, which included lacquer-workers who were known as *urushibe*. It is, however, the sixth century which is crucial to the history of Japanese lacquer and which witnessed the turning-point from lacquer as a craft to lacquer as a highly developed art. Up until the sixth century Japanese craftsmen experimented with the lacquer medium, probably utilizing the sap from the indigenous tree *Rhus succedanea*, whilst surface decoration was of secondary importance to the practical consideration of daily usage. The use of lacquer gained increasing popularity to the extent of receiving official patronage during the Kofun period, but it is a matter of speculation whether or not it would have developed into the highly sophisticated art form of the Edo period (1615–1868) without the events of the sixth century.

Not only did the introduction of Buddhism into Japan, in the mid-sixth century AD from China via Korea, have a far-reaching effect on Japanese culture; it also exerted a considerable influence on the history of Japanese lacquerwork. The Buddhist faith was disseminated in Japan by Chinese and Korean missionary monks, and the prescribed ritual paraphernalia necessary for its practice was either brought over personally by the Chinese monks or was made by itinerant Chinese or Korean craftsmen or even copied by the Japanese. Relations between China and Japan were further strengthened during the regency of Shōtoku Taishi (573–621), for he sought to model Japan on the centralized system of government of the Chinese and, in so doing, embraced its advanced and newly strengthened culture. In 607 the first of many envoys was despatched to the Sui dynasty (581–618) court. This afforded Japanese artists and craftsmen the opportunity to study at first hand the arts of Sui dynasty and subsequent Tang dynasty (618–906) China.

The earliest extant example of Japanese lacquer-

Below: Tamamushi shrine from the Hōryū-ji temple in Nara; *c.* 650. The panels in red, yellow and green lacquer-painting on a black ground depict a story of the Buddha in a previous incarnation.

Above: Upper part of temple guardian; Nara period (645–794 AD). It is executed in the dry-lacquer or *kanshitsu* technique.

Above: Detail from Buddha on page 75; 13th century.

work in a highly developed form is the mid-seventh century Tamamushi shrine in the Hōryū-ji temple. The style and workmanship of the shrine indicate that it was probably executed by Chinese or Korean craftsmen or, at the very least, was indirectly influenced by them. Its name derives from the *tamamushi* beetle whose iridescent wing-cases were set in openwork fittings attached to the shrine. The shrine and its base are executed in black lacquer with Buddhist narrative scenes painted in red, yellow and green lacquer, a technique known as *urushi-e*, 'lacquer picture'. This technique makes use of pigments combined with lacquer instead of water, the medium employed in traditional Japanese painting; the pigments were applied with a brush to a lacquer surface. Since the chemical nature of lacquer is such that it alters the colour of certain pigments with which it is combined, the colours employed in traditional lacquer-painting have been restricted to red, green, yellow, brown and black. When a wider range of colours was needed, the lacquer-artists used *mitsuda-e*, 'litharge painting', a type of oil-painting with which it was possible to obtain additional colours, such as blue and white. The flesh tones of the bodies used to decorate the Tamamushi shrine, for example, were executed in *mitsuda-e*.

During the eighth century the spread and influence of Buddhism increased to such an extent that it affected most aspects of daily life and is particularly reflected in the arts of that period. From the mid-seventh century, for example, the Nara period witnessed the building of numerous temples and monasteries throughout Japan. This resulted in a great demand for their decoration, as well as for shrines, sculptures and other religious items, which greatly stimulated the nascent lacquer industry. Among the few surviving examples are a number of eighth century sculptures executed in the dry-lacquer or *kanshitsu* technique which was known to have been used in Han dynasty (206 BC–220 AD) China. It employed hemp cloth soaked in raw lacquer and then shaped or moulded over a temporary core of clay or wood. When the cloth had dried and stiffened, the core was removed, and the surface could be further lacquered or painted to provide the decorative details. This technique was, however, gradually superseded by the use of carved wood sculptures.

It was, then, the spread of Buddhism and the need for religious articles that provided the greatest stimulus to the increased production of lacquer. This was only made possible by a massive increase in the number of lacquer trees under cultivation. It was only by declaring the *Taihō-ritsuryō*, a code of laws, that sufficient raw lacquer could be produced to meet the new demand. Under the code, promulgated in 701, a department

of lacquer with twenty lacquerers was established under the finance ministry. In addition each household was required to set aside an area for planting and raising lacquer trees, whilst a system of taxation was introduced whereby lacquer was levied as a tax.

Prior to the sixth century, Japanese craftsmen used sap from the indigenous lacquer tree, *Rhus succedanea*. From that period on, the lacquer tree *Rhus verniciflua* was introduced from China, along with lacquer-making skills, and it has been used down to the present day as the sole source of raw lacquer. This tree is widely grown in Japan, particularly on the main island of Honshū.

The chief source of information regarding lacquers of the eighth century is the Shōsōin Imperial Repository or storehouse of the Tōdai-ji temple, which contains the personal belongings of Emperor Shōmu (d. 756), as well as gifts from the court and nobility. Amongst the 150 items which have been classified as lacquerware, seven main techniques can be distinguished, including undecorated black wares and examples of the *kanshitsu* technique.

Lacquer-painting was one of the most fundamental techniques to the decoration of lacquered objects in the Far East. Examples in the Shōsōin reveal three different painting techniques already in use, apart from *urushi-e*: *yūshoku*, *kingin-e* and *mitsuda-e*, the last-mentioned being employed as one of the techniques on the Tamamushi shrine. *Yūshoku* involved applying transparent oil over *sai-e* (painting with pigments blended with glue) and *dei-e* (painting with gold and silver powder blended with glue) in order to protect the painting and raise the ornamental effect. *Kingin-e*, 'gold-silver picture', made use of gold and silver powders which were bound together with glue and applied with a brush to a lacquer surface.

Apart from lacquer-painting, the inlay techniques of *heidatsu* and *raden* predominate amongst lacquerware of the Shōsōin. *Raden* entailed applying large, thick pieces of milky-white mother-of-pearl, which were sometimes cut in advance to the required shape, on to a lacquer base. *Heidatsu* made use of cut sheet-gold or sheet-silver. Both techniques originated in China, where they were forbidden by the Emperor Su zong (756–62) as being too extravagant.

Lacquerware of the Nara period, as represented by examples in the Shōsōin, reflects the strong influence of Chinese art and culture of the Tang dynasty. Indeed, many of the objects themselves were produced by Chinese lacquerers or were direct copies of them. Although many new techniques were introduced from China, it was not until the following Heian period that Japanese craftsmen began to assert their independence as lacquerers and to experiment with new and already existing techniques.

Above: Priest Ganjin, from the Tōshōdai-ji temple in Nara; 8th century. Ganjin's image is executed in *kanshitsu*. The painted details, such as the eyebrows, moustache and stubble of the beard show how much delicacy could be achieved in this technique.

Right: Amida, Buddha of the Western Paradise; 13th century. The statue is carved from wood with lacquer and gilding. The Buddhist temples were important patrons for lacquer-artists who produced shrines and sutra boxes as well as statues. See page 73 for detail.

The Heian period (794–1185)

The establishment of Heian-kyō (present-day Kyōto) as the capital of Japan in 794 marked the beginning of the so-called Heian period, which lasted until the final defeat of the Taira clan by Minamoto Yoritomo (who assumed supreme power in 1185) and which brought to an end an era of political strife and civil wars. During the early Heian period, intercourse with China continued and the influence of Chinese civilization on Japanese culture remained strong. By the later Heian, commonly known as the Fujiwara period (894–1185), the most fundamental aspects of Chinese culture already known to the Japanese had either been rejected or modified. A new, indigenous Japanese culture slowly emerged during this period and China was no longer regarded as the model for all aspects of daily life. The custom of sending official embassies to China was discontinued during 994.

Stylistically, lacquerware of the Heian period may be divided into two main groups. The first, which is represented by a dozen or so surviving pieces, dates from approximately the ninth and tenth centuries. It reflects strong ties with the lacquer of the Nara period, and the influence of Chinese lacquer is still discernible. Examples from the second group, which date from the eleventh

75 Japan

Above: Chest; late 11th–early 12th century. The design of phoenix roundels is executed in mother-of-pearl inlaid into a black lacquer ground with a sparse sprinkling of gold powder.

and twelfth centuries and are described in greater detail below, reflect the establishment and nurturing of a native tradition in the art of lacquerwork which laid the basis for later developments.

The lacquer medium continued to be used for accessories to Buddhism, such as sutra boxes, as well as in the adornment of temple interiors. This is well illustrated by the splendid Konjiki-dō (Gold-coloured Hall) of the Chūson-ji temple in Iwate-ken, dated 1124, the interior of which is decorated with gold lacquer, *togidashi* (a technique which made use of sprinkled gold or silver powders – a form of *maki-e*) and mother-of-pearl. The use of lacquer increasingly pervaded most aspects of life; among many lacquer items were utensils for eating and drinking, toilet-boxes and accessories, writing-boxes, chests and saddles.

During the Heian period, lacquer craftsmen not only employed existing techniques (some of which, such as *kingin-e*, proved unsatisfactory and soon fell into disuse) but also experimented with new ones. Although there are no surviving ninth and tenth century *raden* or mother-of-pearl works, literary references emphasize their great popularity and indicate the esteem in which they were held. According to the *Song shu*, the official history of the Chinese Song dynasty (960–1279), toilet-cases, comb-boxes, reading-desks, writing-tables and saddles, all decorated with mother-of-pearl inlay, were amongst the gifts presented to the imperial Chinese court by the priest Ka-in from the Tōdai-ji temple in 988. Similarly, the diary of Michinaga, a member of the powerful Fujiwara family, mentions his gift of objects with mother-of-pearl decoration to a Buddhist temple in China during the tenth century. Also, a Chinese work of the Song dynasty mentions that 'the origin of lacquerware inlaid with mother-of-pearl may be traced to Japan. Japanese articles are of excellent workmanship and quite different from

those that can be easily obtained on the Chinese market.' Indeed, this indicates the high quality and beauty of Japanese *raden* lacquerwares, for it should not be forgotten that this technique had originated in China. Surviving articles from the later Heian which were executed in the *raden* technique are not uncommon, though mother-of-pearl was more frequently found in combination with gold lacquerwork. This is exemplified by the decoration of two buildings, the Phoenix Hall of the Byōdō-in, built in 1053, and the Konjiki-dō of the Chūson-ji, built in 1124.

The Heian period witnessed the appearance of *maki-e*, 'sprinkled picture', a technique which, above all, serves to characterize Japanese lacquer and to distinguish it from that of China and Korea. Whether the technique originated in China or Japan has been the subject of much controversy. It was in any case Japanese rather than Chinese craftsmen who ultimately perfected the technique, so that the term *maki-e* became synonymous with Japanese lacquer. The *maki-e* technique involved drawing the design in lacquer on to a sheet of fibrous paper which was then placed face down on the lacquer surface. Light pressure of the hand was sufficient to transfer the outline of the design on to the lacquer surface, and the paper was then removed. Gold and silver powders were sprinkled on to this design while the lacquer ground was still wet.

During the Nara period, lacquer craftsmen had begun to experiment with gold and silver powders which were bound together with glue or lacquer and were applied with a brush, as exemplified by such techniques as *kingin-e*. Although the effect was pleasing, such techniques proved unsatisfactory as the designs gradually flaked off. The emergence of *maki-e* at about the same time was probably no mere coincidence for it was a more reliable and successful method of achieving a similar effect. A sword and scabbard in the collection of the Shōsōin are probably the earliest surviving examples of *maki-e*. Although the Tōdai-ji inventory dated 756 adopts the term *makkinru* as being the technique employed in their manufacture, a close examination reveals that they are early examples of true *maki-e*.

Contemporary literary references during the Heian period testify to the great popularity of *maki-e* wares. The sophisticated court of the Fujiwara period was dominated by a group of talented individuals who engaged in cultural pursuits. They produced great literary works in the form of novels and diaries portraying court life, such as the *Genji monogatari* written by Murasaki Shikibu in the early eleventh century. The earliest reference to *maki-e* ware is thought to occur in the mid-ninth century tale *Taketori monogatari*, which mentions 'a house lacquered in *maki-e*'. The most celebrated of early *maki-e* wares is a manuscript-

Above: Tray, shown in colour on page 78.

Below: Tray; probably 19th century. A seated ape holds a branch in gold and black *togidashi*; there are traces of red lacquer on the face. Signed Shiomi Masanari (1646–1719), but probably by a follower.

box in the Ninna-ji, Kyōto, dated *c.* 919. The decoration of scrolls is executed in gold and silver *togidashi*, chronologically the first of three main types of *maki-e* work. In *togidashi*, 'cause to appear by rubbing', the sprinkled *maki-e* design was covered with layers of lacquer of the same colour as the background, usually black, and the surface was then polished down until the design reappeared. The design was thus completely flush with the surrounding lacquer surface and the entire surface was then covered with several layers of transparent lacquer. *Togidashi* produced a rich, smooth and sparkling tonal effect.

The latter part of the Heian period saw the appearance of the second type of *maki-e*, that is *hiramaki-e*, 'flat sprinkled picture'. This involved sprinkling the design with gold or silver powder, as with *togidashi*, but then covering these areas with layers of transparent lacquer thinned with camphor. Finally the surface was polished so that

the design was only slightly raised above the background. The earliest surviving examples are a set of sutra boxes of between 1175 and 1182, made for the Nannatsu-dera, a temple in Nagoya.

Lacquerware of the Heian period is characterized by a new distinctive shape. The hard, angular forms of the Nara period gave way to softer shapes. The box and cover which best characterize these changes have rounded corners and a distinctive recessed rim or *chiri-e*, 'dust ledge'. As the period progressed, the flat lid was superseded by a domed lid (*kōmori*) with bulging side-walls (*dōbari*). The motifs and designs of Heian lacquerware also underwent a gradual change from rich, symmetrical and ornamental decoration to simple pictorial designs with motifs taken from nature. There was as yet, however, no real attempt to portray a scene in its entirety but simply to depict isolated elements or groups of elements from it. Plants or animals, for example, were frequently portrayed without direct reference to their surroundings. At the same time a stylized wave pattern was widely used by lacquer craftsmen and may be considered as the hallmark of late Heian lacquer design.

In the history of Japanese lacquerwork the Heian period is, above all, noted for the beginnings of the *maki-e* tradition. One of the most popular misconceptions regarding Japanese lacquer is that the designs are painted on to the surface. In fact, painted decoration only accounts for a small proportion of Japanese lacquer designs. It is a tribute to the great skills of the Japanese lacquer craftsman that he employed sprinkled powders so skilfully as to produce a detailed pictorial effect.

The Kamakura period (1185–1333)

The final years of the Heian period witnessed not only the decline of the Fujiwara family but also the rise and fall of a distinguished military family, the Taira. In 1185 they were finally overthrown by Minamoto Yoritomo (1147–99), who established the shōgunate at Kamakura, from which city the period derived its name. A system of government was set up which was the pattern for the subsequent development of Japanese history until the restoration of the Meiji emperor in 1868. Successive emperors were rulers in name only whilst the shōgun or military ruler wielded effective power through the military administration or shōgunate. The supremacy of the Minamoto family was relatively short-lived, for early in the thirteenth century power passed to the Hōjō family. Just over a century later the imperial hierarchy and military class were divided into two opposing factions, each contending for supreme power, until the Ashikagas established the Muromachi shōgunate in 1392.

The hallmark of Japanese lacquer is its distinctive use of gold and silver dust and powders, representing its finest achievements. Some of the techniques involved are shown here.

Opposite page: A specimen tray shows the various stages involved in applying *nashiji:* 1, 2. Gold *nashiji.* 3. Silver *nashiji.* 4. Tin *nashiji.* 5. Coating of transparent lacquer, ground roughly (6) with magnolia charcoal. 7. Second coating of transparent lacquer ground smooth (8) with magnolia charcoal. 9. Transparent lacquer applied with cotton-wool, and (10) polished with charcoal and oil. 11. Thin coating of transparent *Yoshino* lacquer, polished (12) with antler ashes and oil. 13, 14. Repeat of 11, 12.

Above: A specimen tray depicting the branch of a lacquer tree shows the stages involved in executing the *togidashi* technique: 1. Outline and veins. 3. Gold dust. 4. Mixture of black and branch lacquer. 5. Black lacquer, ground roughly (6) with magnolia charcoal. 7. Second coating of black lacquer.

Right: This detail of a sample board illustrates the enormous range of gold and silver lacquers obtained by using gold and silver powders of different purity and size and by varying their density and depth in the lacquer.

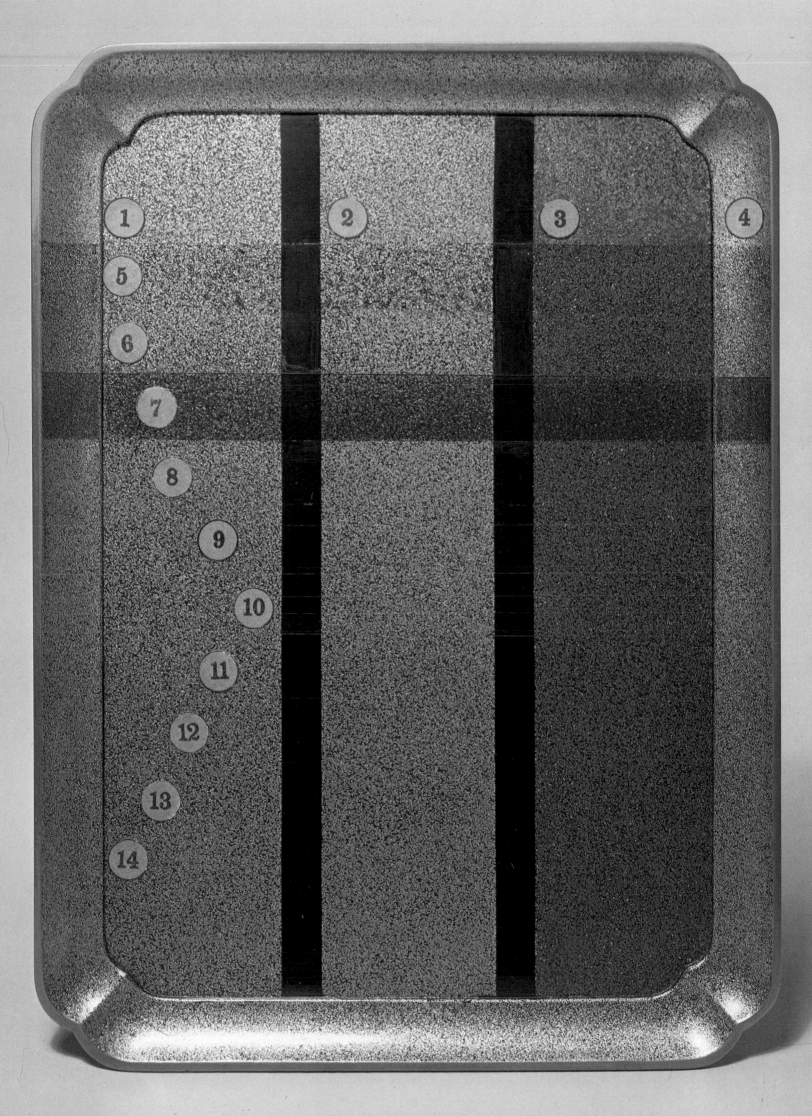

During the early part of the Kamakura period, Minamoto Yoritomo undertook the restoration or rebuilding of the shrines, temples and palaces of the emperor and ex-emperors which had suffered as a result of the internal strife. This provided a considerable impetus to the native arts and crafts which were used in their construction and decoration, including lacquerwork, and the period as a whole is noted for the production of fine works of art.

Up until the Edo period (1615–1868), lacquer-artists usually remained anonymous or were known only through written sources, but, as they rarely signed their works, it was difficult to assign specific objects to them with any certainty. The *Zōei-ki* of the Ōmi Hioyshi-jinja, for example, which dates from 1136, mentions twenty-seven lacquerers. Conversely, the doors of the Mandara shrine in the Taima-dera, dated 1242, not only lists the names of many of the donors, but also the lacquerer, Fujiwara Sadatsune, about whom we have no details. The anonymity of a high proportion of Japanese lacquerers was largely due to the inherent qualities of the lacquer medium which required that much time and effort were expended in the production of a single object.

The processes involved were highly specialized and involved an extensive division of labour. There were three basic stages to the work: the preparation of the base material, the application of the lacquer ground, and the execution of the design by the lacquer-artist. The base material of a lacquered object was commonly wood, well seasoned to avoid warping and splitting; it was also necessary to smooth any joins or natural roughness in the wood and to fill in any cracks before applying a coat of raw lacquer. The object was then passed to another craftsman, who prepared the ground surface by applying numerous thin layers of lacquer of different quality, ensuring that each had completely dried in specific atmospheric conditions and that each was polished to a smooth surface before the next layer was added. The lacquer-artist was presented with a surface which could be decorated in a large variety of techniques; these, too, entailed considerable time and effort.

The underlying political and military instability of the Kamakura period is reflected in its lacquer-ware. The changes in shape during this time are best illustrated by reference to the ubiquitous box and cover in its various forms, and, in particular, to the *tebako*, 'toilet-box'. During the course of the Kamakura period the soft, rounded forms characteristic of the Heian period became increasingly hard and angular. At the same time, the overhanging lid of the box was gradually replaced by a flush-fitting lid, while the proportions of the lid to the side of the box decreased so that the base of the box occupied the greater part of its side elevation. The resulting effect, together with the

fact that the mounts for the tying cords were set low down on the sides, was one of vertical impact, solidity and weight.

The tentative appearance of naturalistic representation in lacquer design of the late Heian period was further developed under the Kamakura, a feature which was itself only made possible by fundamental technical advances and refinements. Lacquerers were now able to reproduce a wide range of gold and silver powders. The lacquer-artist who employed the *maki-e* technique in its fully developed form made use of a bamboo tube cut diagonally at one end, with a piece of fabric glued over the aperture; the fabric acted as a sieve to the powder that was placed in the tube. The lacquer-artist worked with a number of vessels each containing gold or silver powder of different size, shape and purity. Each vessel had its own bamboo tube covered with fabric at one end, the fineness of its mesh being appropriate to the size of the powder. As the artist needed the various types of powder, so these were placed in the appropriate tubes and gently tapped on to the lacquer surface. Frequently, many different types of gold powder were used on a single article.

The lacquerer was thus able to gain a more complete control over his design by selecting precisely the type of powder most suited to the task. Amongst these were to be found *hirame-fun*, 'flat-eye dust', *nashiji-fun*, 'pear-ground dust', and *kirikane*, 'cut gold'. Previously, a mixture of different-sized particles inevitably resulted in designs with soft, blurred edges, whereas the ability to produce uniformly large or small, flat or irregularly shaped particles at will meant that it was now possible to create, for the first time, well-defined hard lines and edges in *maki-e*. This technical development was in itself a prerequisite for naturalistic representation.

At the same time advances were made in three-dimensional representation, as exemplified by the development of *takamaki-e*. *Takamaki-e* ('high scatter picture'), which was chronologically the last of the three main *maki-e* techniques to develop, differs from *hiramaki-e* in that elements of the design were built up with lacquer and charcoal powder so that they were left in relief. A similar effect of surface relief was also obtained at this time by the striking use of mother-of-pearl inlays of varying thicknesses.

The portrayal of scenes from nature, which characterized lacquer design of the early and late Kamakura period, relied on the subtle use of 'shades' of gold and silver to produce a 'coloured' effect. This was achieved by grading the size and type of powders and varying their densities as well as the depth at which they were embedded in the lacquer surface. Lacquer decoration of the mid-Kamakura period was characterized, on the other hand, by a predominance of gold lacquer

Below: Board and tray shown in colour on pages 78 and 79 to illustrate the fine *maki-e* processes which make Japanese lacquer unique.

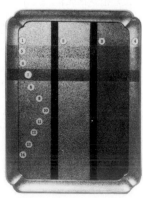

Above: Box and cover; mid-18th century. Plums, camellias and chrysanthemums, rocks, and a stream and waterfall in gold and silver *takamaki-e* decorate the box and cover, which are enriched with encrustations of coral and gold on a black lacquer ground.

alone. Whereas gold had formerly been used to portray elements of the main design on a black (or gold-sprinkled black) lacquered ground, it assumed a new importance both in the background and the main design. The predominance of gold produced a 'metallic' effect which reflected the martial spirit of the age. This coincided with a shift in lacquer design from the naturalistic representation of scenes from nature to the representation of isolated elements from nature, portrayed in a realistic manner but without context or background. Such elements were positioned on the lacquered object in such a way as to avoid pure symmetry, but so as to emphasize the four corners and central decorative field.

The Kamakura period was also marked by the appearance of a new and distinct group of lacquers, known as *Negoro-nuri*. The name derives from wares which were made and used by priests of the Negoro temple, Kī province, from the end of the thirteenth century to its destruction in 1585, although the term has subsequently been used to describe all lacquer of a similar type. *Negoro-nuri* is characterized by monochrome red wares, the surfaces of which were gradually worn away through frequent handling to reveal an underlying layer of black lacquer. Its appeal lay in the simplicity of its forms, the distinctive qualities of the lacquer and the contrasting colours brought about by the worn surface. Although there was nothing new in monochrome lacquers, for it is in itself one of the basic forms of lacquer decoration, the novelty of *Negoro-nuri* lay in the characteristic manner in which the surface was worn away in irregular patches. It was precisely this natural ageing process which was deliberately imitated in later examples of *Negoro-nuri* and which came to be synonymous with it. Although *Negoro-nuri* had its origins under the Kamakura, it was during the

subsequent Muromachi and later periods that the technique came into its own.

Although the Heian period was marked by the appearance of the *maki-e* technique, it was the Kamakura period that witnessed its fruition. Technical refinements resulted in complete mastery of *maki-e*, and by the end of the period the three main *maki-e* techniques (*togidashi*, *hiramaki-e* and *takamaki-e*) had all become fundamental to the repertoire of the lacquer-artist in Japan.

The Muromachi period (1392–1568)

The closing years of the Kamakura witnessed a period of warfare between two rival factions and were known as Nambokuchō, 'southern and northern dynasties'. In 1392 the Ashikaga clan succeeded in subjugating the 'southern line' of the imperial house. Thereupon Ashikaga Takauji established his government at Muromachi in Kyōto, which heralded the beginning of a period of rule that lasted some 250 years. The Muromachi period roughly falls into two halves; the first half saw the emergence of a lavish and brilliant culture amidst the upper levels of Japanese society, which greatly encouraged the arts. Amongst the Ashikaga rulers, Yoshimitsu (1358–1408) and Yoshimasa (1435–90) made the greatest contribution in this respect. Whilst the luxurious lifestyle of those connected with the Muromachi shōgunate developed apace, the remainder of the country was plunged deeper into economic, social and political decline. This culminated in a great civil war, the Ōnin War (1467–77), which devastated Kyōto and which marked the second half of the Muromachi period. Scholars and artists alike fled, taking refuge with the leading *daimyō* (feudal lords) in the provinces, which as a result became the main artistic and cultural centres. During the latter half of the Muromachi period the most important of these centres, in respect of lacquer production, were Yamaguchi in Suō (present-day Yamaguchi prefecture), Odawara (near present-day Tokyo) and Sakai in Settsu (present-day Hyōgo prefecture).

The early fifteenth century is notable for a group of lacquers which were owned by, or were in the style of those owned by, Yoshimasa. They are known collectively as Higashiyama lacquers, after Yoshimasa's residence at the foot of Mount Higashi in Kyōto. One of the most striking features of this group of lacquers is the obvious connection between lacquer design and classical poetry, or literature in general. This is illustrated by examples of *uta-e*, 'poem picture', whereby a few significant written characters of a poem, but rarely the whole text, are cleverly worked into the design in such a way as to be almost undetectable at first glance. Although in such cases the design

of the lacquered object illustrates some more or less obvious scene from a poem, its role goes beyond mere illustration of the scene depicted. In other examples no characters are incorporated into the design but the literary allusion is nonetheless present. The aim of *uta-e*, therefore, was not the realistic representation of a particular scene as an end in itself, but to depict elements of it in such a way as to convey its mood and atmosphere. The full import of such works was thus the exclusive preserve of the educated Muromachi élite.

Other characteristics of Higashiyama lacquers include the influence of painting, as well as the widespread use of *takamaki-e*, often combined and contrasted with *togidashi*. Great prominence was given to the display of the technical skills of the lacquer-artist to produce an elaborate surface of various different techniques. The overriding importance of technique, which became isolated from the shape of the object, did not have a detrimental effect on the pictorial content of the design. Literary sources, moreover, have revealed that Yoshimasa had some of the leading painters and lacquer-masters working for him. The painters included Tosa Mitsunobu (d. 1521), a master of the indigenous *Yamato-e*, 'Japanese picture', style of painting, and Sōami (1472–1525), master of the Chinese style of painting, who produced designs for lacquer-masters such as Kōami Michinaga (1410–78) and Igarashi Shinsai (active 1480). Although there are no surviving examples which can safely be attributed to these lacquerers, they founded important schools of lacquerwork.

During the Kamakura and the first half of the Muromachi periods the influence of Chinese culture was paramount. The renewal of Chinese influence was largely connected with the spread of *Chan* Buddhism from China to Japan, where it is known as Zen; priests made regular trips between the two countries. During the Kamakura period the influence of Song dynasty (960–1279) culture was most noticeable in the realm of Japanese painting and ceramics, with the development of the tea ceremony, while the effect on lacquerwork was minimal. The first half of the Muromachi period witnessed the emergence of a general love of things Chinese. Large numbers of Chinese works of art reached Japan, including porcelain, textiles, lacquer and painting. The influence of painting on lacquerwork is best seen in the new pictorial emphasis in lacquer design, with the main elements picked out against a dark background so that the overall impression frequently resembles that of a painting. Conventions of a Chinese painting are also discernible in such motifs as rocks with holes through them, and the manner in which tree trunks and branches intertwine. Some shapes of early Muromachi lacquerware, particularly those executed in *Negoro-nuri*, also reveal a Chinese influence.

Above: Circular box and cover decorated in *guri* lacquer; early 19th century. The conventional scrolls were carved through the lacquer surface, which is made up of successive layers of black, green, red and yellow lacquer, with black as the final coat.

Left: Inrō, ojime and netsuke; late 18th century. The peonies on a diaper ground are in carved red lacquer. The *inrō* and netsuke are of similar design and appear to have been made in the same workshop, whereas the *ojime*, with storks and flowers in carved red lacquer, is probably of a later date.

The increased volume of trade with China during the Muromachi period, together with a passion for Chinese objects, resulted in large quantities of Chinese lacquer being imported into Japan, including objects executed in lacquer techniques hitherto unknown there. The technique which was to have the greatest influence and impact was lacquer carving. This involved applying numerous thin layers of lacquer, generally in excess of one hundred and possibly as many as three hundred, on to a base material until the desired depth was reached. The lacquer-artist decorated the lacquer by carving through its upper layers, frequently making use of a marker layer in a different colour. The designs employed in carved lacquer reveal strong affinities with those found on Chinese carved wares, with a predominance of floral motifs, as well as figures and buildings in a landscape setting, generally on a diaper ground.

Since the lacquer employed in carved wares was frequently red, the term by which Japanese carved lacquer is most commonly known is *tsuishu*, 'piled-up red'. *Tsuikoku*, 'piled-up black', is the term applied to carved black lacquer. At a time when anything connected with China was in vogue, Chinese carved lacquers were probably the most widely sought-after items amongst Japanese

collectors. This is reflected in the vast terminology used to describe carved lacquer in its various forms. Variety was achieved, moreover, by applying layers of different-coloured lacquer, which could be isolated during carving and used for various areas of the design. One of the most common variants of carved lacquer was a type known as *guri*, 'crook ring', lacquer which was characterized by layers of coloured lacquer superimposed on top of each other in a specific order. The surface was carved with scrolled motifs or curves forming conventional cloud scrolls, executed with cuts of a V-shaped cross-section, to reveal and contrast the various colours below to their best advantage.

A gift of twenty large carved lacquer plates and thirty carved lacquer boxes from the Chinese emperor Yong le to the shōgun Toshimitsu in 1407 testifies to the large quantity of Chinese carved lacquer to reach Japan at this time. It is, however, uncertain when Japanese craftsmen first produced objects by this technique; they worked closely in the Chinese style and it is difficult to distinguish between Chinese and early Japanese examples. Literary sources refer to a Kyōto lacquer-master, Monnyū (active during the second half of the fifteenth century), who was renowned for his carved lacquers, though no examples of his work survive. In addition there was a school of lacquerers, with the name *Tsuishu Yōsei*, who worked almost exclusively in lacquer carving, the reputed founder of which goes back to the fifteenth century, though nothing certain is known about its members until the mid-seventeenth century.

Carved lacquer was, nevertheless, firmly established as a technique in Japan from the latter part of the fifteenth century and remained so for the next four centuries, attaining particular prominence during the nineteenth century, as exemplified in works by such artists as Tamakaji Zōkoku (1806–69).

The complexities and detailed nature of the technique and its decoration is in fact particularly well illustrated by an *inrō*, or medicine-case, reputed to have been made by Zōkoku around 1840, which according to Andrew Pekarik is reputed to have included a design of 55 plants, 30 flowers, 2 rocks, 343 turtles, 433 crabs, 41 fish, 27 snails, 24 dragonflies, 9 flies, 4 wasps, 26 butterflies, 3 beetles, 4 grasshoppers, 4 leeches, 4 crickets, 4 praying mantises, 18 spiders, 5 centipedes, 19 sparrows, 7 herons, 10 kingfishers, 3 geese and 1 swallow! The feat is all the more remarkable when one considers the small size of the average *inrō*.

The application of numerous thin layers of lacquer as a prerequisite for the technique of lacquer carving was a precise and lengthy process which demanded that each layer be completely

Right: Saddle; 17th century. In lacquered wood, it is decorated with stylized lotus scrolls inlaid with mother-of-pearl.

Opposite page: Interior of writing-box; early 19th century. It has two trays, an inkstone and a silver water-dropper. The design of a camellia plant is in gold *chinkin-bori* on dark brown lacquer.

Below: Circular box and cover; late 18th century. The box is executed in *Kamakura-bori*. The manner in which the top layer of red lacquer has been deliberately rubbed down in places to reveal black lacquer below is an example of *Negoro-nuri*.

dried and polished before the next was applied. Therefore it is hardly surprising that, with the enormous popularity of carved lacquerware during the early Muromachi period and with the complex and lengthy processes involved in its manufacture, a simpler and quicker technique was evolved which imitated the effects of carving. The technique is known as *Kamakura-bori*, 'Kamakura carving', after the town of Kamakura in Sagami (present-day Kanagawa prefecture), the most important place of its manufacture. It differs from *tsuishu* in that it is not the lacquered surface which is carved but the wooden base, which is then covered over with a thin layer of lacquer. Although it was initially intended to simulate carved lacquer, in time the full potential of *Kamakura-bori* as a Japanese lacquer technique in its own right was realized.

Although lacquer carving was the most popular technique to be adopted from China, two others made their appearance in Japan at about the same time. The use of mother-of-pearl inlaid into lacquer was by no means new, but the lacquerer acquired from China the knowledge of how to apply finer and thinner pieces than ever before, which gave a new impetus to the technique in Japan. This technique, which involved the use of a blue-green iridescent shell, was known as *aogai*, 'blue-green shell', which should be distinguished from the thick, milky-white pieces of shell characteristic of the *raden* technique. Another technique,

Opposite page, top: Book-rest in the so-called Kōdai-ji style, shown in colour on page 90; late 16th century.

Opposite page, centre: Travelling chest; late 16th–early 17th century. The chest, in gold *hiramaki-e* and *nashiji* on a black lacquer ground, has a design of dewy grasses and paulownia badges.

known as *chinkin-bori*, 'sunken-gold carving', in Japan and *qiangjin* in China was in use in Japan at least by 1433, when *qiangjin* lacquers formed part of the gift from the Xuande emperor (reigned 1426–35) of the Ming dynasty to the shōgun Ashikaga Yoshinori. The technique of *chinkin-bori* involved scratching the design into the wet lacquer surface and rubbing gold into the incised lines. This technique did not achieve the same degree of popularity as carved lacquer and few examples from the period survive. It underwent something of a revival during the eighteenth century when, for example, the lacquerer Ninomiya Tōtei (active 1789–1801) is reputed to have used rats' teeth to incise the lines.

The trade in lacquer between China and Japan during the early Muromachi period was very much a two-way process. Not only were the Japanese introduced to new lacquer techniques but the Chinese were exposed to examples of Japanese lacquer. By the fifteenth century Japanese lacquerers were acknowledged as being masters of their craft, particularly in the field of *maki-e*. This is borne out by various Chinese sources, such as the *Dong hai ji* of the Xuande period (1426–35) which records that 'the father of Yang Xuan . . . used to send people to Japan to learn the techniques of lacquer sprinkling and lacquer painting'.

The last hundred or so years of the Muromachi period were beset by successive conflicts, reflected in lacquer by a general lowering of artistic and technical standards. The influence of Chinese culture in terms of design and technique, so forceful during the early Muromachi, had almost disappeared, whilst at the same time Chinese elements became assimilated into an indigenous Japanese style. A new style emerged which was characterized by an overall simplification as well as a transition from pictorial representation influenced by painting to the more intimate portrayal of certain elements from a scene, usually those in the foreground. Furthermore, decorative features such as leaves or blossoms were frequently depicted as though they had been artificially flattened out, so that something of a two-dimensional effect was produced whilst a realistic portrayal was still maintained.

The Momoyama period (1568–1615)

By the end of the Muromachi period the Ashikaga shōgunate had become weak and ineffectual, and its downfall was imminent. This was achieved not by one of the strong *daimyō* families but by Oda Nobunaga (1534–82), a man of humble birth who had risen to the most powerful position in the land. His rise is not as strange as it may seem, for at this time hereditary rank became increasingly subordinated to power based on wealth, as well as

personal drive and ambition. Toyotomi Hideyoshi (1536–98) and Tokugawa Ieyasu (1542–1616), the military rulers who, along with Oda Nobunaga, dominated the period and brought most of the country under their influence, were men of similar background.

The Momoyama was a short but crucial period in the history of Japan when the hierarchy based on rank and status disintegrated and was replaced by a new social order based on money and the buying power that accompanied it. Those in influential positions were, for the most part, self-made men without the advantages of a sound education. In the realm of the fine arts these new patrons sought objects of immediately pleasing appeal. The emphasis was on overtly decorative objects which spoke for themselves in a striking manner, in a way that was easy to appreciate. Such objects were in direct contrast to the often sober and intellectual works of the preceding centuries, such as Zen ink-painting, pottery for the tea ceremony and lacquerware, which all reveal strong literary affinities. Nonetheless, the different taste and demands of the Momoyama patrons did not have a detrimental effect on the development of Momoyama culture, as it coincided with a particularly inventive phase in most aspects of the arts and crafts.

To this period belong painted screens (*byōbu*) and sliding doors (*fusuma*) with lavish gold backgrounds. There were also striking changes in the textile arts, as illustrated by Nō drama costumes with sharply contrasting areas of design, while in both metalwork and ceramics the emphasis was also on coloured effects. Above all, the Momoyama period produced creative ideas in the field of lacquerwork which culminated in the outstanding achievements of the Edo period.

Broadly speaking, lacquer of the Momoyama period can be divided into three groups: those which continued in the traditional style; the so-called Kōdai-ji lacquers; and Namban lacquers. There is also an additional group which encompassed objects for everyday use. With the emergence of a new social order, the use of lacquered objects was no longer the sole prerogative of the ruling class but fell within the purchasing power of large sections of society, including the rich townsmen, or *chōnin*. New functional shapes appeared which were largely connected with the preparation and eating of food, such as bowls and picnic sets, for the lacquer surface was waterproof and could withstand comparatively high temperatures. Such items for everyday use were generally in the form of undecorated red or black monochrome wares of a type frequently illustrated in Momoyama genre painting. For the most part they continued to be produced throughout the subsequent Edo period almost totally unaffected by the vicissitudes of style and fashion.

The group of wares which best reflect the taste of Momoyama patrons are the so-called Kōdai-ji lacquers. The name derives from the Kōdai-ji temple, in Kyōto, built in 1605 or 1606 by the widow of Hideyoshi, one of the three most powerful men of his time, as a mausoleum for her husband and herself and in which, despite the ravages of successive fires, more than thirty lacquers have survived.

This corpus of wares forms the basis of the Kōdai-ji style, though the term has also been extended to include lacquers which are stylistically similar but which have been preserved in

collections other than the Kōdai-ji.

The predominant feature of Kōdai-ji lacquer is a design of autumn plants and grasses, known as *akikusa*. The plants are in clumps, either freestanding or attached to a small patch of earth, and are portrayed in a naturalistic manner, frequently appearing to sway gently in a light breeze. The plant-heads and leaves, moreover, are often portrayed as though flattened out and turned towards the viewer, which may be seen as a survival from

late Muromachi lacquer decoration. In addition, the design of autumn plants and grasses is often combined with stylized chrysanthemum or paulownia flowers, heraldic devices frequently used by Hideyoshi, for whom many of the Kōdai-ji lacquers were specifically made.

Apart from the recurrent use of autumn plants, the most striking characteristic of Kōdai-ji lacquers is the way in which the surface area is frequently divided by a diagonal line, sometimes incorporating a zigzag. The full impact of this device relied on sharp contrasts in design between the main decorative fields. This is best illustrated by reference to a document-box preserved in the Kōdai-ji temple itself, which reveals three main contrasting features: first, the difference in colour between a predominantly black and a predominantly gold lacquer area of design; second, the use of different motifs, with autumn plants in one decorative field and bamboo occupying the other; third, a contrast in the degree of movement and direction of the motifs, as represented by the swaying autumn plants, which are splayed in several directions, and the stiff, upward-growing stems of the bamboo.

The technical execution of Kōdai-ji lacquers was not a means to an end but a vehicle to emphasize powerful decorative devices. The lacquer-artist therefore employed subtle and relatively straightforward means in the execution of these designs. These techniques included gold *hiramaki-e* and *e-nashiji* or 'picture *nashiji*', whereby *nashiji* ('pear ground', so-called because this type of gold-sprinkled ground resembled the surface of a pear) which was normally used for the background was incorporated into elements of the main design, as well as *harigaki*, 'needle drawing', which involved scratching fine lines into the wet lacquer surface. Although none of these techniques was new, *e-nashiji* and *harigaki* came into common usage for the first time.

Recent research has indicated that lacquer decorated in the so-called Kōdai-ji style was first made in 1586 and continued well into the Edo period, though the most active period of production was between 1592 and 1615. It also appears that certain internal decorative features of Fushimi Castle, built by Hideyoshi in 1594 and destroyed in 1600, were incorporated into other buildings, such as the Kōdai-ji. Although the Kōdai-ji itself has suffered numerous fires, those buildings such as the Mitayama (ancestral hall or mausoleum) that still survive reveal certain internal features decorated in lacquer of the so-called Kōdai-ji style. Inscriptions found on the door to Hideyoshi's shrine date to 1596. As the Kōdai-ji was not completed until 1606 the door was probably an example of an architectural feature which was brought from Fushimi Castle, and it serves to indicate that the style of lacquer decoration which

Right: Book-rest; late 16th century. Chrysanthemums, autumn grasses and paulownia badges in gold *hiramaki-e* and *nashiji* are on a black lacquer ground mellowed by the addition of gold *nashiji* flakes. Some of the flowers and leaves make use of *e-nashiji* (*nashiji* used for the main elements of the design as opposed to the background) on a reddish lacquer ground.

Far right: Lectern of European form; late 16th century. The Jesuit monogram IHS is surrounded by geometric and floral designs in gold and silver *hiramaki-e* on a black lacquer ground, with shaped and un-shaped mother-of-pearl inlay.

Right: Writing-box; 17th century. The flowering plants, grasses and brushwood fence are in gold, brown and black lacquer enriched with shell.

Far right: Tea-jar and cover; 18th century. The flowering plant design is in gold *takamaki-e*, pewter (which has turned white with pewter disease) and mother-of-pearl inlay on a black lacquer ground.

Opposite page: Tiered food-box and cover; early 17th century. The squirrels and grapes in gold *hiramaki-e* and *nashiji* are on a black lacquer ground. The characteristic motifs and devices of Kōdai-ji style lacquers have for the most part been abandoned in favour of a greater range and contrast in the purity and density of gold powders.

has become synonymous with the Kōdai-ji already existed before its construction.

Another significant group of Momoyama lacquers are known collectively as Namban, 'southern barbarian'. The term was used to describe both men and objects which came to Japan from the south, including the Philippines and Java, but later also included the Portuguese, Spanish and Dutch. In the context of Japanese history of art, however, 'Namban' is specifically used with reference to works of art produced as a result of intercourse between European traders and the

Japanese. The earliest European arrivals, first Portuguese, then Spanish and then Dutch traders, were in 1542 or 1543. It was also common practice at this time for Spain and Portugal to send Catholic missionaries to countries that they had recently conquered or explored, in an attempt to convert the people to Christianity; in 1549 the Jesuit Francis Xavier arrived in Japan via India with this end in view.

The Japanese expressed their curiosity about foreigners and the world beyond their shores in their portrayal of maps of the world, foreign

Above: Lectern for use by Christians, shown in colour on page 90; late 16th century.

Below: Writing-box, shown in colour on page 90; 17th century.

Below: Tea-jar and cover, shown in colour on page 90; 18th century.

traders and their unfamiliar articles of clothing and ships, on such formats as folding screens. The Europeans for their part showed a great interest in things from the East, and particularly from Japan. Lacquer, especially, was a great novelty in Europe and became widely sought after by the wealthy for the adornment of their houses. During the first decade of the seventeenth century lacquerware, usually in the form of chests or cabinets, began to appear in great houses throughout England. A flourishing trade developed between Japan and the West based at the port of Nagasaki, in Kyūshū, one of the westernmost ports of Japan, with lacquer as an important commodity. Meticulous records of ships' cargoes, together with personal diaries and letters of the crew and officials, indicate that in the early seventeenth century there was great activity between European merchants and lacquer-masters; it was largely centred on Kyōto, where the majority of lacquers for the export market were produced in a small number of workshops. This is borne out in a letter dated 10 November 1617 from Will Adams, English adviser to Tokugawa Ieyasu, to Richard Wickham of the English factory at Hirado, which was in existence between 1612 and 1623; the letter reads, 'I have sent by this bearer seventeen sundry parcels of contores (contador) and scrittores (escritorio) marked R.W. (Richard Wickham) . . . I have been at meaco [*miyako* or 'capital', that is, Kyōto] and talked with the makeman who hath promised that in short time he will have done. He hath fifty men that worketh day and night: that, so far as I can see, he doth his endeavour'.

Namban lacquers can roughly be divided into two groups. The first includes those which depict Europeans, with great attention focused on details of dress and other features connected with them, such as their dogs or Western guns. These items, which should be considered in the same context as the painted folding screens with European subjects mentioned above, were intended for the Japanese market. The second type of Namban lacquers were those made for, or commissioned by, foreigners. Among this group are objects connected with Christianity which were intended for use by Jesuit missionaries and Christian converts in Japan; they include reliquaries, bible-rests and portable shrines. Although missionaries initially achieved much success in their task, in time Japanese Christians became the object of bitter opposition and persecution. When Christianity was finally forbidden in 1613, and again in 1623, Namban lacquers with religious affinities all but ceased to be made, while many of the existing objects were destroyed.

Namban lacquerwork made specifically for export included objects of a type previously unknown in Japan, such as the cabinet or domed coffer, which was referred to as 'box in fish-sausage shape' (*kamabokogata*), for there was no existing term to describe it in the Japanese language. The majority of export wares conformed to a standard type and design, which frequently allowed for time-saving devices, in order to fufil large orders and keep the price within reasonable limits. Some £20,000 worth of lacquer sold from three ships, the Martha, Sarah and Dorothy, for example, was probably of this type. In addition, certain wares were produced in response to specific orders and, as such, frequently bore the initials or name of the person for whom they were intended. Perhaps the most celebrated example is a box of outstanding workmanship which is

marked 'Maria Uan Diemen', who was the wife of Anton van Diemen (d. 1645), ninth Governor of the Dutch East Indies.

In the manufacture of export wares Japanese lacquerers evolved a curious style which adopted and adapted both indigenous and non-Japanese decorative and technical features. Thus mother-of-pearl inlay techniques from Gujarat and Korea (the latter probably as a result of Hideyoshi's Korean campaigns of 1592–93 and 1597–98) were combined with variations of the Chinese classic scroll, geometric elements from Europe, and purely Japanese features such as the autumn plants associated with contemporary Kōdai-ji wares. The designs were executed in gold and silver *hiramaki-e* and *e-nashiji*, with mother-of-pearl inlays formed of unshaped or pre-cut pieces; or the mother-of-pearl might be deliberately cracked or overpainted with details in gold lacquer.

In his definitive summary and personal interpretation of the fruits of existing scholarship on the subject of Namban lacquerware, Oliver Impey has formulated a chronology of style and shape which distinguishes between a 'Namban' style of the late Momoyama and a 'pictorial' style of the late seventeenth century. Examples of the latter are true export wares and should be considered as outside the main course of Japanese lacquerware. For more information on these and other aspects of the subject, see the section on Japanese Export Lacquer (page 123).

Throughout the Momoyama period, examples of lacquer in a conservative style continued to be produced; these preserved late Muromachi traditions of design and technique, with certain concessions to contemporary ideas and trends. There was a new interdependent relationship between the shape of the object and its decoration. In some instances the design was even positioned in such a way as to be cut off at unexpected angles by the edges of the object. Although this would seem to negate a close relationship between design and object, it reflects a subtle understanding on the part of the lacquerer, which resulted in works of a powerful decorative impact. The tendency, along with others which had their origins in the Momoyama or earlier periods, came to full fruition during the subsequent Edo period.

The Edo period (1615–1868)

With the death of Toyotomi Hideyoshi in 1598 Japan was once again thrown into a period of confusion and civil war. Some two years later Tokugawa Ieyasu (1542–1616), the last of the three powerful rulers of the Momoyama period, defeated his rivals at the Battle of Sekigahara and was subsequently appointed shōgun in 1603. He had a great castle built at the site of his former headquarters in Edo, which gave its name to the period as a whole. The castle at Edo became firmly established as the centre of shōgunal power, while, at the same time, the city of Edo (present-day Tokyo) grew around it.

The long historical Edo period, which encompasses many individual periods, the most notable of which was the Genroku era (1688–1703), did not begin until 1615 with the defeat of any serious opposition to the Tokugawa shōgunate. Ieyasu's prime objective was to consolidate his own position and to ensure that power was passed to his heirs without dispute or conflict. Undoubtedly the greatest threat came from the *daimyō*, and in order to curb their power the shōgunate instigated a compulsory system whereby the *daimyō* were obliged to spend alternate years at the capital away from their estates and their local power base. In order to dissipate any wealth they may have accumulated, they were forced to live on an extravagant scale and to maintain grand households at both centres. It was also customary for their residences to be decorated in a sumptuous manner and to be filled with costly works of art. This, together with the fact that the Edo was a period of peace and prosperity, greatly stimulated the course of Edo arts and crafts. The shōgunate thus succeeded in imposing a costly standard of living on the *daimyō* which drastically curtailed their economic and, hence, political power by a system of 'control through impoverishment'. It was no coincidence that the Edo period was one of peace which lasted some two hundred and fifty years until the restoration of the imperial line in 1868.

By the beginning of the Edo period a series of orders had already been issued, though they were never fully implemented, which proscribed the practice of Christianity in Japan. In 1637 the peasant revolt of Shimabara, which involved many Christians, was the last straw. As a direct result of this, Christianity in Japan was finally forbidden and Europeans were expelled, with the exception of a number of Dutch traders who, along with the Chinese, were permitted to trade from Nagasaki on the island of Deshima. The so-called period of seclusion which followed, far from giving rise to a phase of introverted stagnation in Japanese culture, actually encouraged a re-examination and reinterpretation of traditional ideals, which produced something of a cultural resurgence during the Edo period. At the same time the influence of Chinese culture, which had played a significant role from around 1400 onwards, reasserted itself as the traditional source of external stimuli to native Japanese culture.

When Tokugawa Ieyasu established his new capital at Edo it was little more than a fishing village without artistic traditions of its own. It was some years before the shōgunate could attract to Edo lacquerers of a sufficiently high calibre to

Right: Small chest; 18th century. Irises grow by a stream in gold *takamaki-e* with inlays of coral and mother-of-pearl and encrustations of gold against a lavish background: large irregular flakes of gold are individually set into a gold lacquer ground.

form the basis of a new local tradition of lacquer-work. During the early years of the Edo period, therefore, it is hardly surprising that the supremacy of Kyōto as the centre of the lacquer industry initially remained unchallenged. During the early Edo period much of the lacquerware produced at Kyōto continued to be influenced by Kōdai-ji wares of the preceding Momoyama period, though the use of the diagonal, zigzag line characteristic of earlier works had all but disappeared. Instead it was the distinctive use of gold lacquer (as found on Kōdai-ji lacquers, particularly *e-nashiji*) on a black lacquer ground which persisted and came into its own during the first few decades of the seventeenth century. The lacquerer was thus able to produce a highly successful pictorial effect by making use of the full variety of gold powder techniques at his disposal. These were used in such a way as to produce an effect similar to that of a black and white picture, with all the tones and shades that it was possible to achieve within the range of gold monochrome.

By the late 1630s Kyōto had ceased to be the main innovative and creative centre of lacquer-work, while Edo emerged to take its place. With the establishment of Edo as the new seat of government, Tokugawa Ieyasu, and in particular his grandson Iemitsu, who was shōgun between

1623 and 1651, succeeded in attracting many leading artists to their court. Lacquer-artists such as Tsuishu Yōsei VIII (d. 1654), who was a master of carved lacquer, Kajikawa Hikobei (active 1624–43) and Koma Kyūi (d. 1663) were all provided with official patronage and commissions.

The Tokugawa shōguns, their court circle, and those in influential positions sought to display their wealth and power in a materialistic display of pomp and luxury. They endeavoured to fill their residences with sumptuous works of art, particularly lacquer. Such patrons were not particularly interested in innovation but preferred traditional styles and techniques which were already widely accepted, as manifested in the so-called 'official' style. For the most part this carried on late Muromachi traditions of design and technique which were handed down through the Momoyama period in a slightly modified form and which continued almost unchanged up until the Meiji Restoration of 1868. Examples of Edo official lacquerwork were rich and detailed in their execution, with a profusion of gold lacquer, relying heavily on *takamaki-e*, as well as inlays of metal and semi-precious stones. They were most frequently decorated with scroll patterns, birds, trees, flowers and landscape scenes, often with strong literary allusions, which harp back to a practice from the Ashikaga period. The overall effect of the official style of lacquer decoration was sumptuous and intricate; a peak of excessive technical virtuosity and material cost was reached during the Genroku period (1688–1703). Towards the latter part of the Edo period, lacquer decorated in the official style revealed a general lowering of standards, with creative originality of design suffering at the expense of technical bravado.

There are three main schools of lacquerers associated with the shōgunate and hence with the official style, namely the Kōami, Koma and Kajikawa, all of whom were instrumental in establishing the reputation of Edo lacquerwork. Certain members of the Kōami family, including Chōsei (1506–1603) and his sons Chōan (1569–1610) and Chōgen (1572–1607), had worked for the Momoyama shōgunate in Kyōto. Chōsei received the right to use a seal inscribed *tenka ichi*, 'first under heaven', from Hideyoshi, while at an early age Chōan was commissioned to supply the necessary articles for the enthronement ceremony of the Emperor Go-Yōzei. Nagashige (1599–1651) and Nagafusa (1628–82) were two members of the family noted for their service to the Tokugawa shōgunate at Edo. It was Nagashige, furthermore, who was responsible for the so-called *Hatsune* wedding-set, preserved in the Tokugawa Art Museum, in Nagoya, which is the

apogee of early Edo official lacquerwork. The wedding-set, which comprises more than fifty items of furniture and other utensils, formed part of the dowry of Chiyohime, Tokugawa Iemitsu's eldest daughter, on her marriage to Tokugawa Mitsumoto of Owari. Kōami Nagashige is reputed to have spent three years, that is between 1637 and 1639, in executing the lacquer decoration. The designs used on the wedding-set are taken from the *Hatsune* section of the early eleventh century *Genji monogatari*, 'Tale of Genji'. The *Hatsune* section is symbolic of a happy life and was thus highly appropriate. It also provides evidence of the continuing use of literary themes in lacquerwork of the official style.

Apart from Kyōto and Edo there was a third centre which was noted for its lacquerware during the early Edo period, namely Kanazawa, in Kaga, present-day Ishikawa prefecture. It was customary at this time for leading *daimyō* to employ lacquerers to provide them with the lacquered goods they required. Maeda Toshitsune, the third *daimyō* of Kaga, was no exception and summoned Igarashi Dōho I (d. 1678) from Kyōto, accompanied by his adopted son Dōho II (d. 1691/7) and his pupil Shimizu Kuhei (Kyūbei) active during the early-mid Edo period. The distinctive works they produced, which were of an exceptionally high quality, formed the basis of so-called

Right: Writing-box; mid-18th century. Rocks and peonies line the banks of a stream in gold and silver *takamaki-e*, with *kirikane* on a black lacquer ground. The decoration of the box is in the style of *Kaga-maki-e*.

Strictly speaking, *Kaga-maki-e* was an example of provincial lacquerware, though its exceptional quality put it on an equal footing with that of Kyōto or Edo. At the same time other local centres began to develop their own specific type or style of lacquer, which was generally less ambitious but nonetheless important to the development of Japanese lacquer. Many of these provincial styles were directly influenced by the emergence and subsequent popularity of a group of painted lacquers of the late Momoyama and early Edo periods.

The earliest surviving example of any kind of lacquer-painting in Japan is the seventh century Tamamushi shrine. Later, in the post-Nara period, lacquer-painting all but disappeared as lacquer-artists turned their attention to developing and perfecting gold and silver *maki-e* techniques. Lacquer-painting, however, re-emerged during the late Momoyama period, perhaps partly because of the popularity of Momoyama screen painting, with bold and often contrasting areas of colour, as well as the influence of Chinese coloured lacquers of the Ming dynasty (1368–1644). It may also have been a reaction to a general lack of colour in a tradition which, for centuries, had relied predominantly on black, gold and silver. Although the new painted lacquerware was frequently of a high standard, the use of this technique was largely restricted to articles of everyday use and, particularly, to those connected with food, such as bowls (*wan*) and trays (*bon*). These were intended for the wealthy and powerful, but they served a different function to that of the lavish showpieces decorated in the official style, for practical considerations were of prime importance; it was not worth lavishing expensive gold materials on objects which were, for example, used to serve food. *Urushi-e*, or lacquer-painting, and *mitsuda-e*, essentially an oil-painting technique, were both frequently combined on a single object. This is exemplified by the works of Tanida Chūbei (active 1751–71), one of the most celebrated exponents of Edo lacquer-painting, who was renowned for his designs of floral themes on a red lacquer ground. The unique combination of functional shape, relatively simple technique with colourful decoration of an immediate appeal, high quality and reasonable price ensured the success and popularity of early Edo painted lacquerware.

Another type was known as *Jogahana-nuri*, 'Jogahana lacquer', which derives its name from the town of Jogahana, in present-day Toyama prefecture. It differs from the oil-painting technique, *mitsuda-e*, in that the pigments were bound together with oil or a mixture of oil and lacquer, without the addition of lead oxide, or litharge, as a drying agent. It was reputed to have been brought to Jogahana by Jigoemon, also known as

Above: Sake-bottle for ceremonial use; late 17th century. The decoration is red lacquer-painting, *urushi-e*, on a black lacquer ground. Pine trees, cranes and tortoises are symbols of longevity.

Kaga-maki-e, which was equal in quality to lacquer from both Kyōto and Edo. The Igarashi school itself boasted an impressive pedigree since its founder, Shinsai (*c.* 1480), had worked for Ashikaga Yoshimasa, shōgun between 1443 and 1473. The distinctive feature of *Kaga-maki-e* is the contrast and balance between areas of design, complex in their technical execution, and undecorated areas, usually made up of plain black lacquer and sometimes accounting for over half the decorative surface area. The overall effect is one of restrained elegance and space. Such wares were in direct contrast to official lacquerware, with its detailed and intricate designs.

Below: Writing-box, shown in colour on page 95; mid-18th century.

Below: Detail of writing-box cover; early to mid-19th century. It is in *Wakasa-nuri* of gold, brown and black lacquer.

Yoshinaga, who learnt the technique from Chinese workers at Nagasaki during the late sixteenth century, though none of his works have survived. It is often difficult to distinguish between *mitsuda-e* and *Jogahana-nuri*, so that the term *mitsuda-e* has come to be used indiscriminately to describe all types of oil-painting on a lacquer base.

Other provincial centres which became renowned for their distinctive lacquer techniques during the seventeenth century include Tsugaru, in present-day Aomori prefecture, Wakasa, in present-day Fukui prefecture, and Wajima, in the prefecture of Ishikawa. The technique of *Tsugaru-nuri*, 'Tsugaru lacquer', is reputed to have been introduced by Ikeda Gentarō in 1685. It is characterized by a mottled surface of red, yellow, green, brown and black lacquer. This effect was achieved with layers of different-coloured lacquer on a surface which was made uneven by applying substances such as eggshell, rice or leaves. When the lacquer was finally polished to a smooth finish, it produced a dappled colour surface.

Although the technique of *Wakasa-nuri*, which is said to have originated in the Manji era (1658–61), reveals certain basic similarities, the effect is widely different. Layers of coloured lacquer were applied to an uneven base in the same way, but then thin gold or silver foil was pressed firmly into the hollows and the whole surface was covered with transparent lacquer and polished until it was smooth. Although the predominant effect was of yellow, brown and gold, the coloured lacquer under the foil often showed through in places to produce a striking and distinctive pattern.

Wajima-nuri is very different, a local variant of the *chinkin-bori* technique. Since *chinkin-bori* involved incising fine lines into the lacquer surface, it was essential to provide a firm and durable ground. At Wajima this was achieved by combining lacquer with a special kind of clay that was discovered in the locality during the Kambun era (1661–73). Lacquer-artists thus exploited the advantages of a naturally occurring material to produce their own version of an existing, but not otherwise widely used, technique.

The late Momoyama and early Edo periods were marked by the appearance of a group of highly talented and creative artists, namely Kōetsu, Sōtatsu, Kōrin and Kenzan. They were cultured men who displayed skills and talents in numerous fields and who profoundly affected the course of Edo art in general. Kōetsu and Kōrin had the greatest influence on lacquerwork.

Honami Kōetsu (1558–1637) was not only a talented lacquerer and painter, having studied under the Tosa school, but he was also an expert calligrapher, a gifted potter and a skilful forger and polisher of sword blades. In 1615 he received a gift of land from Tokugawa Ieyasu at Takagamine near Kyōto, where he proceeded to gather round him artists of many different crafts. Amongst members of the artistic community that subsequently developed, there evolved a distinctive concept of composition and design which could equally be translated into lacquerware, paintings or ceramics.

Although Kōetsu was well known as a lacquerer, the true extent of his involvement in the manufacture of works attributed to him is uncertain. It seems likely, however, that he was responsible for the overall design of such wares and for the choice of lacquer technique and the material for inlay. There would have been no shortage of assistants amongst the community in Takagamine to realize his ideas in the lacquer medium. Kōetsu pioneered a style of decoration which combined plain black lacquer and gold *maki-e* with bold inlays of mother-of-pearl, lead, pewter and silver. The overall effect was one of strength, heightened by the new domed profile of the lid, and of simplicity; together they produced a powerful visual impact. Kōetsu and his circle turned for their inspiration to what they considered to be the golden age of the Heian period. This is reflected in the frequent use of literary themes, as exemplified by the *Funabashi* writing-box, the subject of which refers to a tenth century poem about the boat bridge at Sano. The solid silver written characters of the poem are superimposed in relief against a design of boats bobbing amidst waves, spanned by a bold band of lead, representing the bridge. The fact that the pictorial representations and the written characters are inextricably interwoven is well illustrated by the ingenious manner in which the characters for 'boat' and 'bridge', which form the main motifs of the composition, are omitted. Another example of Kōetsu's use of literary allusion, also a writing-box, has a design of a boat, reeds and plovers. Its similarity to one that is illustrated in the *Sanjūroku-nin kashū* (the *Thirty-six Poets*), an anthology of poems dating from 1112, and now in the Nishi Hongan-ji, Kyōto, is unmistakable.

The appeal of Kōetsu-style lacquers lay partly in the fact that they were breaking completely new ground in lacquer design. Their impressionistic manner of portrayal with its use of dull base metals, such as lead and pewter, was also in sharp contrast to lacquerwork of the official style, with its detailed and ornate workmanship and its lavish use of gold lacquer.

Ogata Kōrin (1658–1716) was a great-grand-nephew of Kōetsu and one of his most ardent followers. Kōrin's father was a wealthy Kyōto silk merchant who was also a noted painter and calligrapher in the Kōetsu tradition. Kōrin's younger brother, Kenzan, was renowned as a potter. The artistic skills of the family, however, probably came to full fruition in Kōrin himself.

Right: Writing-box with domed lid; late 17th–early 18th century. The box has a design of waves along a shore, in gold lacquer and applied lead respectively, and has inscribed in silver the text of a poem from one of the classic anthologies. Designed by Ogata Kōrin after Honami Kōetsu.

Below: Inlay could be in high relief, as on the opposite page, or inset into the base and then lacquered and polished down. This tray was made in the 19th century to show the sequence of flat inlay work. 1. *Hirame* over a mixture of black and branch lacquer. 2. Application of coral, shell, etc inlays covered with three coats of transparent lacquer. 3. Coating of Rō lacquer, ground smooth (4) with magnolia charcoal and polished. 6. Coating of branch lacquer, polished with antler ashes and oil. 7. *Hirame*, polished after lacquering. 8. The entire inlaid work polished and the veining of leaves completed.

Opposite page: Writing-box; early 18th century. The decorative motifs are of Chinese inspiration: a Chinese lady with Chinese antiques, including scrolls, a bronze tripod and a celadon vase in ivory, pottery, mother-of-pearl and tortoiseshell with details in red and gold lacquer on a black lacquer ground. Inscribed with the green pottery seal of Ritsuō.

Right: Writing-box; 18th century. The famous 9th century poet Ariwara no Narihira is depicted on a fan in gold *hiramaki-e* with applied silver and tin on a black lacquer ground. The box may have been produced under Kōrin's supervision.

Opposite page, top: Smoking-cabinet in the form of a six-fold screen; early 19th century. The plants are in gold and silver *togidashi* on a black lacquer ground surrounded by gold *fundame* lacquer. On top of the cabinet are a lacquer tobacco-box in the form of an *inrō*, a silver box for ash with a bronze ox, in the form of a netsuke, and a silver stove in the form of a pouch.

Opposite page, bottom: Palanquin; 19th century. The scrolls and badges are in gold *hiramaki-e* on a black ground. The palanquin bears gilt and engraved metal fittings.

He studied painting first under Kano Tsunenobu, and later under masters of the Tosa school, and was greatly influenced by the styles of Kōetsu and Sōtatsu.

Although Kōrin is perhaps best known as a painter, his contribution to the development of contemporary and subsequent lacquerwork is far-reaching, though the exact nature of his involvement with the lacquer medium, like that of Kōetsu, is uncertain.

Although Kōrin carried on the Kōetsu tradition of composition and design, he interpreted and adapted it in a manner which produced lacquer-ware of a more immediate and pleasing appeal. Kōrin made use of large and simple motifs, yet it was precisely this simplicity, this apparent lack of decorative detail, which suggested great depth of detail: he was a master of the understatement. This is well borne out by the *Yatsuhashi*, 'eight bridges', writing-box, probably the best-known item of lacquerware attributed to Kōrin. The design of iris clumps, which are depicted in gold *maki-e* and mother-of-pearl inlay, amidst eight sections of a bridge, portrayed in lead, refer to a section of the *Ise monogatari*, a famous collection of romantic tales from the tenth century. One of the most powerful and striking aspects of the box is the relationship between its shape and the motifs, as well as the manner in which the sections of the bridge link the sides and top surface of the lid and lead the viewer's eyes over the surface of the box. Although the irises are portrayed in a stylized silhouette-form, with no additional naturalistic detail, they nevertheless convey the impression of

lush plants that are actually growing. Therein lies the great skill of Kōrin as a decorative artist.

Ogawa Haritsu (1663–1747), better known by the name Ritsuō, was a contemporary and student of Kōrin though he outlived him by some thirty years. Although his various artistic talents included poetry, wood-carving, metalwork, pottery and painting, Ritsuō is best remembered for his lacquerwork. He owed much to the Kōetsu-Kōrin tradition, with its skilful interaction between lacquer and inlay, though he placed greater emphasis on the inlays themselves. He extended the materials in use to include ivory, jade, coral, mother-of-pearl, tortoiseshell, pieces of carved red lacquer and pottery. Conversely, he produced successful examples of pottery or lacquer which resembled the appearance and texture of other materials, such as wood, stone and metal. Both by way of contrast and in order to show the often colourful and striking combination of inlays to their best advantage, Ritsuō preferred to use a background of plain lacquered wood, woven bamboo, or even rough and decaying wood. Indeed, lacquer often played a secondary role in his works, though he is still primarily classed as a lacquerer. The ingenious and inventive nature of Ritsuō's compositions is borne out by a writing-box dated 1720, with a design of two ink-cakes. One of these is a piece of genuine old Chinese ink inlaid into the lacquer background; the other is lacquer imitating a real cake of ink. This also reflects Ritsuō's passion for Chinese things.

Ritsuō's works were enormously popular amongst his contemporaries and he was succeeded by his most important pupil, Mochizuki Hanzan, who was active around the mid-eighteenth century. The impact of artists such as Kōetsu, Kōrin and Ritsuō was considerable and their distinctive concept of design, together with their use of diverse materials, greatly influenced the subsequent development of lacquerwork. Although they did not found a school in the true sense of the word, perhaps because their talents were unique, they had their followers over the centuries. There were periods during which the works of Kōrin in particular received considerable attention, stimulating the production of lacquerwork in his style. This was partly due to the publication of woodblock-printed books of his designs, particularly during the early nineteenth century, as exemplified by the *Kōrin hyakuzu* (*One hundred sketches by Kōrin*), compiled by the painter Sakai Hōitsu (1761–1828) to commemorate the centenary of Kōrin's death, and again during the early Meiji period (1868–1912), with the publication of the *Kōrin shinsen Hyakuzu* (*New selection of one hundred sketches by Kōrin*) in 1864.

During the Edo period the range of objects to which lacquer was applied was greatly increased. Lacquer was no longer the sole prerogative of the

nobility, who commissioned lavish showpieces; for with the rise of a wealthy middle class, and with quicker and cheaper methods of producing lacquer, everyday lacquer objects were made in increasing numbers. The durability of the material and its resistance to heat, moisture and acids made it an ideal covering for objects connected with the preparation and eating of food, including *sake*-cups and bottles, sweetmeat-boxes, picnic sets, and miscellaneous bowls and trays. It was also used for an enormous variety of other household articles such as clothes-chests and clothes-stands, low writing-tablets and smoking-cabinets, cages for birds and insects, palanquins and domestic shrines and for toilet articles, including combs, brushes, hairpins, mirrors and cosmetic-boxes. Lacquer, being light in weight yet durable, was applied to military accoutrements and paraphernalia. The individual plates of various types of armour, for example, were composed of iron or leather which was then covered with thick layers of lacquer. In addition, parts of the helmet may have been lacquered, together with the sword scabbard, *tsuba* or sword guard, and the saddle

Above: Sake-cup; 19th century. Carp, symbols of perseverance, leap against a waterfall on this cup of gold and red *hiramaki-e* on a gold *fundame* ground.

Right: Sake-cup; 19th century. Executed in gold, black, silver and red *hiramaki-e* enriched with mother-of-pearl on a gold *fundame* ground, the cup shows three figures playing *suguroku* in front of a screen.

and stirrups. Its increasing use in this context reflects the fact that the Edo period was a time of peace during which arms and armour were for ceremonial display rather than actual combat.

The customs and lifestyle of the Japanese were such that covered boxes were the most common containers for both treasured objects and those in everyday use; almost everything in the house was stored in them and taken out only when needed. Boxes appeared in a wide variety of size and shape, serving a variety of functions, and constituted the mainstay of the lacquerer's work. Many were intended for a specific purpose, such as the *bunkō*, 'document-box', or the *suzuribako*, 'writing-box', which was an essential tool of the literate Japanese. The writing-box was most commonly rectangular or square and was designed to contain the necessary implements, such as the ink-cake, water-dropper, inkstone, brushes and knife. Other boxes contained elaborate sets for ceremonies and games; among the most important of the games were the incense game, poem card game, shell game, *shōgi* (Japanese chess) and *sugoroku* (Japanese backgammon).

The *inrō* or 'seal basket', probably the most popular small lacquer item during the Edo period, was to assume a role of paramount importance. Its

Above: Incense set; late 18th century. This set for the incense ceremony in gold and silver *takamaki-e* on a *nashiji* ground is decorated with phoenixes, rocks, a stream, and the paulownia badge of the Ishikawa family of Kameyama, for whom it was probably made.

early origins are uncertain and appear to be connected with similar containers, of Chinese manufacture, to hold either a person's seal or medicine.

In both China and Japan the seal was used as a guarantee of an individual's identity or as a symbol of office, and the boxes held both the all-important seal and the red seal-paste. As early as 1363 the annual inventory of the Enkaku-ji temple, in Kamakura, mentions 'medicine and seal-cases' made of Chinese carved lacquer. These generally took the form of a nest of boxes about 10 centimetres (4 inches) square. At some stage in their development, and certainly by the beginning of the sixteenth century, cords were inserted vertically through either side of the nest and the whole set became smaller and more compact.

The Japanese pharmacopoeia, which owed much to that of China, consisted chiefly of herbs, roots, minerals and anatomical parts of animals, together with new remedies such as *miira*, or powder from ground Egyptian mummies, introduced through European traders during the late sixteenth and early seventeenth centuries. Such medicines were stored in *kusuri-bako* or medicine-boxes, which were in use as early as the eighth and ninth centuries. They were usually just over 30 centimetres (12 inches) square and contained other smaller receptacles for the different types of medicine. At some later date these, like the seal boxes, became smaller and were tied together with cords so that they could easily be carried about. Lacquered objects were intrinsically suited to contain medicines as lacquer helped to preserve them in a fresh state.

At some stage the two types of boxes became inextricably connected, and the ubiquitous *inrō* was the result. The term was employed indiscriminately as early as the fourteenth century to describe both seal- and medicine-cases made of lacquer. These may also have been protected by

an outer bag or basket, which helps account for the term '*inrō*' or 'seal *basket*'. It was probably not until around the late sixteenth century that the *inrō* appeared in its fully developed form as we know it today, generally composed of from one to seven lacquer cases which fit tightly into one another and which are closed at the top with a lid. They are on average between 7 and 10 centimetres (about 2½ to 3¾ inches) in height and are most commonly ellipsoid in cross-section. At either side of the main body are channels through which a cord is threaded. This is arranged in an ornamental bow at the bottom of the *inrō*, while at the top the two threads are brought together and pass through an *ojime* or sliding bead. The two ends of the cord are then secured within a netsuke, or small three-dimensional carving, which was necessary to suspend the *inrō* from the *obi* or sash. Since the traditional Japanese garment, the kimono, had no pockets, it was necessary to find alternative means to carry around everyday necessities. The small pouches or containers, such as the tobacco pipe and pouch, and the *inrō* – known collectively as the *sagemono* – were hung from the sash. The *inrō*, used exclusively by men, was traditionally worn on the right side of the body.

The majority of *inrō* were composed of lacquer over a wooden core, and the processes involved in their manufacture were highly complex, requiring the skills of specialist craftsmen. The numerous stages in the manufacture of a lacquered object, such as drying the wooden base to avoid warping, and applying base and top layers of lacquer with adequate time and appropriate conditions for drying between each, were all the more necessary for the *inrō*: not only did each case have to fit tightly into the next, but it was essential that they could be separated and opened out smoothly, without undue pressure being exerted on any part of the object. It is a great tribute to the precise skills of the *inrō* lacquer-artist that even today many *inrō* still fulfil these stringent requirements.

The standard *inrō* presents two rectangular surfaces, a front and back, which are intrinsically suited to some manner of decoration. The *ojime* and netsuke were an integral part of the *inrō* and corresponded in theme and tone even though they may have been produced by different artists working in media other than lacquer. The netsuke in particular, which was generally executed in ivory, bone, wood or, more rarely, lacquer, has in recent times received much attention as an object of high artistic merit in its own right, particularly in the West, and is often collected separately from the *inrō* and *ojime*. Then too the *inrō* generally suffers more from wear and tear than the two carved pieces.

The Edo period saw the emergence of towns and cities as creative and generative centres. This was partly due to the system imposed by the shōgunate whereby the *daimyō* were obliged to spend alternate years at Edo, along with their families, retainers and servants. It was also partly due to the economic and social upheaval which occurred during the period. Many of the old aristocratic families set themselves on the road to financial ruin in an attempt to maintain a high material standard of living and hence convey a lavish outward appearance of wealth and opulence. The samurai also suffered financially as it was a period of peace and they were therefore warriors in name only, living on small stipends. The merchants and *chōnin* or townsmen, on the other hand, who engaged in trade and industry, prospered at their expense. It was a highly materialistic society in which those connected with financial matters, such as money-lending, and

Right: Inrō; early 19th century. The god of thunder orchestrates a storm while people run for shelter. The *inrō* is decorated with gold and silver *takamaki-e* enriched with *kirikane*, gold flakes. Signed Koma Kyūhaku, probably the work of Koma Kyūhaku IV.

those dealing with procuring and supplying various commodities were in great demand. Although merchants continued to occupy the lowest social order in Japanese society, they assumed a new position of power in the national economy. Denied any political influence, merchants and townsmen directed their newly found wealth to the arts and crafts and to the pursuit of enjoyment and leisure. Money was largely concentrated in urban areas. In Edo, the Yoshiwara district catered for the pleasures of its populace with licensed courtesans and brothels, restaurants, theatres and *sumō* wrestling halls. These are amply portrayed in the woodblock-printed novels and prints of the time.

The merchants and, to a lesser extent, the townsmen, thus emerged as the new patrons of popular culture. Their artistic tastes are reflected in highly ornate works which depict all aspects of everyday life, with a particular delight in the ingenious, unusual or outrageous, often well illustrated in miniature by the *inrō*; the lacquer-artists responded happily to such artistic licence, largely outside the conventions and restrictions imposed on other, more 'serious' objects.

The *inrō* was originally worn by men of the upper strata of society, such as the *daimyō*. As merchants and townsmen became more affluent and as new methods were developed which made it possible to produce a larger number of *inrō* in a shorter space of time, the boxes came within the purchasing power of the middle classes. This drastically altered the role of the *inrō* from a functional container, to hold medicines or the seal, to a fashionable appendage to Japanese dress. By 1778, it was recorded by a certain Ise Teijō that 'nowadays *inrō* are worn not so much because of their use as because they are pleasing and rather extravagant toys'. In certain quarters it became fashionable to form collections of *inrō*. Matsuura Seizan (1760–1841), the *daimyō* of Hirado, accumulated over a hundred sets which were unfortunately destroyed in a fire during his lifetime. In his journal covering the years 1821 to 1841 he recorded:

> 'While I was serving in the government I began to be fond of accessories that hung from the waist and eventually I became a collector. At that time I was frequently invited to the mansions of various important people. On those occasions the attendants would tag along as I went from the entrance to the interview room and they would ask me what I was wearing from my waist that day. Many of them would follow along behind me to get a better look, trying to flatter me with their attention. My own associates would also ask me what I was wearing and when I went to the shōgun's castle people looked in the same way to see what hung at my waist. Naturally it wouldn't have

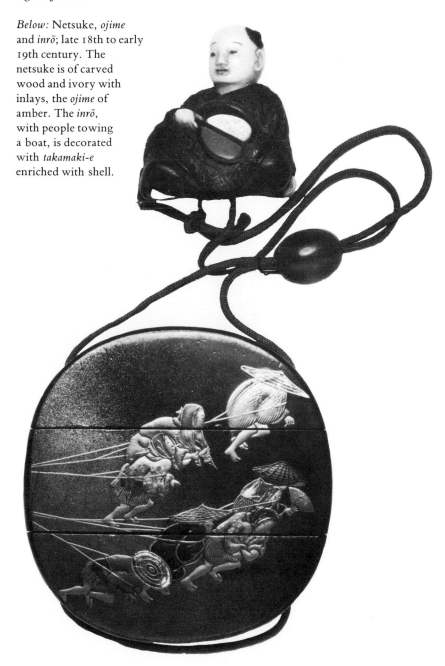

done for me to have worn the same things repeatedly under those circumstances.'

With the adoption of Western dress during the Meiji period (1868–1912), the *inrō* became superfluous and gradually disappeared from everyday use.

This broadly corresponded to an awakening of interest in the *inrō* outside Japan and marked the beginning of many Western collections.

Although the *inrō* lacquer-artist was restricted to a basic form which was dictated by functional requirements, it was possible to make the faces circular, hexagonal or octagonal instead of rectangular, or to expand the elliptical cross-section to form a cylinder. In some extreme cases the entire body of the *inrō* was modelled to represent something else such as a figure, an animal or an insect. Apart from changing the shape of the *inrō* itself, it was also possible to exploit to the full the surface area, which lent itself so well to every kind of decoration; and the disposition of the decoration over the body of the *inrō* could itself be varied. The most common decorative method involved two separate designs, not necessarily connected in theme or subject, on the two main surfaces of the *inrō*. In other examples the *inrō* was decorated with an all-over design with apparent disregard for the outline of the body. More rarely, different patterns, usually abstract or geometric, were used to define each individual case of the body, making horizontal bands of contrasting designs. One of the most successful ways in which the limited surface area was exploited was by extending the design over both main sides of the body either horizontally, vertically or diagonally, often with the centre of the design lying on the cord channels. In many instances this involved drawing the viewer's eye round the body. In a typical scene men pull a rope that disappears over the edge of one side of the body, compelling the viewer to turn it over and discover what is being pulled. Although this device was by no means restricted to *inrō* design, it was nevertheless used on them to particularly striking effect.

The economic and social upheaval of the Edo period made it possible for the merchant class to use their newly acquired wealth to procure the services of some of the leading lacquerers of the day, many of whom produced lacquerware characterized by a profusion of gold *maki-e*, which had previously been available only to the ruling classes. Alarmed at this threat to their traditional position, and spurred on by the fact that gold was in short supply, the latter promulgated numerous decrees banning luxury articles and restricting the amount of gold powder and foil on popular kinds of lacquerware. An edict of 1652, for example, prohibited townsmen from owning furniture and saddles made of *maki-e*, while in 1668 they were forbidden to own *maki-e* at all. In 1724 a further prohibition stated that samurai receiving an income of 10,000 *koku* (1 *koku* was equivalent to 5.2 bushels) of rice a year were entitled only to a light sprinkled design. Such edicts were not always strictly enforced or else were effective only for short periods.

However, gold and silver were in any case expensive and difficult to procure. Describing the work of his grandfather, who was active during the early nineteenth century, the lacquerer Yamamoto Rihei mentions: 'In those days gold was very precious . . . There were silver and gold guilds, and gold was hard to obtain. Aside from what was used at the imperial palace or for the shōgun or other important lords, there was no distribution except for the little the goldsmith shops had, so you could not buy much gold at a time . . . But it was easy for the ruling lords. When one of their daughters married, the gold guild was directed to release whatever gold was needed for her things. If you needed one hundred pieces you asked for two hundred and used the rest elsewhere.' One way round this problem was to use alloys of silver and gold in place of pure gold. In such cases it was sometimes necessary to add some form of colouring agent to the transparent layers of lacquer which covered the metal powder in order to hide the fact that it was not pure gold. In certain extreme cases pure silver or even tin was used instead. The great advantage of the *inrō* in this respect was that, because it was so small, it was possible to use minute quantities of gold and silver to considerable effect. Yamamoto Rihei says of his grandfather's work: 'For the turtle *inrō* he used what [gold] had accumulated on the waste heap'.

Although gold lacquerware continued to be popular and prestigious the problems involved in obtaining the metal encouraged lacquer-artists to develop techniques which relied on other materials. This also coincided with an interest in unusual types of lacquerware. *Zōkoku-nuri*, for example, is named after the lacquer-artist Tamakaji Zōkoku (1806–1869), who worked at Takamatsu, in Shikoku. He specialized not only in carved lacquer but also in the *Kimma* technique. This entailed carving the design on to a black lacquer ground which had already been covered with a rubber solution. The whole surface was covered with red lacquer and left to dry, after which it was washed down to remove the rubber and all the red lacquer except that remaining in the engraved lines which formed the main areas of the design. An adaptation of this technique was known as *Zōkoku-nuri*.

Zōkoku is also thought to have used a technique known as *Zonsei-nuri*, a painted lacquer technique which involved engraving the outlines of the design and filling them with gold dust in a manner similar to that of *chinkin-bori*.

During the latter part of the eighteenth century the *togidashi* technique, and particularly that of *iro-e-togidashi*, 'colour-picture *togidashi*', came into its own. Coloured *togidashi* resembled ordinary *togidashi* except that coloured powders were used instead of gold and silver, and it was not uncommon to combine metal and coloured powders on a single object. During the nineteenth century, however, coloured *togidashi* was increasingly used as the only technique on a lacquered object, particularly to reproduce the effects of woodblock colour prints in the lacquer medium. The use of coloured *togidashi* went hand in hand with the re-emergence of lacquer-painting, which made use of different means to achieve a similar end.

Although materials such as mother-of-pearl and shell had been inlaid into a lacquer surface since at least the eighth century in Japan, the role of such materials was generally of secondary importance to the overall decorative scheme. It was not until the early Edo period that artists such as Kōetsu, Kōrin and Ritsuō made use of an increasing variety of materials, inlaid or encrusted into the lacquer medium, and treated as an integral part of the design. By the nineteenth century such materials included metal ranging from pewter to gold, semi-precious stones, ivory, pottery and shell. Inlays were used to depict minor details of a design, such as the eyes or hands of a figure, and also as its main elements, when the lacquer ground was usually plain (shiny black or gold, for example) so as not to detract from the full impact of the various inlays. Many lacquer-artists had mastered the complexities of the lacquer medium to such an extent that they were able to simulate,

Right: Inrō; mid-19th century. Contrasting diaper bands make up and define the individual cases which comprise this *inrō*. The Somada-style lacquer with minute inlays of gold and *aogai* shell produces a rich, multi-coloured effect.

Opposite page, left: Inrō; mid-19th century. In the shape of a gourd, it is in gold *fundame* lacquer with an inset ivory panel depicting flowers and birds encrusted with shell, ivory, coral and tortoiseshell in the Shibayama style. The wood netsuke represents a demon massaging Shōki, the demon queller.

Opposite page, right: Inrō; late 17th century. Decorated with a bird and flowers in gold and coloured *togidashi* on a black lacquer ground sprinkled with gold, this *inrō* forms one of a set of 100 commissioned by the *daimyō* of Gifu. Signed Koma Yasutada.

The Shibayama school, also founded during the late eighteenth century, made use of a wide variety of different materials, including ivory, metal, coral, jade, soapstone and tortoiseshell, on a lacquer background, frequently of gold. The minute pieces of inlay were sometimes also intricately carved to produce a sculptured effect. The Shibayama family were considerably influenced by the works of Ritsuō, who as already described made use of designs incorporating a large variety of inlays, though the Shibayama preferred minute pieces inlaid in intricate designs.

Both the Somada and Shibayama families produced distinctive work which became synonymous with their names. They also showed a marked preference for small formats, such as the *inrō*, which complemented the minute style of their decoration. As the demand for such works increased during the nineteenth century, lacquerware of the Shibayama type frequently suffered from a general lowering of standards, with a tendency towards fussy and gaudy designs which emphasized little more than the technical skills of the lacquer-artists.

The decoration of Japanese lacquer is extremely

in lacquer, the effects of other materials and textures, such as wood (*mokume-nuri*) or even rusty metal (*sabi-ji-nuri*).

Several schools of lacquer-artists, such as the Somada and Shibayama families, specialized in lacquerwork inlaid with other materials. The work of the Somada school, founded during the eighteenth century, was characterized by thin slivers of colourful iridescent *aogai* shell, inlaid flush, in mosaic form, into a lustrous black lacquer ground to create detailed and intricate designs of landscapes, frequently with buildings, as well as birds, animals and geometric diaper patterns. This characteristic use of shell inlays had much in common with Chinese examples of the same technique.

varied and employs the main themes and subjects found in the decorative repertoire of Japanese art in general. These range from naturalistic representations of animals, human beings and plants to abstract motifs of a purely decorative nature, including comic, gruesome and bizarre scenes. The designs also include references to Shintōism and Buddhism, incidents from myths and legends, actors or scenes from the theatre, exploits of famous warriors, mythical animals such as dragons, festivals and customs, and numerous scenes from everyday life. The essay of instructions for his descendants, written by Kōami Nagasuku (1661–1723) in 1723 mentions: 'Everything in the universe is depicted in sprinkled designs: the dynamic and the static aspects of

Right: Part of a sketch for an *inrō*; *c.* 1740. Two albums of designs were probably compiled for the Yamada family workshop by Yamada Jōkasai's son.

Opposite page: Inrō; *c.* 1900. Three cranes fly across the moon. Signed Hara Yoyusai.

Below: Writing-box; early 19th century. A firefly-hunting party is depicted in gold and coloured *togidashi*.

heaven, earth, and man; the shells and fish; mountains and rivers; a thousand grasses and ten thousand trees; the materials of a house; miscellaneous utensils; all tools; jewellery; the arts; incense; the tea ceremony; cooking; karma; mental impressions. If there is a single one of these things that you do not know you will have difficulty.'

The main schools of lacquer-artists had their favourite sketches and designs which were handed down through successive generations. In addition lacquer-artists frequently made use of designs provided by leading artists of the day. Certain lacquer-artists such as Kōetsu and Kōrin – and Zeshin in the late Edo and early Meiji periods – were themselves painters in their own right, while others simply studied the methods and works of

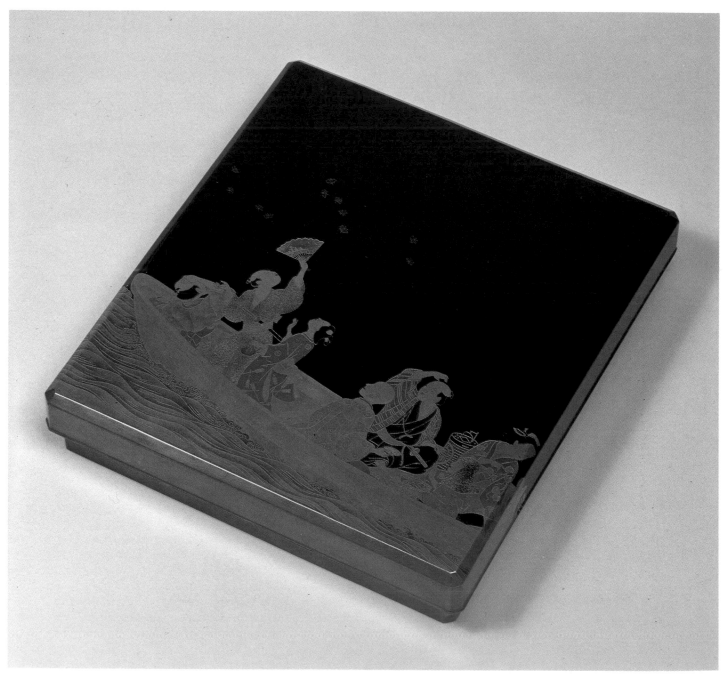

110 *Japan*

Above: Writing-box, shown in colour on page 110; early 19th century.

Right: Inrō of gold *takamaki-e*; late 18th century. The black lacquer ground has encrustations of gold, silver and other metals depicting a famous fight. Signed Kajikawa for the lacquerwork and Hirotoshi for the metalwork.

the main schools of painting. In some instances individual painters produced designs for specific articles of lacquer. The lacquerer Koma Yasutada (1636–1713), for example, was commissioned by the *daimyō* of Gifu to produce a set of a hundred *inrō* based on designs by artists of the Kanō school of painting, each depicting a different bird. In other instances the lacquer-artist simply copied well-known paintings either from first-hand study or from designs in printed sketchbooks. For example the *Hīnagata itoshigusa* ('*An instructional pattern book*'), a guide for *inrō* artists published in 1705, included a number of designs reputed to be the work of famous artists.

Sumi-e togidashi was one of the techniques devised to simulate the effects of ink-painting on paper. It made use of a black powder made from camellia-wood charcoal, which was sprinkled on to the main areas of the design, starting with the darkest areas. When this had dried, the next darkest area was drawn and sprinkled with a lighter tone of black, and so on until the design was complete. The different shades and tones were achieved by adding varying quantities of silver powder to the charcoal. In this way the lacquer-artist was able to reproduce the different ink tones and areas of wash of an ink-painting. When dry, the 'painting' was covered with transparent lacquer and polished down to the picture surface. A number of lacquerers specialized in *sumi-e togidashi*; the most notable was Iizuka Tōyō (active 1764–72), who often made use of drawings by the painter Kanō Michinobu.

Production of woodblock-printed books increased greatly during the latter part of the Edo period and books of designs specifically intended for *inrō* or lacquer in general were available to the lacquer-artist, as well as books of motifs or designs which could be adapted to a variety of media and formats. This explains how almost identical designs were produced in different workshops. The lacquer-artist also adapted and copied popular woodblock prints, frequently employing the coloured *togidashi* technique.

There were still simple craftsmen working in the provinces, well described by the Confucian scholar Ogyū Sorai (1666–1728) and as quoted by Andrew Pekarik:

'I have observed that out in the countryside, when they make layered boxes, the lacquerers are not in a hurry. One lacquer-worker walks a set section of the province and does his work. He lives in one place for twenty or thirty days and applies his lacquer. Then he moves elsewhere and works on something else, calculating how long it took for the lacquer he applied in the first location to dry. Then he comes back and applies the sprinkled design. The lacquer itself has also been bought and prepared in advance. Because the wood bases are made

well ahead of time they are strong and the result is exactly as he wants it.

'A certain retainer of the Tokugawa family, when he was living in Mikawa, had a daughter who would be getting married one day. From the time when she was four or five years old he planned for her wedding day, and the itinerant lacquerer worked on the various furnishings that would be needed. Every year when he came he would add just one or two colours. When I was small I saw what remained of that set. Because all of the parts were made in advance they were indescribably strong.'

The more sophisticated craftsmen, working in the city, had more to worry about. As a result of the time and work that was required to produce a single object, lacquerware was of necessity an extremely costly form of art. In order to avoid the temptation to cut corners in its manufacture and to maintain high standards of quality, it was essential that the most skilled lacquerer had his livelihood guaranteed. This was achieved by a system of patronage by the wealthy and powerful such as the imperial household, the shōgunate, and Buddhist monasteries, as exemplified by lacquers associated with the Kōdai-ji and Negoro temples. It was customary for families of artists to be in the continuous employment of their patrons. The Kōami family, for example, worked for the shōgun and aristocracy for some nineteen successive generations while the Koma worked for the shōgunate for eleven generations. Lacquerers were frequently paid in kind. Kōami Nagasuku wrote in 1720: 'To my great relief I have been given a regular stipend and a place to live'. At the time when Kōami Nagashige executed the *Hatsune* wedding-set described on page 95 the Kōami family were in the official employ of the shōgun Iemitsu and received an annual payment of 200 *koku* of rice. As one *koku* of rice was considered sufficient to support one person for a year, it seems that Nagashige employed many assistants to carry out preparatory work.

The social and economic changes of the Edo period drastically overturned this traditional relationship between the artist and his patron. One factor was the financial impoverishment of many former leading families and the subsequent rise of a wealthy middle class, who acted as patrons of the arts but were interested in buying single items rather than providing sufficient work to employ a lacquerer over a period of several years. Another was the widespread custom of signing individual objects, particularly *inrō*, with the name of the lacquer-artist. In the past, when the lacquer-artist was in the permanent or semi-permanent employ of his patron, it would not have been correct for him to add his name to an object. During the Edo period, however, although many lacquerers, particularly those who worked in the official style, continued to be employed on this basis, others tended to be commissioned for specific individual items or to be employed on a less permanent basis. It became customary for some lacquer-artists to produce at least a few wares for sale through middle-men or through retail outlets. Increasingly, the lacquer-artist had to rely on personal recommendation and also had to publicize his talents by signing his name.

If the lacquerer made use of inlays of another material such as metal, he might also acknowledge this collaboration by adding the name of the metal-worker to his own. Similarly, when the lacquer-artist reproduced well-known woodblock prints, he frequently included the artist's name.

In both China and Japan, part of an artist's training involved studying the working methods and styles of past masters in order to understand better the complexities of the various media. In such instances, an object might be signed with the name of the original artist as well as with the name of the artist who actually carried out the work – but with no intention to mislead.

However, it is an unfortunate fact that some artists even then produced objects which they deliberately tried to pass off as being old or by a past master. This is well borne out by an extract from *Shodō no Shiki* written between 1700 and 1723 which states:

'There was an artist of sprinkled designs by the name of Igarashi Dōho. Since old works of lacquer were scarce, he did many imitations . . . When he imitated old aventurine (that is, gold-sprinkled lacquer), he rubbed in lampblack, then added a coat of lacquer which he wiped away completely. He wiped powdered charcoal in the crevices of the raised areas so that some was left behind. He added lead to the silver and gold . . . and he deliberately aged it. He would place a cover over the piece and smoke it with burning straw . . . But gradually, through experience, even the lowliest itinerant lacquerers learned to recognize the methods of these works called "Dōho fakes".'

It was traditional for a successful Japanese lacquer-artist to train a talented son or close relative to succeed him as head of the workshop and to assume the family name. If there was no suitable relative to take over this position, then an outsider was adopted into the family. The term 'family' was not used, therefore, in the strict sense of the word but was considered instead as a continuous line of talented lacquerers bound together not only by name but also by certain traditions associated with them. The three most important and widely known families of lacquerers are the Kōami, Koma and Kajikawa. In addition, many other names and families were

Right and above (detail): Inrō of black lacquer; early to mid-19th century. The whole inrō is in the form of a cake of Chinese ink, including the cracked surface and worn edges simulating normal usage, depicting a lantern and the seal of Ritsuō. The detail above shows the signature scratched in the lacquer surface: Zeshin saku, 'made by Zeshin'.

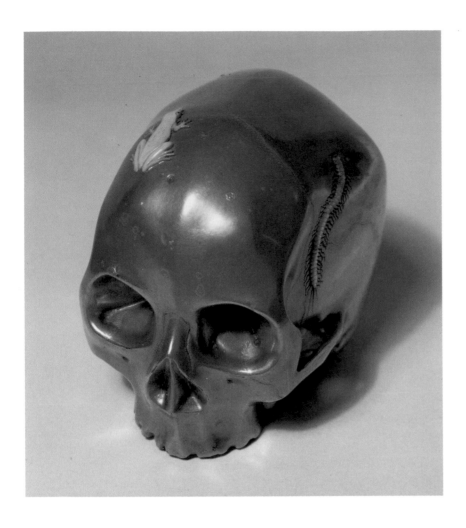

Above: Model of the upper portion of a skull in gold lacquer; Meiji period. The model faithfully reproduces the irregularities and pitting of the human cranium, together with a frog and insect applied to the surface.

Right: Box and cover for writing-paper; Meiji period. Trees and plants stand within a garden wall. The decoration is gold and silver *hiramaki-e* enriched with mother-of-pearl on a black lacquer ground.

prominent during the Edo period. These include Shiomi Masanari (1647–*c.* 1723), a pupil of the Koma school who excelled in *togidashi* and whose *maki-e* work was such that the term 'Shiomi *maki-e*' became synonymous with good-quality lacquerwork, and Yamada Jōkasai (active in the late seventeenth century), who was skilful in many lacquer styles.

Meiji period (1868–1912) and beyond

The fall of the Tokugawa shōgunate in 1867 and the restoration of the imperial line in 1868 marked the beginning of modern Japan. With the abolition of the feudal order, the *daimyō* were divested of their land rights, which had been their source of income, and the samurai were systematically stripped of their privileges. The effect on Japanese art, and lacquer in particular, was devastating. The Tokugawa shōgunate, and the *daimyō*, had been the most important sources of employment for artists of all kinds, but lacquerers had the greatest problem in adapting to the situation since their work, more than any of the other arts, was extremely costly in terms of time and effort.

Although the enthronement of the Emperor Meiji in 1868 in effect marked the end of a period

of seclusion which had lasted more than two hundred years, contact with the West had in fact been established at an earlier date. Some Japanese goods had been exhibited at the Great Exhibition of 1851 in London, and in 1858, for example, a number of countries, including England, concluded commercial agreements with Japan. Just before the emperor's enthronement, in 1867, *maki-e* wares executed by the Kōami lacquerers were sent to the second World Exhibition held in Paris, where they received considerable attention. Unfortunately, the immediate result of renewed contact with the West was a rejection of native traditions in favour of Western ideals, including Western dress. This resulted in a decline in the demand for native arts, and this too had an adverse effect on the lacquer industry.

Under the Meiji government, examples of both old and modern lacquerware were exhibited at the World Exhibition in Vienna in 1873. The following year, the French steamer that was carrying the objects back to Japan sank off the Izu peninsula of Japan. When the boat was salvaged some eighteen months later, the fact that the lacquerware was undamaged by sea-water caused a worldwide sensation.

As a result of the Vienna exhibition, a number of British and Austrian dealers wished to import consignments of Japanese arts and crafts, and the *Kiritsu Kōshō Kaisha* (Kiritsu Industrial and Commercial Company) was set up in 1874 by Matsuo Gisuke and Iwai Kanesaburō, who had travelled to Vienna in connection with the exhibition. To fulfil orders and to ensure that standards were maintained, the company established workshops in Japan where craftsmen produced lacquer, ceramics and metalwork. Branches were subsequently set up in New York in 1877 and Paris in 1878. These organized Japanese exhibits at subsequent international exhibitions, including the Philadelphia World Fair of 1876 and an exhibition in Boston in 1883, and also did much to introduce Japanese crafts to the West until 1891 when the company was dissolved. During the 1870s, many warehouses and establishments specializing in, or dealing exclusively with, 'oriental' goods sprang up in European countries. In Britain the *Furniture Gazette* of 19 October 1878 accompanied an announcement for a forthcoming exhibition of Japanese art with the comment, 'present indications would seem to point to the Japanese as the style of the coming season . . . Everything is already Japanese. The most progressive tradesman in Regent-Street sells *bric-a-brac*'. This was none other than the forerunner of Liberty, the London department store which contributed so much to the Arts and Crafts movement, Art Nouveau and, later, Art Deco.

After the initial rejection of native arts and crafts during the early Meiji period, the enormous popularity of Japanese lacquer in the West contributed towards a re-evaluation and reassessment in Japan. American and European artists became regular visitors, although most were still interested mainly in ceramics; Edward Morse, scientist, natural history lecturer and collector of Japanese pottery, suggested that too many of the finest quality wares were going to museums in the West, and the National Treasures Act was established in 1884 to keep and protect ancient examples of Japanese arts. Partly as a result of this, and partly as a result of the decline in quality and standards of lacquer during the late Edo period, lacquer-artists turned towards styles and techniques of the past. Nakayama Komin (1808–70), for example, made copies of Heian lacquers while his pupil, Ogawa Shōmin (1847–91), reproduced well-known examples of lacquerware of the Nara, Heian and Kamakura periods. Kawanobe Itchō (1830–1910), on the other hand, had entered the official lacquer workshop of the Tokugawa shōgunate, which was run by members of the Kōami school, and continued to work in their traditional style during the Meiji period.

Shibata Zeshin (1807–91), the most talented and well-known lacquer-artist of the late Edo and early Meiji periods, was a leading exponent of the retrospective movement, though this was only as a means to an end and did not in any way detract from his originality as a lacquerer. Apprenticed to the lacquerer Koma Kansai II at the age of eleven, he took up painting five years later under various masters and worked in the realistic styles of the Maruyama and Shijo schools. When Koma Kansai died in 1835, Zeshin took over as lacquer-master of the Koma school.

In order to attain complete mastery of the medium, Zeshin undertook intensive research of lacquer techniques of the past and present. He did not specialize in one particular aspect of decoration, but evolved a style which encompassed the major techniques in the repertoire of the lacquer-artist in Japan. He made particular use of lacquer which simulated other materials, such as an ink-cake, as well as decayed surfaces, such as rusty metal. The range of his technical skills is well reflected by a set of twelve *inrō*, each of which represents a different month of the year. They are executed in sharply contrasting techniques which reflect a microcosm of Zeshin's technical and artistic achievements.

The custom of imitating or reproducing styles or examples of celebrated lacquerware of the past was, however, not always honourable in intention. Exposure to Japanese goods at international exhibitions resulted not only in a general craze for things Japanese but also produced an almost insatiable demand for Japanese arts and crafts on the part of European and American dealers and collectors. Less scrupulous Japanese lacquerers

Above: Inrō depicting the 11th month; 1865. From a set of 12 *inrō* by Shibata Zeshin, each of which represents a month of the year. The *sake*-gourds, orange and prunus blossom are in gold, silver and red *takamaki-e* on green lacquer imitating a decayed surface. See also pages 118 and 119.

Opposite page: Box for sweetmeats; mid-19th century. The box is in the form of an insect cage of gold lacquer with mother-of-pearl inlay. Signed Nakayama Komin.

seized upon this golden opportunity to produce deliberate fakes, particularly during the late nineteenth and early twentieth centuries. In the majority of cases, there was little attempt to disguise the use of modern gold powders, for example, or to match styles with appropriate shapes of the same period and it is comparatively easy for experts to distinguish these fakes from genuine examples.

The decline in standards of late Edo lacquer and the loss of patrons during the early Meiji period, together with the impetus provided by foreign buyers who often had no real knowledge of the craft, all had an unsteadying effect on lacquer-artists, whose works often reflected an unhappy compromise between native and alien cultures. To help overcome some of these problems and in an attempt to offer some form of practical guidance, the government, and other bodies, established institutions such as the *Nihon Bijutsu Kyōkai* (Fine Arts Society of Japan). The *Nihon Shikkō Kai* (Lacquer Artists' Association of Japan) was founded in 1889 by Ogawa Shōmin, together with other artists, and issued a regular journal and organized competitive exhibitions.

Particularly instrumental in providing practical

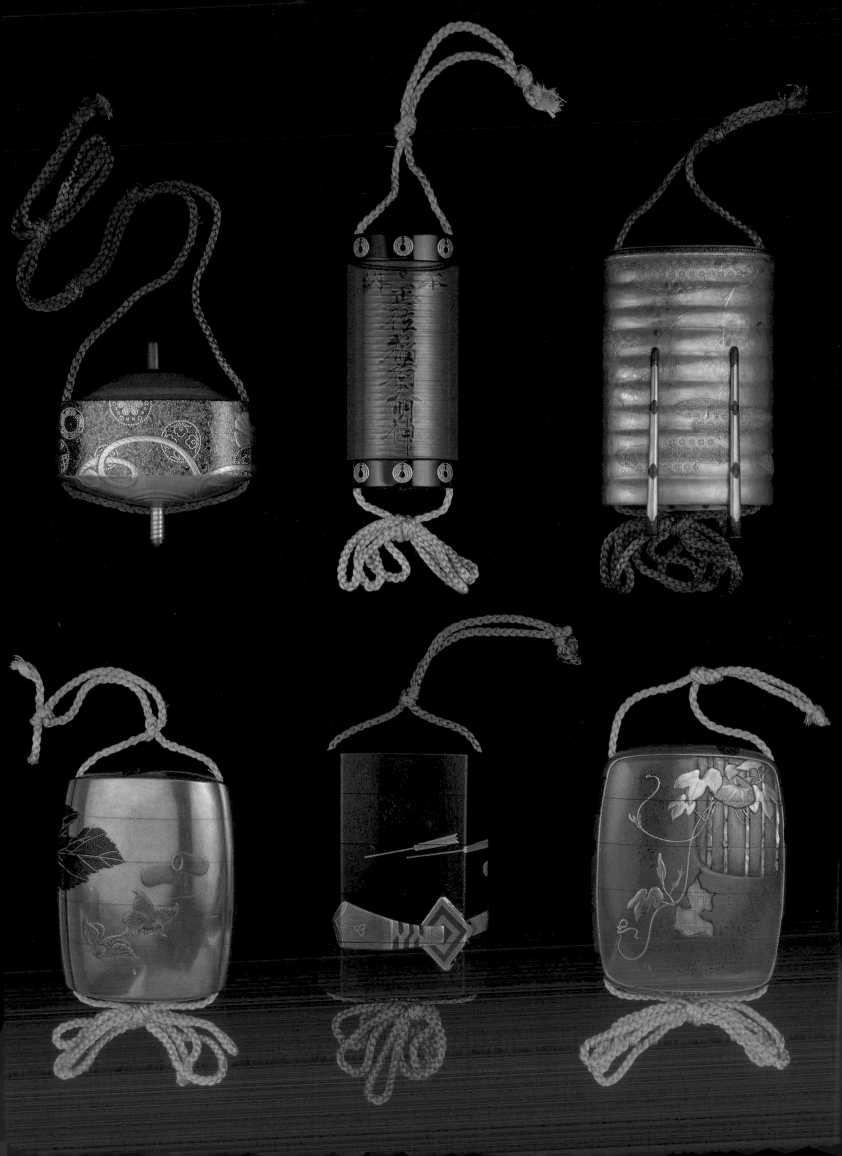

help, however, was the Tokyo Art School founded in 1888 with Ogawa Shōmin as head of the lacquer department from 1890, followed by Kawanobe Itchō and Shirayama Shōsai (1853–1923). Technical schools were also set up in various parts of the country with lacquerwork an important part of the curriculum. These, together with the Tokyo Art School, became the new training ground for lacquer-artists, replacing traditional family workshops or those supported by the *daimyō* or shōgunate.

Direct help also came through official channels. In 1890, for example, Zeshin was appointed court lacquer-artist, a position later filled by Kawanobe Itchō and Ikeda Taishin (1825–1903), in 1896, and Shirayama Shōsai in 1906. The construction of the imperial palace in Tokyo between 1886 and 1889 provided the main source of employment for the most talented lacquer-artists of the period, including Zeshin, Itchō, Shōsai and a host of other artists and assistants.

The National Treasures Act in 1884 encouraged the foundation of the Tokyo, Kyōto and Nara museums which not only protected the objects themselves but also helped to increase the general public's appreciation of the art.

There was also the beginning of serious scientific research into both the nature of lacquer itself and new uses to which it could be put. One of the most profound innovations, largely due to the work of Rokkaku Shisui (1867–1950) and Ishii Kichijirō, was the extension of the traditional range of colours to include vivid ones such as orange and violet, using a base of bismuth chloride. Attempts to find an alternative to the wooden base for export wares, which tended to warp or split in countries with different atmospheric conditions, also bore fruit with the successful use of a light metal base. The Pilot Fountain Pen Company, for example, advised by the lacquer-artist Matsuda Gonroku (1896–), exported fountain-pens made of ebonite covered with lacquer and decorated in *maki-e*.

Lacquer was also found to be a suitable medium for decorating ships' interiors, as it was not adversely affected by sea-water. In 1931, part of the interior decoration of the s.s. Terukunimaru was carried out in lacquer by Matsuda Gonroku. He was also commissioned by the Nippon Yūsen Kaisha Line to decorate the steamships Brazil Maru, Kasuga Maru and Nitta Maru, all of which were completed by 1940.

The technique of lacquer-painting on paper, an innovation of the Meiji period which was perfected by Zeshin, should be distinguished from other lacquer-painting techniques, such as *urushi-e* and *mitsuda-e* (lacquer- and oil-painting respectively on a lacquer or wood ground). Zeshin was trained as both a lacquerer and painter and began experimenting with lacquer-painting on paper

Left and above: Inrō; 1865. The *inrō* illustrated here form a set representing the months of the year. Signed Zeshin. See also page 116.

Right: Hanging scroll; late 1870s. In its close resemblance to an ink-painting, this lacquer-painting is testimony to Zeshin's skill as both a painter and lacquerer. Signed Zeshin.

Right: Set of three trays; *c.* 1980. The trays are in the form of connecting wheels and are decorated with rice sheaves in gold *hiramaki-e* on a black lacquer ground. Made in Kyōto by Suzuki Mutsumi.

Opposite page, above: Portable water container; 1981. Blades of *tokusa* grass are in gold *hiramaki-e* on a black lacquer ground. By Suzuki Mutsumi.

Opposite page, below: Tea-jar and lid with mother-of-pearl mosaic; 1977. The tea-jar is in the *nakatsugi* form, that is, cylindrical with the diameter slightly wider at the top to avoid the optical illusion that it widens towards the base. The base and interior of the jar are of silver *nashiji*. The jar was made in Kyōto by Kuroda Tatsuaki.

comparatively late in life during the early 1870s. He succeeded in producing a type of lacquer which was sufficiently flexible when dry to allow the paper to be rolled or unrolled, and applied this highly viscous medium in such a way as to capture the spontaneity of ink-painting. In 1878, he was awarded the first of many prizes for a lacquer-painting on paper exhibited at the National Industrial Exhibition.

To commemorate the enthronement of the present emperor in 1928, a group of leading lacquer-artists including Akatsuka Jitoku (1871–1936), Rokkaku Shisui, Uematsu Hōbi (1872–1933), Gonroku and Mizoguchi Saburō (1896–1973) were commissioned to produce lacquerware as commemorative gifts for members of the imperial family. In addition, some 400,000 men and women over the age of seventy were presented with gold *maki-e sake*-cups.

The 1950s mark something of a turning-point in the development of modern Japanese lacquer-work. At about this time lacquerers found a new

self-confidence and an instinctive awareness of their art. They largely worked in a manner which, although indebted to the past, was no longer bound by it, and confidently adapted their art to the twentieth century. Decoration for its own sake was no longer the sole objective of lacquer-work, as it had been during the latter part of the Edo period; the shapes and forms of objects came into their own, complemented by subtle surface decoration. Although the *maki-e* tradition was still very much alive under the guiding force of Gonroku, as exemplified by the works of Suzuki Mutsumi (1942–), other techniques came to the fore including *chinkin-bori*, *kimma-nuri* and lacquer inlaid with mother-of-pearl, as well as carved lacquer. The work of Tsuishu Yōsei XX (1880–1952), in particular, exerted a considerable influence over the subsequent development of lac-quer-carving in Japan. He exploited the potential of 'horizontal' carving whereby elements of the design were carved in flat planes with additional surface decoration carved in low relief. This was in marked contrast to traditional Japanese lacquer carving in which complex and intricate designs were carved in such a way as to emphasize their verticality.

In 1954, the establishment of the National Commission for the Protection of Cultural Prop-erties was instrumental in developing the course of modern lacquerwork in Japan. One of the provisions of the commission was to select 'kokuhō', or National Treasures, including lac-quer, for special protection. In addition, the commission recognized the intangible cultural products of human activities such as music, dance, drama and the applied arts, which were of sig-nificant historical or artistic value. Traditional lacquer techniques which are considered to be of particular importance are designated Important Intangible Cultural Properties, and are realized through 'Holders' or artists who have attained a particularly high standard in one or more of the various techniques. In recent years, Holders of the Important Intangible Cultural Properties have included Kuroda Tatsuaki (1904–), renowned for his work in mother-of-pearl, Mae Taihō (1890–1977) for *chinkin-bori*, Isoi Joshin (1883–1964) for *kimma* lacquer, Akaji Yūsai (1906–) for the *kyū-shitsu* technique, jointly with Masumura Mashiki (1910–), Otomaru Kōdō (1898–) for carved lac-quer and Matsuda Gonroku (1896–) for *maki-e*.

Since 1954, the Japanese Arts and Crafts Associ-ation, in conjunction with the commission, has organized arts and crafts exhibitions (Nihon Dentō Kōgeiten) of works by Holders of the Important Intangible Cultural Properties.

Today, exhibitions in Japan, London, New York and Paris are often based on small collec-tions of the highest quality wares, uniting tra-ditional methods with fluid, simplified designs.

Mutsumi Suzuki and Kuroda Tatsuaki work together in a 'family' and their work is represented in museums.

In present-day Japan, therefore, lacquerwork is still very much alive and represents a highly sophisticated form of art, a far cry from the simple, coated objects of the protohistoric period. Although lacquer carving has become associated mainly with Chinese lacquer, all the forms of *maki-e* have become synonymous with Japanese lacquerwork and Japanese craftsmen remain the unchallenged masters of this technique.

Right: Cabinet; 1943. It is decorated with cranes against stylized water in red, black and gold *hiramaki-e*. The necks of the birds are in eggshell, on a woven and lacquered bamboo ground. Made by Matsuda Gonroku.

Above: The Ambras cabinet; *c.* 1585–95. The decoration is of the earlier Namban type: geometric patterns in rather large pieces of mother-of-pearl. Such cabinets were imported into Europe and often set on legs or stands to show them off nearer to eye-level.

Japanese export lacquer

Most European palaces, mansions, châteaux or Schlösser contain one or more large black lacquer cabinets, usually decorated in gold lacquer-painting with a landscape design on the paired doors, the sides, the interior of the doors, and the drawer fronts that are revealed when these doors are open. Usually these cabinets are raised on elaborately carved and gilded wooden table-stands.

While the stands are invariably European, the cabinets themselves are either true Japanese export lacquer or Chinese or European imitations made in the seventeenth or early eighteenth century. The oriental pieces were usually trade goods, made to order in shapes conformable to European usage and taste, and shipped as items of commerce

to Europe. Examples made in Europe are not lacquered, but japanned.

Trade between Japan and Europe began with the arrival of the Portuguese, the first Europeans to reach Japan, in 1542. At first the Portuguese held a virtual monopoly of the Japan trade, shared only with the Chinese. Around 1600 this monopoly was broken by the Dutch and, briefly, by the British. By the 1630s the Dutch had taken over the monopoly, shared, as always, with the Chinese, and both the Portuguese and the British had withdrawn. This near-monopoly was to last into the nineteenth century.

The Japanese began to make lacquer specifically to European order, for the export market, in the latter half of the sixteenth century. At first this was heavily decorated with inlay of pearl-shell, but by the second decade of the seventeenth century there was a reduction in the amount of pearl-shell used in favour of increased pictorial decoration. A transition period of some twenty years is followed by the settling down of an export style of lacquer in the 1650s that was to last until the break in trade of the 1680s and after. This was a style of gold lacquer pictorial decoration on a black ground, sometimes with the use of *nashiji* (aventurine lacquer) or other borders.

Towards the end of the seventeenth century the Dutch ceased to buy Japanese lacquer in quantity. Throughout the eighteenth century there was only spasmodic trade in export lacquer from Japan, though there was a slight revival in the late eighteenth and early nineteenth centuries and a much greater burst of activity at the end of the nineteenth century. The great heyday of the Japanese export lacquer trade was, perhaps, 1580–1680. Chinese imitations of Japanese lacquer were sent to Europe until well into the eighteenth century.

Namban lacquers

The word *namban*, meaning 'southern barbarian', was used in Japan indiscriminately not only of Europeans (and even people from South East Asia) but also of anything appertaining to Europeans. Hence it can mean not only objects made to European order in European shapes but also things depicting Europeans.

For example, there is a series of screens depicting Portuguese ships landing in Japan; these are Namban *byobu*. Similarly there are other objects, among them lacquers, depicting the Portuguese. The Japanese lacquerers often let their sense of the absurd (an enduring and endearing trait in Japanese humour) run away with them, and the Portuguese are depicted in the most grotesque manner. However, as far as lacquering is concerned, it is not so much the depictions of foreigners but the foreign style that is important.

The use of pearl-shell inlays in a coarse, thick lacquer ground was nothing new; it was much used in contemporary Jiajing and Wanli China and in Korea. It was the style that was new and this seems partly to have been based on Chinese models but also partly on a style brought in by the Portuguese, that of the lacquers of Gujarat in India which were themselves heavily influenced by both European and oriental models. Areas of pictorial decoration were broken up by bands of geometric patterns into separate zones. This was to become one of the characteristics of the new, so-called Namban style. Because the shapes used for the Namban style were usually European, being pieces intended for export, the banding often corresponded to the leather or metal decoration on the European models which the Japanese

copied. The two most commonly used shapes in Namban lacquer, the coffer and the fall-front scriptor have bands of decoration around the edges and, in the case of the coffer, across the half-cylinder lid, dividing the total area into two or three divisions.

Inlay of pearl-shell did not provide either a sufficient nor, usually, an accurate enough decoration, and much use was made of overpainting in various shades of gold lacquer, often raised above the surface of the black background or of the pearl-shell itself. This element, at first mere pattern-making but becoming increasingly pictorial, not only came to take over the whole decoration of the later export pieces, but also may well have drastically influenced (or even created) the Kōdai-ji style, hence becoming a decisive element in later Japanese lacquer in general.

Quite when this Namban style begins is unclear, but various indications lead us to believe that its origins lie in the mid-sixteenth century. One of the Jesuit Fathers in Japan, Luis Frois, comments in a letter of 1569 that the *de facto* ruler of Japan, Oda Nobunaga, had in his possession 'Cordova leather skins, hour-glasses and sundials, candlesticks and tapers . . . the finest glassware . . . and many other different kinds of things that I do not remember. All this is in such abundance that he has twelve or fifteen chests, like those of Portugal, filled with these things . . .' Frois does not say Portuguese chests, but chests like those of Portugal. Presumably, then, these were Japanese imitations of at least the shape of Portuguese chests of some sort.

There are two types of 'chest' which might answer this description. The first is the fall-front scriptor or escritorio, now often called a *varqueno*, which comes from a shape supposedly invented in Nuremburg, resembling the centre part of some chests found in the sacristy of southern European churches. Here, a hinged fall-front reveals small drawers that usually surround a cupboard, or a deep drawer, the front of which is often decorated in the architectural form of an arch. These drawers may or may not be regular or even-sized. In the Japanese (Namban) version of this chest, the door and carcase are usually panelled, so that there is a raised edge; this is sometimes true of the drawer-fronts also. The hinges of the front are usually very simple in design, though there are usually elaborately pierced gilded or silvered copper hinge-mounts and lockplates. The door usually folds to below the level of the base of the cabinet and there is no form of foot – this makes the chest awkward to use.

The second candidate for Nobunaga's chests must be the coffer. This is also a European shape, being originally of wood, metal or leather, and it is typically rectangular with a half-cylinder lid that hinges at the back. Japanese examples vary

Above: The Ambras cabinet, shown in colour on page 123; *c.* 1585–95.

Right: Retable; *c.* 1610.
The initials IHS are in
mother-of-pearl, in the
early Namban style.

Below: Fall-front cabinet,
shown in colour on page
126.

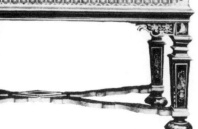

Above: Detail of the
Gripsholm coffer; *c.*
1614–16. The geometric
borders and spandrels,
and the lacquer-painted
decoration in the
cartouche are typical of
the Namban style.

from very small – a few centimetres in length –
to over 1.5 metres (5 feet).

There are examples of both types that have a
certain dated provenance in Europe; while dates
are only *terminus ad quem*, they do add some
substance. The Ambras cabinet was inventoried as
being in the possession of the Archduke Ferdinand
of the Tyrol in 1597, while the Gripsholm coffer
was presented by the States General to King
Gustavus Adolphus II of Sweden in 1616. The
Ambras cabinet is unusual in shape: it has no fall-
front door, nor is it of panelled construction.

Typically, decoration in Namban style is of
three types. These can be well seen on the Ambras
cabinet and the Gripsholm coffer. The three types
of decoration often, but not always, occur together and typically form zones of decoration.

Borders are usually geometric; pearl-shell is cut
into shapes and inlaid in a regular manner to form
a pattern. The most common type is probably the
overlapping circle formed by an arrangement of
thin, elongated ovals of shell, but squares or
triangles also occur. Such patterns may also occur
on the main decoration, often as spandrels around
a cartouche, when the shell may be carefully cut
and patterned, as in the Gripsholm coffer, or
randomly broken, as in a crazy paving.

The second type of decoration is a floral or
other painted pattern, using roughly shaped pieces
of pearl-shell, that is crude in execution and
design. This is usually used as a secondary pattern, but on the Ambras cabinet it is the major
decoration. It is also often used on the sides (as in
the Gripsholm coffer) or on the inside of the fall-
front of cabinets.

Thirdly there is the more pictorial decoration
within, at first, a cartouche though (as in the
Ambras cabinet) this may not be present. It is
clearly visible on the Gripsholm coffer within a
double, shaped cartouche on the front and on the
domed lid. This style of lacquer-painting is better
executed and more painterly in style. As we shall
see, this style became more and more important
and eventually took over the whole decoration at
the expense of the other two styles.

It was this Namban style of lacquer that came to
Europe in the sixteenth and early seventeenth
centuries. In 1584 the Jesuit Father in Japan,
Alessandro Valignano, sent an embassy to Europe
which presented some Japanese lacquer to Philip II
of Spain. In 1610 the Dutch ship de Roode Leouw
met de Pijlen landed at Texel with nine chests of
lacquer. In 1613 Captain John Saris bought for the
East India Company of London, in Japan, '1 case
of Trunckes, . . . two smalle scritoryes and a
Trimming box'. These he later (1614) described in
a letter as 'of a most excellent varnish' and
mentioned also 'Cupps and Dishes of all sortes'.

Other Namban lacquer shapes still exist today:
dishes, mugs with handles and lids, backgammon

boards, comb-cases and a particular group of
church vessels and implements inlaid with the
insignia of the Society of Jesus. Because of the
eventual persecution of Japanese Christians, it is
unlikely that this group of lacquers would have
been made after the 1620s.

The transition phase: early seventeenth century

It is not clear when the true Namban lacquer style
ceased. In fact, of course, it did not actually stop
but changed in various ways in a normal process
of evolution into the style that we shall call
pictorial.

This transition phase is not one of a simple line
of change, but one where different things change
at different times and in different ways. Fortu-
nately these changes can be seen by comparing
existing pieces with the shipping documents of
the Dutch East India Company (Vereenigde Oostindische Compagnie – VOC). This is particularly
easy when we use pieces that are inventoried in
early collections – as were the Ambras and
Gripsholm pieces. And here we are fortunate
enough to have the large and meticulously cata-
logued Royal Collection of the Kings of
Denmark.

In general, there was a gradual phasing out of
the use of pearl-shell, and increasing use of the
painterly style seen in Namban lacquer. At first

Above: Cabinet. The fall-front door is typical of Namban lacquers. The original European piece on which the cabinet is based was probably a writing-desk.

The three cabinets on these pages show some of the variety possible within a very simple shape. Scrolling ivy leaves were a common motif, and Greek columns were often adapted for the central drawer, rather like the central fittings in a secretaire of the period.

this is confined within a cartouche, and it is the loss even of the cartouche that heralds the final phase of the development of the pictorial style. Changes in shape are also important. Fall-front cabinets were clearly found to be impractical, and the fronts were split vertically down the middle and hinged at the sides to form the paired doors that became the standard type thereafter. Namban cabinets with paired doors are very uncommon, but their very existence shows how early was this innovation. In some cases this division of the doors was, as it were, incomplete; the decoration does not conform to the new shape.

While pearl-shell clearly was becoming less widely used, it did not in fact disappear totally, and cabinets from the end of the seventeenth century can be seen where the decoration is still

almost entirely in pearl-shell. Occasionally ray-skin (shagreen, or *same* in Japanese) was used instead of areas of pearl-shell or of secondary painting.

In an intermediate cabinet from the second quarter of the seventeenth century, there is no pearl-shell at all. There are some new techniques, while the main decoration descends directly from Namban lacquer. But here the centre deep drawer or cupboard of the interior has been copied on a larger scale to produce the main lay-out of the outer doors. The small arch has become quite large, is split down the middle by the division of the doors and is covered with the sort of decoration found on Namban borders, but in lacquer-painting without use of pearl-shell. Under this arch is a cartouche in which landscape and a

Above: Arch-front cabinet; *c.* 1640. The cartouche shows a landscape and dragon, painted in lacquer.

Right: Cabinet with open, hinged doors; *c.* 1650.

127 *Japan*

splendid dragon are painted in thickly raised lacquer. This is more proud of the surface than on earlier lacquers. Even more unusual is the technique of the spandrels, in imitation wood-grain. Additional indications of the date of this cabinet are given by the interior decoration of the doors which is remarkably similar to the Kōdai-ji style, and by the fact that the interiors of the drawers are lacquered not in the black of previous time but in red. In the VOC documents of 1637–43 it is stipulated that the interiors of cabinets and coffers should be red or green.

Another piece that probably comes from this early date is a curiously shaped chest in the Royal Collection in Copenhagen, with a flat lifting lid above small drawers enclosed within doors. This is inventoried for 1673. However, we know it was in Denmark before 1668, because a motif on it was copied for a 'lacquer room' at Rosenborg which is known to have been finished before that date. Indeed it may well have been given to Queen Sofie Amalie by the VOC in 1666. It also corresponds to the description of some pieces imported by the VOC in 1634 (*kisten met schuyttlaeden*). A similar cabinet now in England has a certain amount of pearl-shell inlay, lacking in the Copenhagen piece.

Captain Saris in 1613 referred to '1 case of trunckes' and it seems possible that the Namban coffers – which come in many sizes – may have been sold one within the other for easy packing. No such series as early as 1613 exists but, again in Copenhagen, there is a series of six coffers, similarly decorated, that fit one within the other, like Russian boxes. These are sparingly decorated, with some use of pearl-shell. In the Dutch shipping documents, coffers with half-round lids are described as *coffers*, while the flat-topped kind are called *kisten*. As the word *coffer* disappears in the 1630s, it is reasonable to assume that these coffers are of the transition period. In the Danish inventories these half-round lidded coffers are *schrijne*, while flat-topped ones are, again, *kisten*.

The flat-topped chest or *kist* appears in the documents for the first time in the 1630s. The earlier examples have a lid that overlaps the base by a considerable margin. Later *kisten* have lids that fit more snugly.

The high point of the lacquer trade

The trade in Japanese lacquer as demonstrated by the VOC documents begins to increase greatly in the early 1630s. The first big order seems to have been from the Dutch 'factory', i.e. station, in Siam in 1631 for '150–200 small cabinets'. In 1634 the Hirado office bought '52 coffers; 72 scriptors large & small; 2 chests-with-drawers; 1 table'. In 1635 Hirado office bought '149 cabinets large & small; 186 Coffers; 51 lacquered chests (*kisten*) large & small; 10 gaming boards; 10 lamps with shades; 10 shaving basins'. In the 1650s and 1660s orders are sent for quite large quantities of lacquers. In 1658, for instance, thirty cabinets were

Opposite page, above: Cabinet or chest with lid and drawers. This strangely shaped piece is an odd amalgam of East and West, and is probably from a relatively early date when European forms were not completely understood.

Opposite page, below: Cabinet. The landscape scene is in *takamaki-e*.

Below: Coffers; early 17th century. They fit into each other for easy packing.

ordered; in 1659, fifty; in 1660, 1661 and 1662, a hundred each year; and so on.

One of the features of the trade of this time seems to have been the use of Japanese lacquer as presents to the rulers of the various countries in which the VOC was trading. Particular attention was paid to gifts for the Great Mogul. In 1656 Bengal ordered, '1 *norimon* (Japanese 'carrying-chair'); 1 women's palanquin; 1 elephant's howdah; 4 saddles; 178 shields'. The carrying-chair was a model much used in Japan and, according to the traveller Peter Mundy, imported from Japan for use in Goa in India (1637). At least one had come to Europe; Prince Christian of

Anhalt seems to have seen one in Rosenborg Castle in 1623. The shields would have been leather, made in Bengal and shipped to Japan to be lacquered – probably a special order.

The cabinets of this period are occasionally panelled, but more usually they are flush-doored and flush constructed on the carcase and drawers. Usually the cabinet is mounted on a low, slightly splayed foot a few centimetres high. This innovation – it seems never to occur on Namban cabinets – may date from the 1630s; the arch-fronted cabinet referred to earlier shows unmistakable signs of having had just such a foot, now removed. The central interior drawer was moved, usually to one side at the bottom, and was no longer decorated in a different manner from the other drawers. The decoration, in shades of gold lacquer, was often slightly raised from the surface (*takamaki-e*). It was usually a landscape in a style vaguely reminiscent of the Kano school of painting. Invariably the doors have better-quality decoration than other parts of the cabinet. In the mid-century considerable attention was paid to the decoration of the top of the cabinet; the sides (and even the back) were also decorated, but less skilfully or elaborately. Later the back was undecorated and even the top may be plain lacquer.

In the 1660s there were nearly always one or more borders around the main pictorial design on the doors, usually of aventurine lacquer (*nashiji*) but sometimes geometric patterns of some elaboration; some even echoed the overlapping circle designs of the Namban style. Borders gradually disappeared, and were uncommon by the 1680s when the picture covered the whole surface.

Despite its popularity, lacquer never made much profit for the VOC. Shipping space was too much in demand for it to be imported in great quantities. It is worth noting that when, in 1664, the VOC imported 101 pieces of lacquer into Holland they also imported (officially) some 45,000 pieces of Japanese porcelain. (The use of the word 'officially' is important – the permitted private trade by VOC officials was quite considerable.) Japanese-made lacquer cabinets were therefore not all that common; this is borne out by the admiring comments made by various travellers, or visitors to great houses. On 20 April 1661, for instance, Samuel Pepys saw in the Duke of York's closet 'among other things two very fine chests covered with gold and Indian varnish, given him by the East India Company of Holland'. In 1679 John Evelyn saw in the Portuguese Ambassador's House in London 'rich (Japan) cabinets of which I think there were a dosen'.

During the 1660s imported cabinets had their drawers fitted with smaller items for shipment. In 1665, for instance, 2,675 small lacquered boxes were imported, and in 1680, 3,846. Few of these seem to have survived.

Later in the seventeenth century and well into the eighteenth century, the Chinese imitated the Japanese in production of these cabinets. Even in the eighteenth century these were recognized as of lesser quality than the Japanese.

In the 1680s the Dutch began to find Japanese lacquer too expensive and cut down on orders for Holland; it does not appear in the books of the Company in Holland after 1693. Yet the VOC continued to order lacquer as presents. In 1697 the order was for '52 shields with flower work without any animals, birds etc.; 20 with birds; 122 long oval betel-boxes all with flower work of which 91 flat-bottomed and 31 egg-shaped; 85 trays for the same; 12 betel-boxes finely aventurine lacquered; 25 round trays; 20 square trays; 12 nests of fruit-boxes (3 or 4 in a set); 2 small black chests of drawers with flower work . . .; 20 pieces one size smaller'.

Japanese records of transactions with the VOC are entirely lacking save for the years 1709–13. Here one can find that the Dutch continued to buy small amounts of lacquer; these pieces were not made to order but were normal Japanese products. Many may have been for the private trade of VOC officials and therefore not recorded in the VOC documents. I have only been able to trace six items that may have been export-type cabinets listed in the Japanese documents for those years.

According to the records, the Dutch did not buy lacquer from the Chinese until 1733. Clearly the Chinese lacquer brought into Europe at the end of the seventeenth century was shipped by other East India Companies.

Private orders

So far we have been concerned with trade goods – pieces made to order, certainly, but made in quantity for resale in Europe or in the various Asian countries in which the VOC traded. But there were two other ways in which lacquered objects from Japan could reach Europe.

East India Companies other than the Dutch were trading in Eastern waters. It was only with Japan that the Dutch had the European monopoly and even here they shared that trade with the Chinese. Other European nations were, therefore, able to buy, from the Chinese, Japanese lacquers which the Chinese had bought in Japan.

This 'route' accounts for some of the Japanese lacquers (and porcelain) found in Europe. For example, the Royal Collection in Denmark has a large group of small lacquer pieces, some of which were clearly not intended for export to Europe. These include boxes of all sorts, trays, pillows, ṣake-cups and a portable picnic set. This latter piece, most parts of which are inventoried

Left: Picnic set; *c.* 1650. This was probably not intended for export to Europe.

Above: Shield; *c.* 1668. Of Indian origin it was lacquered in Japan. Most known shields from this period bear the coats of arms of VOC officials.

Above right: Large dish; *c.* 1680. Of Japanese lacquer, with Chinese scenes, the dish is thought to be one of two presented to Louis XIV of France by Constant Phaulkon.

for 1674, is clearly of an earlier date. There is also a lacquer tea-bowl which arrived in Europe before 1665 and which imitates *raku* earthenware, complete with drips of 'glaze'.

The other source of lacquer imported into Europe was the special order. Much the most famous piece of this type is the van Diemen box. It is one of a small group of lacquers – some nine or ten pieces – which share certain characteristics. Of these, by far the most important is quality; all are of a quality far higher than that of export trade goods. (It is important to note this distinction: although these are pieces made for export, almost certainly to European order, they are not normal trade goods.) Another characteristic is the subject-matter of the lacquered decoration, which is in almost all cases not merely pictorial but refers directly to classical Japanese literature. The van Diemen box and its pair, the now dismembered Buys box (both ordered for wives of high Dutch officials in the East) were probably commissioned by someone with access to the Koami workshops; this would not have been the case for the normal pattern of trade. A detail of the van Diemen box is on page 93.

If we do not know who commissioned the boxes, at least we know for whom they were ordered. But one fine-quality piece whose provenance is a mystery is a six-fold lacquer screen which so closely imitates a painted *byobu* that even the back is lacquered in imitation of the patterned paper that normally covers the back of such screens. It depicts a rugged landscape and may well date from around 1660.

Much easier to understand are the shields and dishes with lacquered coats of arms. The shields are round and made of leather; they were made in Bengal and shipped to Japan to be lacquered. In 1656 Bengal ordered 178 shields, in 1663, twenty-five, in 1675, 150. Of those few that are known today, most bear the coat of arms of some official

of the VOC, and all can be dated to the third quarter of the seventeenth century. A typical example bears the arms of Constantijn Ranst who was the VOC's Chief Merchant in Deshima in 1667–68 and Governor of Bengal from 1669 to 1673. Around the arms fly birds among randomly spaced twigs, and there is a narrow border of gold lacquer with slightly raised leaf-work. The back is of gold and silver *nashiji*. Shields are not used in Japan. This Indian form of shield must have been much appreciated by men such as Ranst, for it was surely very expensive, but it is not known what purpose it served.

Another order was that placed in 1680 by the adventurer Constant Phaulkon, who was then in control of Siam, for, *inter alia*, '2 pairs very costly large Japanese dishes, 2 pairs smaller dishes'. These were to be among Phaulkon's presents for Louis XIV and his court, sent with his ambassadors in 1686.

The eighteenth century trade

The Dutch alone were in a position to buy Japanese lacquer in the eighteenth century. The Chinese had no need to, for they could imitate it more cheaply than they could buy it, even though their imitations were of inferior quality. The VOC bought Chinese lacquer spasmodically between 1733 and 1763, mostly small items, but gave it up as unprofitable. They also continued to buy a few small items of Japanese lacquer for the intra-Asian trade throughout the eighteenth century.

This was not a trade to Europe; after the sale of the collection of the Chevalier Antoine de la Rocque in 1745, when the *marchand-merciers* of France attempted to cater for the craze for Japanese lacquer, the cataloguer, Gersaint, could not find recently imported pieces in Holland, much less offer them for sale.

On the whole, these collectors, who included

Charles, Duc de Lorraine, and Madame de Pompadour, did not want export lacquer – they wanted the better-quality pieces, usually those made for Japan. The van Diemen box belonged successively to Madame de Pompadour and the Duc de Bouillon before it was bought by William Beckford in the early nineteenth century.

This craze for lacquer shows itself, in France in particular, not just in the number of collections, but also in the mutilation of lacquerwork. In the seventeenth century lacquer had been used for wainscoting or panelling, but in the eighteenth century it was used for inlay in furniture, in smaller items such as pen-stands, and even in snuff-boxes. So highly prized was the lacquer that it was often reused when the furniture into which it had been inlaid went out of fashion, when it would be taken out and refitted to another piece. If the lacquer did not fit a desired shape it was bent; if it did not suit the design it was 'improved', and if it was too small it was enlarged. 'Improving' and enlarging were achieved by the use of varnish such as *vernis Martin*.

Dutch officials working in Japan continued to order lacquer, among other curiosities. One of the most interesting of these men was Johan Frederik, Baron van Reede tot de Parkeler, who was Chief Merchant in Japan in 1786 and 1788. Among the pieces he sent back to Holland were 'an extra fine lacquered Japanese medicine-box such as the Japanese wear at the side of their waistbands' – an *inrō*. He also sent 'two oval portraits of Frederick

II or the Great, one of which is lacquered with colours and a ditto ditto inlaid with mother-of-pearl or nacre'. Other sets of similar lacquer portraits copied from different books exist; one such (of Gustavus III of Sweden) is actually dated 1788, and the fact that van Reede was Chief Merchant in that year adds to the probability that he was in some way concerned with this curious enterprise.

Other European prints were also copied. Indeed, one workshop in Japan seems to have specialized in such copies. Topographical prints (as various as views of Amersfoort and of the Ka'aba in Mecca) and battle scenes seem to have been popular. Four depictions of the battle of the Doggerbank (1781) engraved as prints in 1782 by Ballier after designs by J. F. Reitz were copied in

Right: Panel illustrating the Battle of Doggerbank; 1792. This is part of a series; see page 135.

Above: Portrait of Gustave Adolphe of Sweden and (*right*) two portraits of Frederick II; late 18th century. Large pieces of furniture became too unwieldy to ship to Europe, and later lacquer imports were often small *objets d'art*.

Above: Tray; *c.* 1785. The scene is taken from a contemporary print.

lacquer. Each is signed by the lacquerer Sasaya and dated 1792. Also by Sasaya are panels of lacquer inlaid into a *secretaire à abattant*, which depict the invasion of Holland by Russian and British troops in 1799. As Dr Christiaan Jörg comments: 'This genre of lacquerwork suddenly enjoyed a certain degree of popularity . . . Various Dutch merchants made use of their privileged position in Deshima to place orders and to ship this lacquerwork in the context of the officially permitted private trade.'

This use of the private trade was, as we have seen, a practice of the Dutch throughout their tenure of the partial monopoly of the Japanese trade. That this monopoly was ended by the arrival of Commodore Perry's 'black ships' in Uraga bay in 1853, with the subsequent Treaty of Kanagawa which opened Japan to the West, is well known. Subsequent exports from Japan, including vast amounts of inferior work, were due to a different kind of Western influence – the great period of export lacquer was over.

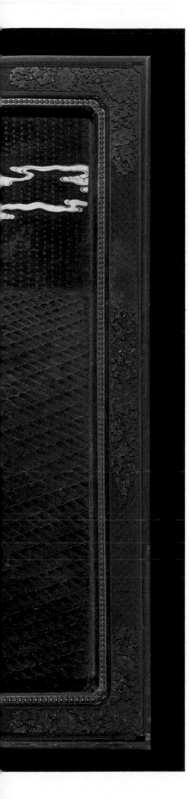

Above right: Two battle-
scenes; 1792. These
lacquer panels were
intended to be hung as
paintings, and are based
on a series illustrating the
Battle of Doggerbank
(see also page 133). Series
like these were produced
to celebrate
contemporary events.

4

The Ryukyu Islands

The chain of thirty-six islands
known in Japanese as *Ryūkyū* and in Chinese as *Liuqiu* is strung out across the Pacific
Ocean in a curve linking the southern tip of Kyushu with the north-eastern shore of
Taiwan. Today they are integrated into the Japanese administrative system as
Okinawa Prefecture, named after the largest and best known of the group. However,
from the early fifteenth century to the annexation by Japan in 1879 the Ryukyus
formed a separate kingdom with a distinct culture and artistic traditions
open to influences from China, Japan and South East Asia. Lacquerwork was one of the
most accomplished achievements of this little known state, an art which has only
in recent years begun to be recognized and distinguished from the products of
its larger neighbours.

Above: Round, handled basket
incorporating basketry panels

Opposite: Detail from cosmetic-box on
page 139; 15th century.

It is now generally accepted that, despite the intrinsic poverty of the Ryukyu archipelago, the profits of trade and a lucrative role as intermediaries supported a Ryukyuan 'golden age' in the fifteenth, sixteenth and seventeenth centuries. During this period lacquerware of a sophistication and variety rivalling that of China and Japan was produced on the island of Okinawa. Initial reluctance to view such a remote and underpopulated spot as the source of high craftsmanship has now given way in Japan to enthusiastic ascription of a large number of fine pieces to a Ryukyuan provenance. Perhaps this process has gone rather too far in some cases, and a true assessment of the place of the Ryukyus in the complex history of artistic interaction in East Asia cannot yet be arrived at. However, enough securely provenanced and datable Ryukyuan pieces survive in Japan to dispel any image of the lacquerware as provincial or crude.

Geography has given to the Ryukyus the role of intermediaries between China and Japan. History records an early period of Chinese political and cultural influence from the late fourteenth century, followed by an era in which Japan acted as the islands' political overlord, after a formal recognition of vassalage to the Shimazu family, Lords of Satsuma, in 1609. Ryukyuan lacquer reflects these two periods, but the position of go-between was never quite lost, with the Ryukyuan artisans continuing to cater, in the Edo period (1615–1868), for the Japanese taste for exotic *karamono*, objects in a Chinese or Chinese-inspired style. They may also have catered for the Chinese taste for exotic lacquer by supplying either Japanese or Japanese-style goods via the Ryukyuan settlements in the Chinese port cities of Fuzhou and Quanzhou.

The origins of lacquering in the Ryukyus remain obscure, the confusion being compounded by disagreement over whether or not the lacquer tree itself is native to the country. It seems likely that *Rhus succedanea* and *Rhus ambigua*, varieties of the tree also known in South East Asia, are part of the native flora, but that *Rhus verniciflua* is a later introduction. The rival claims of China and Japan as the source of the transplant owe as much to national pride as to the paltry available evidence. *R. verniciflua* may have arrived in the twelfth century with Japanese refugees from civil wars, or may have come from China much earlier. It was certainly well established by the early fifteenth century when a Chinese ambassador travelled to Shuri, capital of Okinawa, to bestow the Chinese surname Shang (pronounced *Shō* in Japanese) on the family which had unified all the Ryukyus. His orders included instructions to acquire raw lacquer sap from Okinawa, which implies the existence of a lacquer industry there a mere forty years after the Ryukyuans had been described in a Chinese text as eager buyers of Chinese carved red lacquerware. But the lacquer trees of the islands seem to have had an uneven subsequent history. They were important enough to be taxed all through the seventeenth century until 1699, but by 1719 sap was being imported *from* China. In 1888 the administrator Ishizawa Hyōgo, author of the very important *Ryūkyū Shikki Kō*, 'A Study of Ryukyuan Lacquerware', could claim that the tree was no longer known to grow on the islands.

Incised gold lacquer

Whatever the origins of the trees used, the first identifiable pieces of Ryukyuan lacquer certainly draw technical and stylistic inspiration from China. They are executed in a technique known in Chinese as *qiangjin*, 'incised gold', and in Japanese as *chinkin*, 'sunk gold'. Grooves are formed in the lacquer surface by a V-shaped stylus, gold leaf then being laid into the grooves to form the design. In China, such workmanship is described in texts of 1366 and 1388, while actual pieces datable to around 1315 are preserved in Japanese temples. Very recent excavations in China have extended our knowledge of *qiangjin* lacquers to the mid-thirteenth century.

The *chinkin* lacquers of the Ryukyus were probably well developed, under Chinese influence and possibly even under the direct stimulus of

Below: Cylindrical box; 15th century. The design of flying peacocks and peony scrolls shows Chinese influence. The box has been converted into an incense-burner; the metal liner and perforated cover are probably Japanese.

immigrant Chinese craftsmen, by the mid-fifteenth century. A now lost diplomatic gift of a *chinkin* sweetmeat tray to the Japanese shōgun Ashikaga Yoshimasa in 1458 is likely to have been a native product. Korean envoys reported the presence of gold-decorated lacquerware on the islands in 1478. The earliest actual pieces of Ryukyuan lacquer with any sort of provenance are hence not surprisingly decorated by *chinkin*. These are two tall circular boxes, containers for ceremonial jewellery, traditionally given in 1500 by King Shō Shin to a priestess of Kume Island for her help in suppressing a revolt on the southern island of Yaeyama. The ground is of green lacquer, with a design of flying birds and flowers in gold. Though Chinese influence is obvious, the decoration, executed with a mass of short, regular lines of gold, is assured and has already developed independent features. The thick hatching of the gold is unlike Chinese work, as are the distinctive diaper backgrounds against which the birds are set. These backgrounds are built up on a simple grid at 45° to the main design, and help to distinguish Ryukyuan from Chinese pieces.

By 1500 *qiangjin* decoration was falling out of fashion in China. In the Ryukyus by contrast it continued to find favour, and a group of objects with similarities to the Kume Island boxes can be dated to the later fifteenth or early sixteenth centuries. These include dishes on high pedestal feet, some of which carry the heraldic device of the royal Shō family, and tiered boxes with matching stands. Such pieces are often found with gold decoration over a striking red ground, a style which continued into the early seventeenth century. A deep dish exists marked with the title of the Chinese Wanli emperor (1573–1619), while tiered boxes of red *chinkin* can be seen on contemporary Japanese screens depicting the arrival of European 'southern barbarians' bringing exotic trade goods.

From the late sixteenth century *chinkin* began to be used in association with *mitsuda-e*, 'litharge painting', on lacquer to produce an effect perhaps imitating Chinese polychrome *tianqi* or 'filled-in colours' lacquerware. A tiered box presented to the Shimazu family by the Ryukyuan king in 1585 is the earliest datable example. Both types probably continued to seem agreeably exotic to Japanese eyes throughout the Edo period, and both continued to be made. Among the very important dated patterns published by Ishizawa in 1888 is a piece of pure gold-on-red *chinkin* from 1860.

Painted gold lacquerware, a technique called *haku-e*, may have originated in the desire to find a quick substitute for the laborious *chinkin* process. There are also clear links with South East Asian lacquer styles (undoubtedly familiar to the far-ranging Ryukyuan merchants of the sixteenth century) and to the Chinese porcelain of the middle of the Ming dynasty (1368–1644) decorated with gold leaf and admired by the Japanese under the name of *kinrande*. Again a red ground was preferred, and Chinese influences are pronounced in the eighteenth and nineteenth century examples, both as regards shapes and decorative schemes.

Mother-of-pearl inlaid lacquers

The shorelines and coral reefs of the Ryukyu Islands are a rich source of the molluscs whose iridescent interior shell-layers have been used to decorate lacquer surfaces in China since earliest times. Hence it is not surprising that the diplomatic gifts presented to the Chinese emperor on the establishment of formal relations in 1372 should include a considerable amount of raw shell. This material continued to feature in lists of presents in the fifteenth century, together with bowls, basins and sword scabbards decorated with mother-of-pearl inlay on a red ground. Such a colour scheme is rare in Japanese lacquer of the period and so it seems likely that these finished pieces, like the raw material, were native Ryukyuan products. However, no actual objects of such an early date have been identified.

The first pieces of Ryukyuan mother-of-pearl lacquer to bear a reasonably secure provenance date from 1611, two years after the kingdom

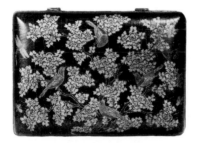

Above: Cosmetic-box; 15th century. The decoration shows birds on peony branches with, at the sides, butterflies and dragonflies. See page 136 for detail.

Right: Ceremonial fan; 18th century. The decoration is in raised mother-of-pearl with painted gold landscapes.

Above: Square tray with separate stand; 18th or 19th century. Decorated in browns, yellows and reds; the *I ching* emblem of *ying* and *yang*, symbolizing duality, is on the tray and there are landscape panels on the stand.

Right: Tiered box; 18th century. Large pieces of inlaid shell, particularly in the floral borders, decorate the hexagonal sections. There is a landscape scene on top, and the edges are strengthened with twisted wire.

Lacquers inlaid with mother-of-pearl required formidable specialization, with five different types of shell, seven different undercoats and three grades of shell-polisher.

submitted to Japanese political tutelage. They include a calligraphic tablet executed on a black ground surrounded by a diaper formed of intersecting circles, and a low table in which large chips of shell are inlaid in a red ground to form a sparse scene of a pine tree and a wall. The tablet would be very difficult to distinguish from a contemporary Chinese piece but for the decoration of the table, which has a distinctive feel.

Despite the difficulties of identifying objects in this technique – in which the confusion between what is Ryukyuan and what is Chinese is most acute – mother-of-pearl inlaid lacquers were certainly still of great importance in the early seventeenth century and after. In 1612, attendant on the Shimazu reorganization of taxation on the islands, the first mention occurs of the *Kaizuri Bugyōshoku* or 'Office of the Supervisor of Shell-Polishing'. A man called Mō or Fuyimo (Japanese scholars disagree on the reading of his name) was appointed to the post in that year, the implication being that this specialized workshop had been in existence for some time.

One surviving object is generally singled out as the product of the *Kaizuri Bugyōshoku*. This is a rectangular box, fitted with an internal tray and used for the storage of writing-paper. The decoration on the top and sides is of waterfowl swimming, flying and diving among reeds and small islets, and is done with large pieces of shell on a black ground. The style is reminiscent of Chinese painting of the early seventeenth century, but the box itself has been dated to around 1700. Other pieces in a related manner are known, including table screens and writing-boxes with both black and red grounds. The red ground was not widely favoured by Japanese craftsmen, nor did they use twisted metal wires in their designs. The Ryukyuans may have acquired this last technical feature from the Chinese, or possibly from the Koreans, with whom they shared motifs such as squirrels on bunches of grapes, common on Yi dynasty ceramics and lacquer. Cultural relations between the Ryukyus and Korea have hardly been studied at all, but it is known that the Ryukyus were one supply source for the tortoiseshell which was popularly used in Korea as a lacquer inlay. The Korean fondness for external strengthening devices was not imitated, but an individual way of reinforcing exposed edges (for example, on table screens) was evolved by using large triangular chips of shell in rows, with the pieces pointing in alternate directions.

Lacquer bowls decorated in mother-of-pearl inlay with five-clawed dragons were considered suitable to present to the Qing emperors in the course of Ryukyuan 'tribute missions' to China in 1725, 1740 and 1788. Again it is the size of the pieces of shell, allowing full play to the blue-green sheen of the material, that is the most distinctively

Ryukyuan feature of the wares ascribed to this period. Whether or not they were thought to represent the finest the kingdom could produce, lacquers decorated in mother-of-pearl seem to have led the field in the eighteenth century. Of the sixty designs dating from 1714 and after reproduced by Ishizawa, thirty-seven are for pieces of this type.

Painted lacquer and other types

In painted lacquer, from the early eighteenth century at least, a Ryukyuan synthesis was successfully achieved between Chinese and Japanese features. Such wares, decorated in both coloured true lacquers and vegetable-oil-based pigments, had been well developed in southern China by the late Ming dynasty. The Ryukyuans took the technique and certain decorative elements, such as the common motif of birds on flowering branches, and applied them to objects more suited to Ryukyuan and Japanese ways of living. These included the personal medicine-cases called *inrō* (also made with mother-of-pearl inlay), boxes for inkstone and writing equipment (*suzuribako*), and tiered boxes for foodstuffs with matching trays. In this last category the design might be set against a ground of sprinkled gold in imitation of Japanese *nashiji*, and it was often spread across the whole height of the box. This way of handling the surface also shows Japanese inspiration, the Chinese tendency being to treat each tier as a separate field of decoration. Some Ryukyuan painted lacquer can be difficult to distinguish from Chinese workmanship, but one pointer is a distinctive palette of colours, with a green which has often degraded to grey in the passage of time.

The early eighteenth century seems to have been a time of innovation in the craft of lacquering on Okinawa. Ishizawa gives 1715 as the traditional date when the major Chinese style of carved red lacquer (*tsuishu* in Japanese) was introduced by Kise Jōshō. This looks like an example of the East Asian fondness for ascribing changes in craft techniques to one named artist, and carved lacquer may have been practised earlier.

As in Japan, lacquer carving never achieved the importance it did in China. Ishizawa's earliest design in this style is dated 1748. In 1788 a mission was sent to Fujian on the orders of the Shimazu overlords to acquire further expertise, suggesting that the technique was not yet fully under control. From the early nineteenth century onwards come a large group of pieces, Japanese in form but decorated with carved lacquer built up in thick layers by the use of lacquer putty, then coloured in a variety of shades of brown, yellow and green as well as the more standard red.

According to tradition the beginning of the eighteenth century saw the introduction of the

Above: Ceremonial fan shown in colour on page 139; 18th century.

lathe for the construction of the wooden cores of objects, previously bent or carved by hand. Credit for this is given to Samejima Rokurobei, an immigrant from Japan and founder of a line of lacquer-workers, who was active in the Wakasa district of the town of Naha, chief port of Okinawa. Wakasa (probably named after the Japanese lacquer-making district of the same name) was and remains the chief centre of the craft on the Ryukyu Islands.

Fang Hongde, a craftsman who may have been a Chinese immigrant (alternatively he may have been Bō Kō-toku, a Ryukyuan with a Chinese-style name), is the traditional inventor of *tsuikin*, the Ryukyuan lacquer technique most associated with the islands in the Japanese mind. *Tsuikin* means 'piled-up brocade', and the word is used today to cover two different but related processes. One is the inlaying of various hardstones, soapstone, woods and stained ivory into a lacquer surface to form a picture in high relief. In China this was called *Zhou zhi*, 'Zhou work', after its eponymous late-Ming inventor, who is probably a convenient fiction. The other, more widespread, process is the use of coloured lacquer putty (lacquer mixed with burned earth or powdered whetstones) to simulate this colourful, even garish effect by appliqué work. In 1718 a table screen decorated by means of the first process was presented to the Tokugawa shōgun, the earliest piece of *tsuikin* with Ryukyuan associations, though it may actually have been made in China. The inlaying of rare (and presumably imported) materials was never as common as the cheaper and simpler putty simulation, which became the dominant form of Ryukyuan lacquer in the nineteenth century.

The rule of the Shō kings on Okinawa was ended by the Japanese in 1872. Sixteen years later Ishizawa Hyōgo could still claim that lacquerware was 'the principal product of the Ryukyu Islands', though one that was declining in relation to the manufacture of rice spirits. As elsewhere in Meiji Japan, the administration sponsored industrial exhibitions late in the century to stimulate craft production, but the quality of Ryukyuan lacquer declined steadily as the islands became merely a Japanese backwater.

Appalling devastation was visited on the islands, Okinawa in particular, in 1945 during the last months of World War II. Craftsmen, objects and records all perished in great numbers. Though some efforts were made in the years immediately after the war, it is really only with the return of the Ryukyus to Japanese administration in 1972 that attempts have been made to study and revitalize the art of lacquer in the islands. *Tsuikin* and mother-of-pearl inlaid wares are today the principal survivors of that rich tradition.

5

South East Asia

Although lacquerware is well established in most South East Asian countries today it is very difficult to trace the development of the craft, for its early history is obscure and little existing material can be dated further back than the eighteenth century. While it is generally agreed that the use of lacquer as a watertight or protective layer on wooden and woven containers has been common since prehistoric times, the origins of the more sophisticated decorative techniques remain a matter for debate and speculation. Tropical conditions render the survival of any lacquered object extremely hazardous, however, and so the lack of early evidence is not surprising.

Above: Flat box and cover; Burma, 18th–19th century.

Opposite: Detail from cabinet on page 147; Thailand, early 19th century. The motifs derive from Khmer temple reliefs.

A variety of local traditions support the theory that lacquer techniques were brought to the area from China. One such story involves a mid-fifteenth century ambassador from Hanoi to China, who is said to have returned with Hunan lacquerware: for that reason the ambassador, Tran-tuong-Cong, is today the patron of the Vietnamese lacquer-workers' guild. A Burmese story has it that decorative lacquer was brought to Pagan – where the lacquer industry is still centred – in 1058, from 'the east', but an immediate association of this source with China is made doubtful by the fact that the nearest Chinese province, Yunnan, has a lacquer tradition unlike the Burmese one. A recent suggestion that the Vietnamese tradition was the inspiration for the rest of South East Asia is supported by the use in Burma of a Vietnamese word, *yun*, for lacquer, and by a Thai story which puts the original source of their work to the east of their country among the Lao, on the trade route to Hanoi.

The early history of the manufacture of lacquer from tree resins is as obscure as that of its use, although the region's forest products have been used for trade since Roman times, and its peoples have long exploited the mineral and vegetable oils. The modern customs, however, provide an insight into the necessary preparatory stages.

South East Asian craftsmen have never had access to the sap of *Rhus verniciflua*, used by their Chinese, Korean and Japanese counterparts. Their three main sources are *Rhus succedanea* (also a secondary source for Chinese lacquerers), *Melanorrhea laccifera* and *M. usitata*. Other vegetable varnishes exist in the area, but none is used for the production of true lacquer. The trees from which the resin is obtained grow in the drier forest zones up to about 1,000 metres (3,200 feet) and are

not deliberately cultivated – although in some places they appear to be protected by local forest laws, for they are used not only by charcoal burners but also by carpenters.

Burmese gatherers, at least, avoid the flowering season when the resin is of poor quality and will not take a good polish.

The tapping itself is usually carried out by making V-shaped incisions and inserting small bamboo cylinders to catch the resin. The matured resin is black, which can be intensified by adding iron sulphate or softened with indigo, while the addition of cinnabar (red mercuric sulphide) or, less successfully, red ochre produces red lacquer. The resin of another tree, the gamboge, is added to produce a yellow lacquer; finely ground orpiment in a gum base and diluted with oil is sometimes also used.

Green and brown shades are produced by colour mixtures, while tonal variations in all the colours are achieved by using further additives, and by the use of a wide range of vegetable oils and resins as bases.

In considering the products to which such lacquer has been applied it is important to remember that the borders of South East Asian countries today are very different from those of the past, and so it is difficult to attach a precise country of origin to much of the evidence. Such divisions seem the most useful in this context, and are used to differentiate the wares of Vietnam, Thailand and Burma, but it should be remembered that they are necessarily tentative.

Four main techniques are found throughout South East Asia; of these the finest is the use of gold decoration on a black ground. Most such pieces come from Thailand, and a few have a brown or red ground rather than the predominant black. Incised and coloured wares mostly originate from Burma, where the technique is known as Pagan ware. Relief decoration is also common in Burma and found in other areas as well: the standard of such work is very high and certainly excels that of China, where it is thought to have originated. The last technique, mother-of-pearl inlay, is used throughout the region.

Vietnamese lacquer

Although wood has been the most frequently decorated surface in Vietnamese work, metal, paper, basketry and cloths such as silk are also found, and all these require lacquer of different qualities. The tapped resin is stored in covered baskets of woven bamboo, which have been waterproofed with lacquered paper or with paper soaked in persimmon oil. The resin separates into five distinct layers, with the lowest providing a base for crude varnish and fillers, and the next a caulking material for boats and baskets. The top-

Below: Twelve-sided pedestal bowl; 18th century. The mother-of-pearl inlay, used throughout South East Asia, is applied to a black lacquer ground which covers a base built up from cane rings.

most layer is reserved for special applications, and the second and third – *son nhat* and *son nhi* – are most commonly used for decorative work after further filtering.

Lacquered and cut leather was used for the saddles and harnesses of mandarins' horses, and also in the decoration of their carrying-chairs. Sometimes whole sheets of solid lacquer were relief-carved, and panels were painted with coloured varnish and enhanced with mother-of-pearl and metallic detail. But it is the decoration on wood which most typifies the work of this region, and which can be seen at its best on screens, containers and furniture.

Great attention was paid to the quality of the joinery in such items, and the final product was valued for its smoothness of finish as well as for its decoration.

The object was first covered with a thin coat of fine sawdust mixed with filtered lacquer and filler. This, in turn, was rubbed down with pumice and covered with a mixture of lacquer and finely filtered clay: further layers of carefully graded lacquer followed, each polished with appropriate powders and 'cured' in a warm, damp atmosphere. If the final surface was to be black the last polishing was with charcoal; in this case the surface finish could be compared to that of porcelain. Decorative additions were most usually achieved with gold or silver leaf or with fine sheets of tin, and a heavy-grade lacquer was used as the adhesive. Where silver or tin have been used a thin layer of translucent lacquer covers them to prevent tarnish.

From the fifteenth century onwards lacquer was used increasingly on wooden sculpture, and existing pieces as well as newly carved items were treated in this way. This had the effect of protecting the sculpture as well as adding a decorative finish, and both Taoist and Buddhist images were coated with polychrome lacquer. Whole shrines were made in lacquered wood, and lacquered figures were added kneeling in attitudes of constant prayer and adoration. In some cases stone figures were similarly treated, and these were not always of Vietnamese origin: some Cham sculptures were converted to Vietnamese use by means of a lacquer overlay. One fine example of Vietnamese work, however, is a figure of the many-armed *bodhisattva* Quan Am. It is dated to the late fifteenth or early sixteenth century, stands about 3.5 metres (11½ feet) high, and is in the Ninh Phuc temple in Tay Ninh.

Thai lacquer

It is generally agreed that Thai lacquer reached its greatest splendour during the eighteenth century, when the Thai capital was at Ayudhya. The production during this period of gilded lacquer-work on wooden chests, cupboards and caskets is unequalled, and almost all of this work was designed for a single purpose: the housing of Buddhist scriptures.

The scriptures were written on rectangular strips of palm and secured between two boards, with cords inserted through holes at either end of each bundle. The bundles' standard length of 70 centimetres (27½ inches) made their storage in regularly sized containers possible, and these were generally cupboards with a trapezoidal elevation. The two sides, the double-fronted doors – and in some cases the backs as well – were richly ornamented and the oldest examples also stand on a carved base. Later the base was replaced by four feet which sometimes curve inwards and terminate in lion's-paws resting on a sphere: an unmistakably Chinese device.

The manuscript containers are all characterized by fine workmanship and costly production techniques, befitting their sacred purpose. The decorative motifs naturally include scenes from the life of Buddha, but it is more surprising to find episodes from the Thai version of the Hindu *Ramayana* epic. (Rama is an incarnation of the Hindu god Vishnu, and the poem deals with his life and that of his queen, Sita.) This may, however, be explained by Rama's association with kingship: the Thai dynasty of kings since 1781 are all referred to by the title of Rama.

The most striking panels show the *nariphaka*, a tree whose fruit are women in various stages of maturity. Spirits of the air pluck the ripened fruit, while erotic scenes are depicted around the base of the tree. The *nariphaka* tree occurs in a metaphorical context in Buddhist scripture, and this has been suggested as a reason for its appearance on the containers. Other designs include single figures of either a spirit or a god on each panel, or an overall pattern based on spiral floral work enclosing tiny figures. These derive from the decorative reliefs carved on the stones of the great Khmer temples at Angkor and elsewhere in both Cambodia and Thailand. One such motif, the rice-flower, shows a variety of forms which can be used to date the objects on which they appear. In general the greater the area covered with gilding – and thus the less definition of reserved areas – the later the date: the earliest examples have roughly half-and-half black lacquer to gold leaf decoration.

Other dating criteria depend on the frequency of different motifs. The reign of the Sino-Thai King Phya Tak (1767–81) produced a large number of Chinese themes, while the fall of Ayudhya to the Burmese in 1767 is preceded by the production of manuscript cases in the form of inverted and truncated pyramids with flared or curved tops. Another group of containers which also shows Chinese influence is decorated with

Right: Detail from black lacquer coffer (*below*) with all-over gilded decoration; Thailand, 17th–18th century. The detail shows the elaborate and imaginative use of floral and animal motifs. Thai lacquer reached heights of great splendour during the 18th century.

Pieces like this coffer, made at Ayudhya, and the cabinet on the opposite page were often made to house Buddhist scriptures.

coloured lacquer applied with a brush, and finished with gold leaf.

The craftsmen capable of producing such objects were always few in number, and were therefore associated with the court, or with provincial centres where members of the royal family or powerful officials were stationed. Less costly items were produced in painted and gilded wood, while low relief carving highlighted with glass mosaic was reserved for the more expensive objects. Carving ornamented with mother-of-pearl on a lacquer base was highly prized, but the finest of all were the gilded lacquer containers.

This last technique involved the application of successive coats of resin lacquer on a wooden base. A pattern was pounced on to the final surface with powdered chalk, leaving a dotted outline on the black. A protective yellow fluid was painted over the parts which were not to receive the gilding, and the gold leaf was applied to the unpainted areas, with as much precision as possible, using thumb pressure and a cotton pad.

Right: Cabinet; Thailand, early 19th century. The gold decoration, sometimes continued on the back, was carried out in a technique called *lai rot nam*, 'designs washed with water'. Note the contrasting red lacquer on the base. See page 142 for detail.

architecture, and on the guardian figures which stand before many monasteries and temples.

Burmese lacquer

Some of the earliest remaining evidence of South East Asian lacquerwork is to be found in Burma, although its authenticity as home-produced art is disputed. One circular teak box painted in a mixture of lacquer and yellow ochre from the Mingala pagoda in Pagan is said to date from the thirteenth century, and a statue of a twelfth century king in the Ananda pagoda is made from layers of material soaked in a lacquer-like material wrapped around a cloth core. But no more positive evidence attests to the widespread use of lacquer before the seventeenth century.

In Burma, as in Thailand, lacquer is obtained from *Melanorrhea usitata*. And, as elsewhere in the region, Burmese lacquer has architectural as well as decorative uses, is employed as a waterproofing agent, and is used in the manufacture of furniture and containers. But the typically Burmese use of lacquer is as decoration on a flexible base: indeed, only the coarsest wares are produced on a solid wooden base. Cups and boxes of any distinction are made from woven basketwork of bamboo strips, and the best pieces have a weft of horsehair.

The bamboo framework to which the lacquer is applied is prepared carefully, and woven on a wooden form: that with a horsehair weft is extraordinarily flexible, and the edges of such a cup can be pressed together without cracking the lacquer or destroying the vessel's shape. An initial coat of lacquer is followed by a sawdust, lacquer and rice-water paste, and then by further layers of lacquer and bone-ash, until the glossy black surface is ready for decoration.

Boxes for clothes and toilet articles, make-up boxes, betel-boxes with trays and compartments to hold the leaves and other ingredients, containers for hair-pieces or head-dresses, as well as tiered food-containers and wooden trays, have all been made in this way. Only the wooden trays (often large enough to carry food for a family) were never highly regarded, and were thus seldom decorated, although they are often handsomely coloured in red or black.

In order of popularity the colours used in decoration are red, yellow and green, and two main methods of using colour seem to dominate. One technique described in the nineteenth century involves the application of thick lacquer with a brush to form a raised pattern on the black body, from which it is distinguished only by its height. The whole object was then coated in red lacquer, and later turned on a lathe to expose the black raised pattern beneath. The underlying basketwork in some cases produces another pattern.

The addition of a third colour was achieved

Above: Modern Thai lacquered wooden pieces, simple and striking in design and colour.

With the gold leaf in position the container was treated with absorbent paper, rinsed under running water and wiped to remove any remnants either of the gold leaf or of the protective paint. The whole process is known as *lai rot nam*: designs washed with water.

As well as the manuscript containers, Thai craftsmen produced lacquerwork which reflects that of other parts of South East Asia. In particular coloured lacquer was much used on wooden

Below: Wooden panel; 19th century. The moulded decoration is made from a mixture of lacquer and black ash; the scrollwork was made separately in individual pieces.

Much of this typically South East Asian relief work was manufactured in Mandalay, Burma.

with a freehand engraved line, often using no more sophisticated a tool than a nail fixed to a piece of bamboo. Further rubbing removed any colour not firmly fixed inside the incised line, and a final lacquer coating was polished with fossilized wood. (Work of a lower standard was finished with a paddy-husk polish instead, or with an abrasive leaf.)

The second method used incised lines alone, with each colour added in turn and separately rubbed down. Some evidence suggests the existence of a third method similar to that found in China; in this, successive layers of different colours are applied and incised to reveal a multi-coloured pattern, but it is not yet clear that such work was carried out in Burma.

All Burmese engraving has been – and indeed is still today – done freehand without preliminary pouncing, and it is an impressive sight to watch a bowl being inscribed with a linear design around its circumference which returns unerringly to its starting point. Outline human figures, which have increased in frequency in recent years, are begun at the eye! Boxes carrying the signs of the Zodiac and the planets (there are eight, rather than nine) are also commonly produced.

Gilded lacquer is made by the same method as that in Thailand, and lacquer is the standard adhesive for gold leaf and glass mosaic popular in architectural decorations. (The traditional Burmese history, *The Glass Palace Chronicle*, is named after a hall decorated in this style, in which the scholars who compiled the history held their meetings.) Coloured lacquer has also been frequently used on beams, rafters and other structural elements of wooden buildings.

Although the lacquered leather seen in Vietnam does not appear in Burma, the Burmese made considerable use of moulded lacquer. The base was a mixture of resin and bone-ash or ground paddy-husk and remained malleable for some time. The craftsmen used both fingers and horn tools to mould flowers and sprays either in individual patterns or in a repeating motif, and these were then applied to the object to be decorated with a lacquer adhesive, or sometimes modelled *in situ*. Such work was usually gilded, and forms the base of small shrines and pagoda platforms. The same method was used in some areas to decorate chests which housed scriptures, and was further embellished with glass mosaic.

Many such designs were given special names, indicating the frequency of their use. One such name, *Yodaya*, commemorates the sacking of Ayudhya, from where the Burmese derived much material which was incorporated into their existing culture. Another design, called the running deer pattern, is said by its undulating line to replicate the path of a hunted deer in the forest.

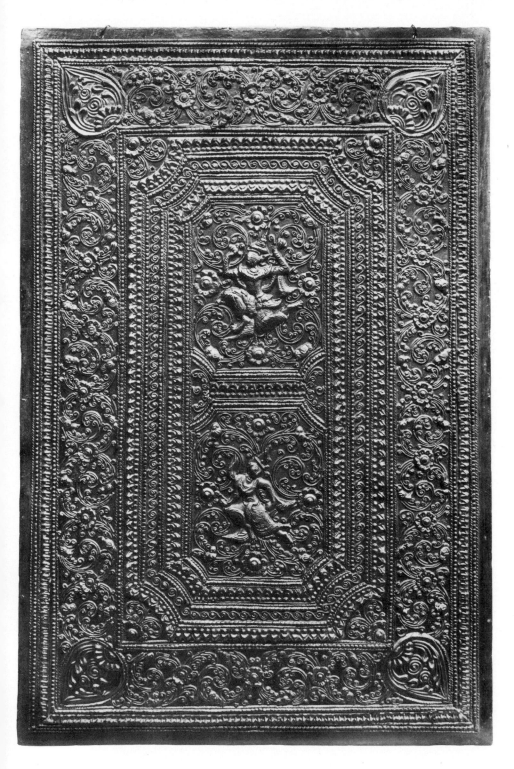

6

The Near East, the Middle East and India

The Islamic tradition is one of the world's richest sources of inspiration for the decorative arts. Pottery, glass, carpets, mosaics, and bronze and copper wares all show its influence at some time in their development. Lacquerwork is no exception. Indeed, motifs on the very early European examples, in mid-sixteenth century Venice, were inspired by those of the Near East.

Lacquer was a particularly useful material in the Islamic world. In its primary role, as a preservative, it protected wood from insects and fierce heat. At the same time it created a marvellously colourful background for the elaborate painted decoration which is so typical of Near and Middle Eastern art.

Above: Large pen-box; India, 17th century. Signed by the outstanding master Rahīm Dakkāni, the box has three cartouches of ladies, on its top, and sprays of leaves in red and gold on the base.

Opposite: Book-cover for prayer-book written in Arabic and Persian; Persia, 18th century. The rich colour scheme is characteristic of the second half of the century. The basic design has scattered flower-heads with scrolled stems.

For centuries, Western scholars misunderstood the technique used by Islamic craftsmen – a major stumbling block to assessing their work. Like their European counterparts they did not have access to the sap of *Rhus verniciflua*. Their use of lacquer for preservative and decorative purposes was based on indigenous materials, and may in fact have grown out of Egyptian or Byzantine crafts rather than oriental models.

In addition, fragments found in excavations are difficult to analyse and date; there are few written references, and even these are ambiguous as the ancient Persian script can be interpreted in many different ways.

Nonetheless, there is no ambiguity about the beauty of Iranian lacquerwork, which reached its height from the seventeenth to nineteenth centuries. Used particularly freely in the architectural structure of wall and ceiling panels, it also provides a rich background for fascinating painting, in miniatures, of domestic and court scenes that are unsurpassed in their delicacy and in their decorative colour.

Lacquered or varnished? The history of the technique in the Near and Middle East in early Islamic times

Work of such intricate beauty might suggest the existence of a wealth of related historical research, but in fact the reverse is true: lacquer-painting of the Near and Middle East has been a much-neglected subject. Articles relating to specific objects have been published in recent years, but as yet there is no definitive study on the history and development of the lacquer decoration of the Islamic world, and the origins and techniques have generally been treated in a cursory fashion by scholars, particularly in connection with book-covers.

The origins of Islamic work have been the subject of considerable debate. For many years it was thought that the influence of the Far East had been predominant; Maurice Dimond's article in the *Encyclopedia of World Art* reflects this thesis. But in recent years many differences between the two schools have been identified. Professor Ernst Grube's detailed study of a lacquered panel painting highlights one aspect of these differences, and since it throws light on the debate it will be useful to quote his description of the technique and materials used:

> While in China true lacquer was used as the painting medium, in the Muslim East it would appear that the painting itself was never carried out in lacquer. Rather, a surface to be decorated with what is generally called 'lacquer painting' but should more correctly be called lacquered (or varnished) painting, was coated with a chalk

or gipsum base. This basic coating was covered with a tinted varnish that came close to being lacquer and which can at times actually be called lacquer. On this lacquer or varnish base the design was painted, first in gold (in 13th-century Anatolia, 15th-century Herāt, 16th and 17th-century Turkey), later in polychrome tempera (16th- and 17th-century Iran and India), and, in still later times (Qāğār period in Iran, 18th-century to early 20th-century) in water colours. The varnish or lacquer base gave the pigments a special brilliance heightened by the fact that, after they had dried, they were covered by colourless, transparent varnish. The painted design, in other words, was placed between two coats of varnish, and attained an intensity and luminosity of colour that was difficult to achieve in any other medium. It was because of the similar effect, rather than the technical similarities, that these lacquered paintings were often confused with the actual Chinese lacquer painting and simply called 'lacquer paintings', which they are not.

There is, however, evidence of further techniques. A Persian scholar, Dr Kiani, recently claimed that Persian artists were familiar with true lacquer from early Islamic times. His evidence is based on the history of the Persian word *lāk* or *lāki*, used for a material produced from both vegetable and insect substances. Vegetable *lāk* was made from the sap of a tree, while the insect version was collected from the fluid of a red insect called *germez*. Dr Kiani has pointed out that the word *lāk* denotes a colouring or painting material, or a coating material used to protect objects, especially those made from wood. But, in Persian, *lāk* also means 'a red pigment used by painters'. This suggests its use not only as the protective layer identified by Professor Grube, but also as a painting medium.

Another technique was recorded by an Arab historian who lived in Cairo at the beginning of the fifteenth century. According to his research in the rooms of the tenth century Fatimid royal palace of al-Hakim, there were walls decorated with the portraits of poets painted on 'lacquered wood'. The Arabic term used is *khashab madhūna*: literally, 'varnished wood'. There is, therefore, evidence that lacquer was used as a protective material, and also as a pigment; and that, in Egypt, decorated wooden panels were varnished.

Modern Iranian lacquer-artists claim that the methods they use are entirely different from those used earlier in Persia. The same claims are made for two recent periods: the Safavid of the sixteenth to the early eighteenth centuries, and the Qājār of the late eighteenth to the early twentieth centuries. But even early techniques can be shown to be distinct from those of the Far East. A leading Chinese dealer and lacquer expert has identified twenty-two different methods known in the Far East: of these, only one was used by Near Eastern lacquer-artists, and that only seldom. This is the fabric technique, where the wood or *papier mâché* object is covered with a textile such as linen or silk, and coated with a layer of lacquer.

There can be little doubt that there is probably only the most tenuous of connections between lacquer-workers of the Near and Middle East and those of the Far East, and continued support for the influence of Chinese or Japanese lacquer is difficult to maintain. The most recent research looks instead towards other ancient centres of the art; close contacts between Byzantine and Persian lacquerwork may lead to the discovery of a common origin for them both. The varnishing techniques of the ancient Egyptians, and the somewhat later Buddhist reliquaries of East Turkestan, are possible sources for such an origin although supporting evidence for this theory has yet to be supplied.

The results of the Kozlóv expedition in northern Mongolia in the 1920s threw fascinating light on the search for such links in Central Asia, the original home of the Turkic people. During the excavation of tombs near the Selenga river a number of objects dating around 100 BC to 100 AD were discovered, including gold, bronzes, textiles and carpets. The fragment of a lacquer vase, almost certainly Chinese, was also found.

The excavators mention, however, that 'the outer surface of some of the coffins were lacquered, but only a small area survived on the bottom of the coffins, where it was in close contact with the underlying carpet. This was black lacquer decorated with a goose flying through clouds and the design was painted in red, yellow, green and brown.'

Later studies have claimed that this work is not Chinese, and was probably executed under an outside – and possibly Persian – influence. This has still to be proved, but it is certainly true that neither the colours nor the technique used are those of Far Eastern lacquer of the period – around 100 BC to 100 AD. Other lacquer-paintings untypical of Chinese craftsmanship have also been discovered in Central Asia by Sir Aurel Stein.

We do know, however, that lacquer of some kind, lacquered painting and varnishing were used in early Islamic times. An Egyptian collection has been assembled from excavations in Old Cairo and Qus, in Upper Egypt. More examples have been discovered at al-Qusayr on the Red Sea, where several pieces have been recovered during the 1979 and 1980 seasons, the latter including a cylindrical box without a lid. Most of these Egyptian objects were painted in black and red, but green and yellow colourings also occur. Some of the decorative details were incised rather than painted, with the incisions cutting through the pigment down to the wood. All these objects can be dated to the late Ayyubid period (the mid-thirteenth century), or the early Mamluk period (the late thirteenth to early fourteenth centuries). The wooden panels included in these discoveries are thought to be of the type mentioned earlier, which decorated the walls of the Fatimid palaces in Cairo: the Ayyubid and Mamluk palaces had similar decorative work. Objects used by the Egyptian ruling class of this period also carry such decorations.

Two small wooden objects were discovered at Nishapur, in Iran, during the Metropolitan Museum's excavations: the fragment of a box punched with small dotted circles, and a bone figurine, painted red. The fragment of a thirteenth century cylindrical wooden box came to light during my own excavations in Iran, at the Islamic site of Ghubayrā in Kirman Province. It was painted in black and red, with simple and somewhat crude scrollwork incised through the black pigment down to the wood. (This technique is, perhaps, a deliberate imitation of contemporary *sgraffiato* pottery wares.) The most remarkable piece, however, was discovered in 1978, shortly before the outbreak of the Iranian revolution, in the palace and caravanserai complex of Robat-e Sharaf in north-eastern Iran, on the ancient Silk Route. It is a wooden box, found in two pieces and painted in black, yellow, red and green. The upper narrow band consists of intertwined scrolls, while the wide central band contains seven human figures, each holding a musical instrument. The outline of the figures and the scrolls are incised rather than painted – just like the Ghubayrā box and some of the Egyptian pieces. The figure-work and other decorative details recall the designs of twelfth century metal and pottery. This elaborately decorated wooden box represents a comparatively early and well-developed example

Below: Base of wooden box; Persia, 12th century. Painted in black, yellow, red and green, and varnished, this piece was excavated from the site of the palace and caravanserai of Robat-e Sharaf just before the Iranian revolution, in 1978.

of painted work, and it is probably varnished or lacquered. The Iranian revolution made it impossible to carry out chemical analyses on either this or the Ghubayrā box, to establish whether the coating was *lāk* or varnish, but preliminary examinations indicated the presence of some kind of protective layer.

The connection between Byzantine and Islamic lacquerwork is supported by the existence in Turkey of a thirteenth century Quran stand, a so-called *rahla*, dated 1279–80. The elaborately carved decoration shows scrollwork, a double-headed eagle and sphinxes, and it is covered with a protective layer of *lāk* or varnish. We can assume that this example, made in Anatolia under the Seljuq rulers, was not unique. But we cannot be certain that the Turks brought this art with them from Central Asia (even with the evidence from Mongolia and Central Asia), or that during their migration they introduced this technique into Persia and to other parts of the Near and Middle East. It is possible that such works may have been made in Asia Minor by Byzantine artists well before the advent of the Turks, and that their knowledge was handed over to Turkish craftsmen. This, however, seems less likely, and the archaeological evidence from Central Asia, Mongolia and Persia supports the initial conclusion. Whichever was the case, it is clear that both Turkish and Persian artists played an important role in the development of this lacquer technique in the Islamic world.

Persian book-bindings of the fifteenth to eighteenth centuries

There is a gap of almost two hundred years between the Turkish Quran stand and later Persian known lacquerwork. The date 1479 appears on a cenotaph in a shrine near Sārī in the Caspian region of Iran. We know that a number of Egyptian vessels have been dated to the late thirteenth and early fourteenth centuries, and it is hardly likely that there was such a long gap in workmanship only in Turkey and Persia, and even more unlikely that the technique died out. Nevertheless, the next pieces date from the latter part of the fifteenth century, and apart from the cenotaph these are all book-bindings.

During the Timurid period from 1370 to 1506, but especially after Timur's death in 1404, the city of Herat became the capital of the Empire, and a major artistic centre. Splendid illuminated manuscripts were produced in the *atelier* of Herat, which received support both from Timur's son Shah Rūkh, and his grandson Bāysunqur. The *atelier* not only created the richly illuminated manuscripts themselves, but also their book-covers: in fact it was here that the earliest lacquered bindings were made.

The earliest-known surviving example of these bindings decorates the covers and the flap of Jalāl al-Dīn Rūmī's *Mathnawī*, a collection of fables, legends and poems which was copied in 1483 for the last Timurid ruler, Sultan Husayn Bayqara. The lacquer decoration surrounds a stamped, moulded and gilt-lobed central medallion. Similarly moulded and gilt quarter-medallions decorated the corners and the border. The lacquered surface is black, ornamented with dense floral scrollwork in gold which is reminiscent of the decoration on the famous Ardebil carpet of 1539.

Two more early lacquer-painted book-covers are the binding of Husayn's *dīwān*, a collection of poems, of 1492, which carries motifs of golden scrollwork and birds, and one that decorates the covers and the flap of Amīr Khusrau Dihlawī's *Hesht Bihisht* (the seventh paradise). The latter is the first known to have been executed in polychrome lacquer enriched with mother-of-pearl inlay. The previously traditional stamped and gilt medallions on the centre and corners have gone; instead, the entire surface is covered with black lacquer and the design is painted in gold and other colours. Within the central lobed medallion is a blossoming tree, with two mythical Chinese animals, the *chi'lins*, underneath it and pairs of fishes in the pendants above and below.

The Safavid dynasty replaced the Timurids at the beginning of the sixteenth century, and the royal *atelier* with most of its outstanding artists was moved to the Safavid capital of Tabriz in north-west Persia, a move which had far-reaching consequences. Immediately after the Safavids came to power in 1506 war broke out between them and the Turkish Ottoman empire, and the Safavid army of Shāh Ismail was defeated at the battle of Chaldiran, near Tabriz, in 1514. The Ottomans occupied Tabriz, and some of the Safavid artists were forcibly removed, together with numerous manuscripts, to Constantinople. There they played an important role in setting up the imperial school of painting and calligraphy, and must have carried their lacquer binding techniques and decorative traditions with them.

In Safavid itself, lacquer binding continued to develop. Gold and black decoration was carried on for a time, but the decorative themes became ever more elaborate, and landscapes and human figures played an increasing role in the design. Shāh Tahmāsp (1524–76) moved his capital from Tabriz to Qazvin, and later, Shāh Abbās I (1588–1629) to Isfahan. The royal artists and library moved with the capital, and we may presume that later book-covers were made in these two cities. A pair of book-covers showing a bearded prince killing a dragon in a landscape, was probably made in Isfahan. It bears the signature of the artist Rezā and the date of 1612.

A few sixteenth century book-covers present

Right: Binding of Avicenna's *Canon*; Persia, 1632. The cover depicts a patient having his pulse taken by a physician who is obviously suggesting fresh fruits and herbal drinks. The gold on red painting is rare, and the details of the landscape and figures typically Safavid.

the unusual colour combination of gold on red, but these are very rare. The binding of a copy of Avicenna's *Canon* is more colourful. Avicenna or Ibn Sina (980–1037) was a physician, philosopher and theologian, a prolific writer whose works were appreciated long after his death. A copy of

his *Canon* and its beautiful binding is dated 1632. Its covers show scenes of patients consulting physicians. The figures, their garments, the landscape and shrubs, and every other detail of the decorative design, are typical of the seventeenth century Safavid style.

Above: Pair of doors in cream lacquer with polychrome decoration; Persia, early 18th century. Garments and headgear of the figures under the arches date these doors, one of two pairs from this period in existence today.

The later Safavid period: seventeenth to early eighteenth centuries

When Shāh Abbās I moved his capital to Isfahan in 1598 he built new mosques and palaces, and the miniatures and frescoes with which these were decorated provided work for the painters who moved with the court. Some of these artists also worked in lacquer, and one, Maulānā Muzaffar Alī, a famous sixteenth century painter and cal-ligrapher, is mentioned in a Persian treatise.

A large number of lacquered objects have survived from the beginning of the seventeenth century. An unusual group is a set of sixty-one bows, made of wood and painted in lacquer. A few bear artists' signatures. One bow with an elaborate floral design is signed by a female artist, Zeyneb bint Husayn, and probably dates from around 1600. The only bow with a decoration of figures is signed Sulaymān, and dated 1609.

Another unusual object is a *papier mâché* canteen painted in lacquer. On one side the decoration shows a garden party, while the reverse has a hunting scene. This canteen was first attributed to the second half of the sixteenth century, but its style is that of the seventeenth, and it was therefore probably made in Isfahan. Canteens such as this were used to contain liquids; the lacquer layers prevented evaporation and leaks. They were expensive items, and so were restricted in use to the ruling class.

The second half of the seventeenth century and the beginning of the eighteenth century were dominated by the works of two artists who were probably brothers: Muhammad Zamān and Hājjī Muhammad. Both men contributed paintings to several manuscripts and albums, but they excelled at lacquer-paintings. One large pen-box in the Keir collection bears the punning signature *Yā Sāhid al-Zamān*, 'Oh Lord of Time', attributed to Muhammad Zamān; it also bears the date of 1663. The picture inside the lid depicts Europeans in a landscape. This is probably one of Muhammad Zamān's early works. A casket showing a princess at her toilet surrounded by European figures is signed with the same signature, and may be one of his last works, since it is dated 1714.

Some interesting speculation surrounds Muhammad Zamān, who is said to have been sent by the Shāh to study European painting in Rome, where he became a Christian and assumed the name of Paolo Zemān. His return to Persia was shortlived because of his conversion, and he is said to have travelled to India and to have found patronage in the Mogul court. These claims, however, have recently been challenged.

Hājjī Muhammad was most certainly influenced by Muhammad Zamān. As far as we know, he mainly produced large pen-boxes, called *qalamdān-e bozorg* in Persian. One of the earliest of these is dated 1673. It has an elaborate floral design in gold over a brown background, and on the top are three medallions, the central and largest one containing the portrait of a woman. His last known lacquer work is a large pen-box painted with erotic scenes, which bears the date of 1712.

An interesting casket is dated 1609. It is richly decorated with figures in Safavid dresses, and indeed the entire decoration of the casket is in

Right: Detail of door with polychrome decoration on black; Persia, 19th century. The painting imitates Safavid work, a highly admired earlier period (see below).

Right: Door; Persia, 17th century. Figures in panels, with the rest of the surface covered with gold dust, are typical of the early Safavid period.

Safavid style. But recent research suggests that the casket may not be original, but rather a somewhat later copy – including the date – of an earlier Safavid object.

The Safavid period ended with the Afghan invasion of Persia in 1722, and a bronze ewer that has lacquer-painted decorations showing young couples under a blossoming tree may represent one of its last works.

Doors, walls and ceiling panels: Persia, Turkey and Syria, seventeenth to nineteenth centuries

The walls and ceilings of the palaces and private houses in Isfahan – and probably in other cities as well – were decorated with wooden, lacquer-painted panels. Doors were made and decorated in the same way. Unfortunately very few palaces or houses survive in Iran with their original Safavid panelling, but a number of lacquer-painted doors from that period exist in both public and private collections. Their use in palaces and houses is illustrated in a number of miniature paintings such as the *Saray* or *Fâtih* Album which contains a monastery scene from the fifteenth century, including a balcony door in this style. In Isfahan, Shiraz and other cities, decorative panels were also installed during the Qājār period in the early and mid-nineteenth century. In the reception room of a house in Isfahan the walls have richly decorated panels, some of which show the main square of the city. The stalactite semi-dome, the vaults and the entire ceiling are decorated in the same way. The room also has two pairs of doors executed in Qājār style.

The lacquered doors in existence show either a solitary figure or a young couple in a central medallion on each wing of the door; further figures appear above and below in square panels. The rest of the door's surface is covered with gold dust (known in Persian as the *marqash* technique) on a brownish-red background. A young man holding a typically Safavid long-necked bottle in his right hand and a small cup in his left hand, comes from another similar door. Doors of this type most probably date from the seventeenth century.

Later doors have central panels filled with large figures, under a lobed arch. Young couples appear in the square panels above and below, while the frames are decorated with intertwined floral scrolls over a gold background. Only two pairs of these doors are known today. The garments and headgear of the figures indicate an early eighteenth century date for both pairs.

A third pair of doors has been the subject of considerable controversy. The evidence all supports a late Safavid dating within the second half of the seventeenth century, for its decoration is

entirely in Safavid style. The details recall contemporary miniature paintings, book-bindings, lacquerwork and textiles, and the quality of the painting certainly matches that of Safavid lacquerwork. The medallion on the left wing probably represents the fugitive Mogul emperor Humāyūn being entertained by Shāh Tahmāsp in his court in Persia. But recent research now suggests that this door, and several others in the same style, are later, probably of the mid-nineteenth century, perhaps representing a deliberate attempt to reactivate and imitate Safavid work. During the Qājār period everything Safavid was highly admired and respected, and in great demand. Qājār artists, in response to this demand, produced doors, mirror-cases and caskets correct to the most minute detail. These objects were not made with the intention of forgery, but instead represent a sincere admiration for the earlier work.

The practice of decorating the walls and ceilings of private houses with lacquered wood panels had spread from Persia to Turkey and Syria. The ceiling over the throne of the Ottoman Sultan Mehmet III is decorated with lacquered painting, and dates from the end of the sixteenth century. The design includes cloud patterns, palmette flowers (called *hatayi* in Turkish), naturalistic motifs, and a dragon fighting a *semorgh*, a mythical Persian animal. This is thought to be a genuine Turkish work, and is so far the earliest known Turkish-Ottoman example of the technique.

In Syria the reception rooms of some houses in Aleppo and Damascus were covered with lacquered wood panels like those in Isfahan, and a number are still preserved in their original settings. Some panels were exported, and a few even reached public and private collections in the West. The so-called 'Aleppo' room comes from a private house in the Christian district of Aleppo, and was made between 1600 and 1603. Its extensive decoration is comparable to Safavid miniature painting. However, there are also Christian scenes in the design, and many Arabic inscriptions, and it has been suggested that the room's artist must have been a Persian living in Syria. The decorative details, and the fact that the inscriptions are in the *Nastaliq* script, so popular with Persian calligraphers and painters, and not in the *Dīwānī* style practised by Turkish scribes, supports this theory.

Another of these rooms, the *Nūr al-Dīn* or 'Damascus' room, is dated 1707. A third, another 'Aleppo' room, seems to be much later in date, probably from the first half of the nineteenth century. Similar rooms, which betray a strong Turkish influence, have panels dated to 1775. The architectural details in the design represent buildings of Turkish style, including *türbeh* shrines, while the floral decorations of tulips and carnations on others seem related to sixteenth century Turkish *Iznik* pottery.

Syrian lacquer was clearly produced under either Persian or Turkish influence. There is no evidence of an independent Syrian style for lacquered painting of panels or smaller objects.

The earliest known Turkish-Ottoman lacquerwork is the late sixteenth century ceiling decoration of the throne of Sultan Mehmet III, described in the previous section. The fine detail and execution suggest a sophisticated level of craftsmanship, and the thirteenth century Quran stand already mentioned supports that theory. It, too, could hardly have been an isolated piece, but unfortunately no other contemporary specimens are known.

During the later Ottoman period, between the seventeenth and nineteenth centuries, a large number of lacquer pieces were produced in Turkey. Most come from just two places, Edirne and Constantinople, and the majority are signed and dated. One prominent artist, Mustafā Edirnevi (or Mustafā from Edirne), was active from 1756 to 1766. Book-covers, pen-boxes and large panels were among the objects painted by the Edirne artists with naturalistic floral motifs or architectural subjects. An exceptionally beautiful book-cover is signed Hajji Dede, and dated 1756.

Another, with rich floral decoration, is signed Châkerî. Yet another by the same artist states that he made it in Constantinople in 1744.

Turkish lacquerwork, still largely unknown today, was made until the beginning of this century. It may have started under Persian influence, but gradually an indigenous Turkish style evolved, with a tendency towards naturalistic treatment of floral and vegetal patterns. The later impact of European artistic styles, and particularly of rococo, can also be seen but in architectural representations actual Turkish buildings are depicted: mosques, *türbehs* and palaces.

Indian lacquerwork

Even less is known about Indian lacquer than Turkish. Apart from twentieth century pieces, objects date from the period between the seventeenth century and the late nineteenth century, but the only modern study has been restricted to the earlier work. It has been assumed that lacquer-painting was introduced to India from Persia during the Mogul period, but it is possible that the damp Indian climate destroyed earlier examples. It is unlikely that lacquerwork was ignored in India before the Moguls, and some pieces may be discovered in a private collection or the reserve stores of an Indian museum.

Contacts with Persia were certainly strong in the seventeenth and eighteenth centuries, but it has also been suggested that Deccan painting from southern India must have influenced not only Indian, but also Persian, lacquer-artists. Rahīm

Left: 'Damascus Room'; Syria, 18th century. Sumptuous lacquered wood panels like the ones in this room were used in reception areas. Some are still in their original settings.

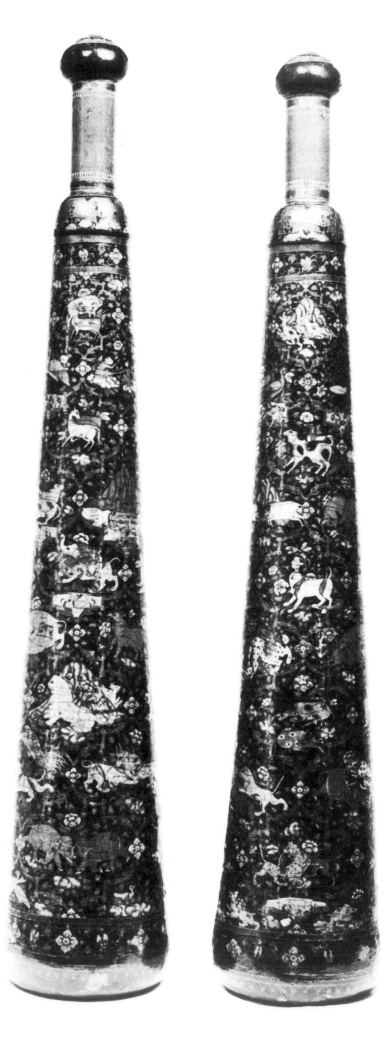

Dakkāni, an outstanding master of the late seventeenth and early eighteenth centuries, may have travelled to Persia and influenced the work of artists there. A *papier mâché* casket is attributed to him, and a pen-box bearing his signature has been dated to the late seventeenth century.

A richly decorated pair of wooden book-covers is covered with lacquered paper. Both covers carry identical decoration, of a tree painted in gold over a black ground, with a gold scrollwork frame. The decoration inside the frame shows a bouquet of flowers on each side, over a red ground. These covers can be dated within the eighteenth century.

A large pen-box is decorated with red and green figures painted over a gold ground. The sides show hunting scenes, while on top there are horsemen, two footmen, a woman seated under a tree, a fox, birds and a grazing horse. Over the grazing horse is written the artist's signature: *amal Azīz Saad*, 'the work of Saad'. It dates from the first half of the nineteenth century.

Kashmir was one of the major centres for lacquerwork, and various utensils and decorative objects were produced there. The designs and the colour combinations are the same as those on Kashmiri textiles. A pair of strongman's clubs (*mīl-i zūrkhāne* in Persian) were made for the Persian market in Kashmir during the late nineteenth century. They are wooden, and richly decorated with a variety of animals and birds, including a sphinx with a typically Indian head. During the last hundred years, however, lacquerwork in Kashmir and in other parts of India has catered mainly for the tourist trade, and that has meant an unavoidable decline in quality.

Persian lacquerwork during the Zand and Qājār periods: mid-eighteenth to early twentieth centuries

Ten years after the Afghan invasion in 1722 the Safavid dynasty died out. A leader called Nadir came to power, drove out the Afghans in 1727, and proclaimed himself Shāh in 1736. A new dynasty, the Zand, emerged in 1750. They moved their capital south to Shiraz, but their power was limited to Fars Province and to the regions around it. Then the Qājār Agha Muhammad Khan proclaimed himself Shāh and united the country again, moving the capital to Teheran. With the reign of Fath Alī Shāh (1797–1834) a new and comparatively prosperous era opened in the long history of Persia: the Qājār period, which lasted until 1924. During the time of the Zand dynasty, and afterwards under the Qājārs, the political and economic conditions were once more favourable for artistic activities. Some artists remained and

Above: Pen-box; India, early 19th century. Red and green figures on a gold ground.

Opposite page: Strong-man's clubs; India, late 19th century. Rich decoration on black.

Below: Mirror-case with portrait; Persia, 19th century.

worked in Isfahan while others moved to Shiraz, but later most of them joined the new Qājār capital in Teheran.

Under the influence of European styles many artists started to paint in oil on canvas, but miniatures were not completely forgotten and artists used a new medium: water-colours on lacquered surfaces. Interest in lacquered objects gradually increased during this period, and there was a great demand for mirror-cases, book-covers, caskets, letter-boxes, pen-boxes and even for panel paintings.

Mirror-cases

Mirror-cases have been known from the Safavid times. They were used by women for the application of cosmetics, and for storing love-letters, and had an additional role at marriage ceremonies, when they were placed in front of the bride as a sign of purity. Examples include one signed Alī

Above: Detail of a mirror-case; Persia, 18th century. The meticulously painted floral design with a bird shows the artist's skill with minute detail.

Left: Mirror-case; late 19th century. Mirror-cases have existed almost unchanged since Safavid times. This rich design is restrained and elegant.

Right: Mirror-case; Persia, first half of 19th century. The inside top cover, depicting a loving young couple, is part of a series of Persian wedding-scenes.

Mirror-cases became even more popular later in the Qājar period, and a large number of them have survived. One has the inscription *Yā Sādeq al-Waada*: 'Oh he who speaks truly in his promise.' According to one expert this is the punning signature of Muhammad Sādeq. However, the case is dated 1810. Muhammad Sādeq worked during the second half of the eighteenth century, and would have been dead by the time it was painted. The cover presents a young couple, entertained on a terrace by musicians and dancers; the back cover has a variation of the same scene, and inside the top cover is a design with a young couple alone.

Another example has a carefully drawn and painted floral decoration including a bird: the so-called *gul va bulbul* design. Inside the top cover a young couple appears, and above them is the same punning inscription – *Yā Sādeq al-Waada* – and the date, 1789. This particular piece is an excellent demonstration of the artist's style, his love of portraits and his talent for devoting great attention even to minute detail.

Some of the mirror-cases depict dervishes; an octagonal example shows a dervish sitting under a tree talking with two young men. A woman sits behind the tree and a bearded old man with a long pipe is shown in the foreground. The picture is signed *Yā Shāh-e Najaf* – 'Oh King of Najaf'; an inscription which is attributed to Najaf Alī, an eminent lacquer-artist of the middle of the nineteenth century. Several of his works have been studied and analysed, and it is interesting to note that some of them are decorated with Christian scenes. A mirror-case bears the same signature and the date 1855.

An entirely different subject, treated more elaborately in a rather overcrowded way, decorates the top and back cover of a mirror-case. A Persian wedding with all its festivities is shown on three levels, with the main event taking a central place. Portraits of four young women decorate the corners within circular medallions, and a loving young couple appear inside the top cover. This was once considered to be the work of Najaf, or perhaps of his son Jafar. The detail, however, is much closer in style to the work of Najaf's younger brother, Muhammad Ismail of Isfahan, who according to one expert was a *naqqāsh bāshi*, a Painter Laureate, responsible for a number of outstanding lacquerwork objects. One of these, a mirror-case, represents the meeting of Tsar Nicholas I and Muhammad Shāh in 1838 and is dated 1854. There are a number of similarities between the two objects which indicate the hand of a single artist.

Book-covers
Gold decoration on a black ground was still favoured for book-covers in the second half of the

Rezā Abbāsī, an outstanding artist of the Safavid period, and dated 1625. Another bears the signature Naqqāsh Ghulām Ibrāhīm Alī and the date 1720. Yet another is signed by the great painter Muhammad Sādeq, who was active during the Zand and the early Qājar periods. This case is decorated with a hunting scene. Sādeq excelled in painting portraits of Qājar princes and princesses, and young lovers.

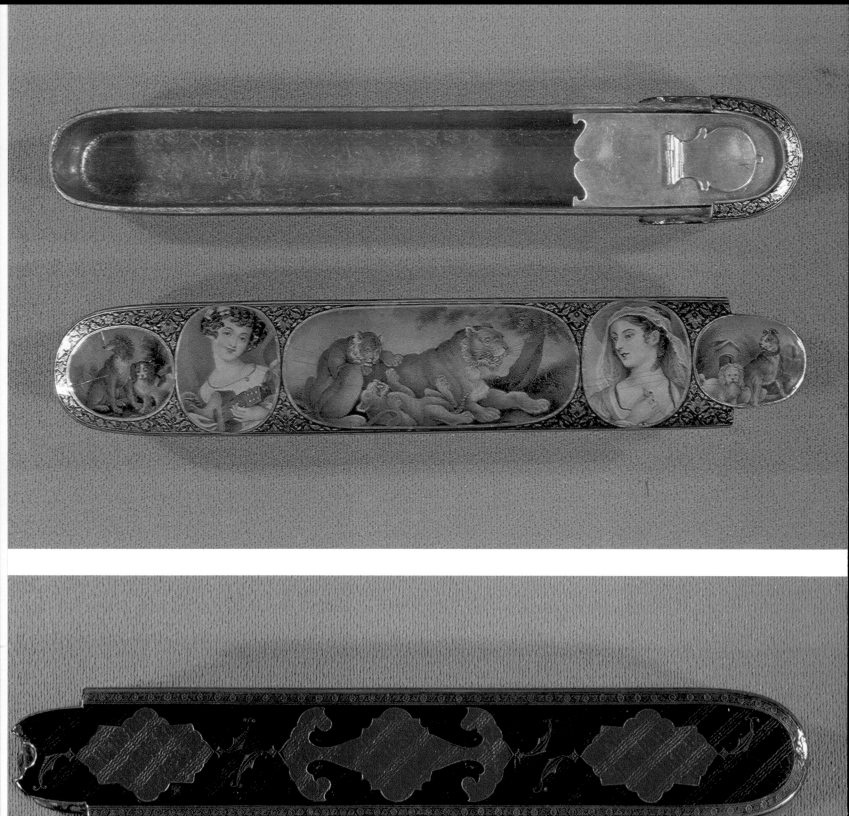

the battle cannot be identified. It is signed by Mubarāk ibn Mahmūd, an artist active during the first half of the nineteenth century. Another box, showing women (or, perhaps, fairies) picnicking with an old man in a landscape scene, bears the inscription *Yā Shāh-e Najaf* – the signature of the artist Najaf Alī – and the date 1854. The sides are decorated with portraits: young girls, women, and an old man.

A box which features lions in an elongated central medallion, and the portrait of a young girl and a dog at either end, may represent the transition from elaborate scenes to portraits. This is an extremely fine piece, with a gold inkwell. It is not signed, but it can be attributed on stylistic grounds to Abbās Shīrāzī, who was active during the second half of the nineteenth century. Pen-boxes with portraits and gold scrollwork include some delightful work, and the portraits of solitary figures – mostly women, and sometimes Europeans – are charmingly painted with great finesse and attention to detail, as in the work of Lutfullah Hamzawī. Another example from this group shows the Madonna and Child inside an oval medallion with roses above and below, while the pattern of scrollwork on a gold ground mirrors that of the previous box. The side landscapes recall the Holy Land. This box can be dated to the third quarter of the nineteenth century, and may be the work of one of Najaf's pupils.

Pen-boxes with floral and bird decoration in the *gul va bulbul* style can be divided into two further categories: those which are painted in polychrome, and those which are brush-painted in black over a brown background. There are a limited number of examples of the latter type, but most are signed and dated and this evidence shows they were made by a small group of artists at the end of the nineteenth and the beginning of the twentieth centuries. A box decorated with flowers, and two birds perching on the branches of a central bush, is signed *Kamtarīn Jawād*, 'the humble Jawād', and dated 1900. Several of Jawād's works have been identified, including the first letter-box discussed in this section.

The last group of pen-boxes are those on which the decoration gives a 'cloudy' or marbled effect, a

Opposite page, above: Pen-box; Persia, second half of 19th century. The lid of this extremely fine piece features lions in an elongated medallion.

Opposite page, below: Pen-box; Persia, 1860. It bears the signature of Abū Tāleb. The top and sides are decorated with gold wavy lines, and cartouches and medallions.

Left: Pen-box; Persia, late 19th century. Great attention to detail marks the portrait and the gold scrollwork.

Above: Casket; Persia, late 18th century. The Shāh at a lion hunt is featured on this casket painted in reds and gold by a court artist.

Right: Panel painting; Persia, early 20th century. This hunting scene in an Indian landscape is probably by Sania Humāyūn, a well-known artist who specialized in large formats; it could have been set in the 18th or 19th century. The panel was hung on the wall like a painting.

technique sometimes used alone, or superimposed with other designs such as coloured cartouches and pendants. This style was introduced towards the middle of the nineteenth century, and used by only a handful of artists, led by Abū Tāleb. A pen-box decorated with gold wavy lines on a dark brown ground, and with cartouches and medallions on the back, carries his signature, *Abū Tāleb al -Mudarris*, ('*Abū Tāleb*, the Teacher') and the date 1860.

Caskets, instrument-boxes and large panel paintings

Large lacquered caskets were used in Safavid times to store documents and letters, and remained popular until the present day. They are made either of wood or *papier mâché*, and the domed or flat lids are attached with hinges. Several examples from the late eighteenth century exist, including one with decorations that relate to the court, life and reign of Fath Alī Shāh. One scholar has devoted an entire article to the court painting of this period, for not since Sassanian times in the early seventh century had courtly paintings assumed such significance. The Shāh's court included a number of artists, of whom Mīrzā Bābā was the leading exponent. Their subjects centred upon the Shāh enthroned, the Shāh hunting and the Shāh in battle, and two are represented on this casket, as they were on the pen-box mentioned earlier. On the top of the lid the enthroned Shāh is shown at the coronation of prince Abbās Mīrzā. The raised medallions on the sides of the lid feature court scenes and portraits of women, while on the side of the casket Fath Alī Shāh is pictured at a lion hunt. The casket has neither signature nor date, but can be attributed on stylistic grounds to Muhammad Sādeq. However, it may be the work of Mīrzā Bābā since

some of the side portraits and scenes recall those on a casket dated 1804 which is the acknowledged work of this artist. The casket can be attributed to the very end of the eighteenth, or the beginning of the nineteenth century.

Dense scrollwork decorates the top of a rectangular instrument-box which originally belonged to a physician. It may be the work of a member of the Imāmī family, who worked during the second half of the nineteenth century. The beautifully elaborate decoration of another casket may also be attributed to one of the Imāmīs. A domed lid recalls the shape of earlier Safavid examples, and the figural decoration, scrolls, tree, flowers and the clothes the figures wear are all in Safavid style. But the designs are all painted on *marqash*, gold dust background, which was not introduced until the middle of the nineteenth century. The casket, together with the physician's instrument-box, and the lacquer-painted door mentioned earlier, were all made in Persia during the second half of the nineteenth century in deliberate imitation of the earlier Safavid style.

Large oil paintings on canvas became fashionable in Qājār times, and the court painters of Fath Alī Shāh – and of his successors Muhammad Shāh (1834–48) and Nasr al-Dīn Shāh (1848–96) – were responsible for many. The same artists also painted lacquered panels of various sizes. These depict historical scenes, the life of the Shāh, courtly life and religious themes, and are made of *papier mâché* with a lacquered surface, in the technique described by Professor Grube. The paintings on this surface were coated with a layer of clear varnish. An unidentified battle scene was thought to have been made during the first half of the seventeenth century, but further research has led to a re-attribution within the second half of the nineteenth century, when a Qājār school of painters worked in the traditional Safavid style. One of the most outstanding was Sania al-Mulk, who painted tableau portraits of officials, Europeans and religious leaders. He died in 1866. Another artist who painted in large format was Sania Humāyūn, active at the end of the last and at the beginning of this century. A panel painting that represents the battle between the Ottoman and Safavid armies at Chaldiran in 1514 may be an example of his work.

The works of Sania Humāyūn represent the last important phase in the long history of Persian lacquer. Regrettably, modern examples show definite signs of a decline in quality. Here and there we may come across an outstanding piece of work, perhaps ordered by the last Shāh or a foreign collector, but mass manufacturing has generally made a sad impact on the art. The love, patience and enthusiasm that is reflected so clearly in the works of the past is very rarely apparent.

Below: Doctor's instrument-box; Persia, second half of 19th century. The rectangular box is decorated with dense scroll-work, in the Safavid style.

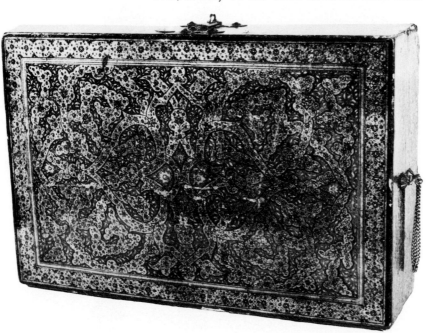

7

Europe
and Russia

Lacquer first became fashionable in Europe in the late sixteenth century.
Introduced through Venice, the process of applying painted, varnished decoration to
traditional objects was used by European craftsmen until about 1630, when its
popularity waned for about thirty years.

When lacquer came into vogue again in about 1660 – to remain in fashion
throughout the eighteenth and nineteenth centuries – interest was at first concentrated
on the Far Eastern style. Enough pieces were never imported to satisfy the demand,
and craftsmen in Europe therefore learnt to produce passable imitations of real
lacquer, and to copy oriental forms and motifs. It was only at the end of the
eighteenth century that wares became more obviously European.

Above: Japanned tin study for a memorial
to Earl Howe; late 18th century.

Opposite: Desk in blue *vernis Martin*; 18th century.

Very little early European lacquer seems to have survived, though references in contemporary inventories, diaries and trade descriptions indicate that the demand for lacquerwork was fairly widespread throughout Europe. Towards the middle of the seventeenth century references to lacquer production seem to subside. At this time a number of books and reports were published of journeys to the Far East. Descriptions of oriental customs, dress, and life in general whetted the European appetite for more information about this colourful alien world. Ships began to arrive, their holds laden with strange porcelains, silks and lacquer objects. In 1644 the diarist John Evelyn travelled to France, and in Dieppe his eyes grew wide at the glorious treasures being unloaded from ships which had successfully navigated the dangerous trade routes from the East. 'Whatever the East Indies affords of cabinets, porcelain, natural and exotic rarities, are here to be had with abundant choice,' he wrote. His interest did not wane, and in 1664 he listed in his diary everything he saw in a group of Eastern artefacts collected by a Jesuit.

The Portuguese were, in fact, the first to gain footholds in Japan and China – Kyushu in 1542 and Macao in 1557 – but these were taken away when the Portuguese came under Spanish domination in 1581, and Spain controlled the Pacific sea-lanes. The Dutch had also started a Far Eastern trading company in 1609, doing business with Japan and India.

The English established their East India Company in 1600, but the Spanish still controlled the trade routes to the orient, and the East India Company was not over-successful until it was re-organized under Charles II in 1698. The French set up their *Compagnie des Indes Orientales* in 1664, though they carried on only a fraction of the total European trade.

It is now difficult to conceive of the impact that lacquerware from the East had on Europeans seeing these bright, highly coloured objects for the first time. Their rarity and desirability combined to push prices to ridiculous heights, and people were constantly searching, like medieval alchemists, for the recipe for a passable imitation. During the seventeenth century it was erroneously believed that Indian shellac was the basic ingredient of all oriental lacquer. In France, England and Italy tests were made on imported pieces to find out the constitution, but identification of the substances used proved beyond the capabilities of the learned scientific bodies of the day. Father Filippo Bonanni, who procured specimens of resin sent from China to Cosimo III of Tuscany, published his findings in 1720 in his *Trattato Sopra la Vernice*; he was the first to give the correct constitution of lacquer, but he stated that the resin used was untransportable and that

the tree it came from was impossible to grow in Europe. He recommended shellac, the substance already most used by lacquer-masters, as the best substitute to use when manufacturing copies of oriental lacquer.

In England in 1688 John Stalker and George Parker published *A Treatise on Japaning and Varnishing*, which gave both lacquer recipes and designs, albeit rather naive, for the decoration of lacquerware. This and Bonnani's tract were the main sources of information until the publication in 1772 of Sieur Watin's *Le Peintre Doreur et Vernisseur*.

Many different terms were used to describe what we now call lacquer, and little differentiation seems to have been made between the oriental variety, derived from the sap of the lacquer tree, and its European imitations. In the Low Countries the generic term for both was *lac-werk*; the French described them as *vernis de la chine* or just *vernis*; and the Germans used the term *Indianish werk*. The English called their imitations Japan work as well as japanning.

Until the mid-seventeenth century it was difficult for European lacquer-workers to find sources for the decorations they wished to apply to their work. All too few of them had access to genuine oriental pieces in any quantity, or even to oriental vases. In 1655 Martin Martinius published *Novus Atlas Sinensis*, an illustrated description of China. Other publications followed. The most influential at this time was probably a report by Johann Neuhoff in 1665. After the flight of the last Ming Emperor in 1644, the Dutch government had decided to send an embassy to Peking and Johann Neuhoff was sent as steward to the ambassadors; on his return he published an account of his travels, with accompanying engravings taken from his drawings, under the title *Gesandtschaft der Ost Indischen Gesellschaft*. Next came *China Monumentis Illustrata* by Athanasius Kircher in 1667, based on information gleaned from Jesuit missionaries, and *Asia* by Johann Christian Bernn in 1681, together with a spate of other books by authors climbing onto a fashionable bandwagon. Many were rehashes of books already published, and some accounts seem to have been rooted solely in the vivid imaginations of the writers.

Up to 1700 the Chinese were considered to have extremely high standards of both thought and craftsmanship, and the scholar Gottfried Leibniz, influenced by oriental philosophy, seriously considered promoting China as a sort of Utopia; but all this ended in 1704, when a papal bull was issued condemning the moral lessons to be derived from the teaching of Confucius – or at any rate the lessons that the Jesuits had derived from them. In addition, travellers in the orient brought back more and more tales of ridiculous customs

Right: Venetian mirror; *c.* 1575. In wood and gilt, the mirror is architectural in shape with Islamic-style motifs.

and strange morals. This led to the eighteenth century *chinoiserie* designs as distinct from earlier decorations which had been more closely imitative of oriental prototypes.

Augsburg and Nuremburg were the two great print-producing centres in Germany, and many *chinoiserie* designs were disseminated from there. Paul Decker published a series of designs for lacquerwork. In England William Chambers and Matthias Darly, amongst others, published *chinoiserie* designs. In France, Daniel Marot used Chinese motifs in the early eighteenth century, and in Italy the firm of Giovanni Antonio Remondini furnished printed designs to Venetian japanners for three generations. Drawing from all these sources, Robert Sayer in London published a volume of 1,500 *chinoiserie* designs in about 1760.

Information about European lacquer-workers is erratic. About some we know a great deal and about others little more than their names. In some cities the Masters joined guilds, such as London's 'Patentees for lacquering after the manner of Japan', Amsterdam's *'Verlakkers'* and the Venetian *'depentores'*; but the guild archives, where they still exist, give very little information beyond their members' names.

Japanning or lacquering also had a strong amateur following, especially in the eighteenth century among fashion-conscious society ladies with time on their hands. Sir Horace Walpole obviously did not approve of this hobby and once expressed his horror at 'two vile jars that look like the modern japanning by ladies'. One lacquer-master at the Prussian court even complained about Queen Sophia Dorothea's attempts at the art, which he always had to re-do for her.

The impoverishment of Europe after the Napoleonic wars caused a slump in the luxury crafts that had catered to the brilliant courts of Europe. The production of lacquered tin products at Pontypool and Usk continued, however, well into the nineteenth century, and so did the *papier mâché* industry at Birmingham in England, at Brunswick in Germany, and in Russia.

Italy

Fine textiles, metalwork, earthenware, exotic jewels – and oriental lacquer – first came to the West through Venice, Europe's historic gateway to and from the East. Consequently it was the Venetians who first tried to imitate the technique of lacquer. A document of 1283 setting out rules for *depentores*, the guild for painters, miniaturists, gilders and anyone else who used a brush, is the earliest written work which mentions varnishing caskets and furniture. Although the date when varnish was first used to decorate rather than simply to protect such objects is unrecorded, it is known that the Venetians were copying Persian

Below: Lacquered book-binding; 16th century. Decorative motifs on the earliest Venetian lacquerwork were derived from Moresque and Persian originals.

lacquered book-bindings by the mid-sixteenth century, and using the same motifs to decorate small caskets and cabinets.

At the end of the century Wolf Dietrich von Raitenan, Bishop of Salzburg, ordered a number of lacquered shields from Venice for his horsemen. A toilet casket commissioned by Archduke Ferdinand II of Tyrol (1529–96) for his *kunstkammer* at Ambras is probably also Venetian work of the same date. These are the earliest pieces that can definitely be ascribed to Venetian lacquer-workers, and the decorative motifs are derived from Moresque and Persian originals. A late sixteenth century lacquer table, at Ambras, may also be of Venetian origin.

A mid-sixteenth century painting attributed to Bernardino Licinio shows a Venetian lady at her toilet. Open before her is a lacquered box for her combs and utensils; some of these are on the table next to the box, which is decorated in the Persian or Turkish manner with stylized scrolled foliage. Boxes of this type still exist and are probably of Venetian craftsmanship.

A series of small picture- or mirror-frames worked in lacquer and inset with panels of coloured marble are closely related to these caskets. They are architectural in design and the motifs are very Islamic in feeling, probably derived from Persian book-bindings. The small cabinets with leather-covered exteriors and lacquered interior façades, again architectural in conception, and

Opposite page: Detail from the Venetian chest of drawers on page 176; 18th century. The rich, rococo decoration has *chinoiserie* figures and very European sprays of flowers in swags and scrolls.

Below: Private theatre in the Italian Embassy, Paris; it incorporates pieces from an 18th century lacquer room in Palermo. See page 177 for detail.

containing drawers, are of the same period. (These were copied in France.) Also related are a group of sumptuous caskets inset with rock-crystal or marble panels within an elaborate architectural framework decorated in lacquer, and probably intended as containers for papal gifts of linen to new-born royal children.

Fine musical instruments were often considered as precious objects and were sometimes decorated in lacquer. Several examples of virginals still exist, as well as a wonderful harp made for Duke Alfonso II of Mantua in 1587 and embellished with a mixture of Renaissance and Moresque designs on a painted lacquer ground.

Venetian lacquer in the late seventeenth to early eighteenth centuries

By the 1630s lacquer production in Venice seems to have come to a halt, and not much is known about it in Italy until a Frenchman, Misson, visited Venice in 1688 and recorded a flourishing lacquerware business. The art had probably become fashionable again in the 1660s: at about this time Father Coronelli had produced a specially durable varnish to cover globes, consisting chiefly of sandarac (resin from a tree native to North West Africa), which remained one of the most popular ingredients of European recipes.

Despite Misson's mention of a thriving trade, however, it is difficult now to find many pieces that were made in Venice in the latter half of the seventeenth century. Much of this work must have been thrown out and later destroyed as unfashionable, presumably in the century that followed. But some pieces do exist. These include a cabinet-stand, an armchair, a stool, and a table and chair which formed part of the furnishings of a villa at Longio belonging to the Giovanelli family. All are lacquered in green and decorated with *chinoiserie* designs partly inlaid with mother-of-pearl. The use of mother-of-pearl inlay combined with lacquer seems to have been a Venetian idea at this time, copied from the orient, and harks back to the sixteenth century, when bone inlay was sometimes incorporated into lacquer pieces.

By this time goods from the Far East were being imported directly to northern Europe rather than via Venice, which had been the major port of entry a century earlier. This may explain why both the overall design and the decoration of Venetian lacquer objects and furniture from this period are similar to those of northern European pieces. Examples of furniture made of the fir-wood normally used in Venice resemble English or Dutch work in structure and the use of Far Eastern decorative motifs and *chinoiserie*.

Eighteenth century Venetian lacquer

By the early eighteenth century, bureau cabinets, among the most popular pieces of furniture in the Low Countries, had also become fashionable in Italy. The upper section of these cabinets had cupboard doors enclosing shelves or sometimes a more elaborately fitted interior, while below was a hinged, sloping front that fell forward to form a writing surface supported on two pull-out *lopers* (runners) with drawers or, more rarely, cupboards below. Several Italian examples decorated in imitation of oriental lacquer survive. These, with their lively colouring and shapely outlines, are usually very distinct from their northern cousins.

A typically Venetian product, first seen in the late seventeenth century, is a stand in the form of a Moor or 'blackamoor', usually holding aloft a shelf to support a candelabra or vase. Sometimes upright, sometimes crouching, sometimes standing on their hands (with the shelf supported on their feet), these figures remained popular well into the eighteenth century, were revived in the nineteenth, and are still made today.

The technique known as *lacca povera*, which put imitations of oriental lacquer within reach of amateurs, was also used by professionals in Venice. Firms of printers, particularly that of Giovanni Antonio Remondini, produced sheets of motifs and of scenes with landscapes and figures, which would be cut out, stuck to a screen, box or other piece of furniture, and then painted and varnished until the appearance of lacquer was produced.

Venetian commodes were the most eccentrically shaped in Europe, and lacquered examples are no exception. They were painted in vivid blues, greens and reds and were weighed down with marble slabs or wooden tops painted in imitation of marble. By the 1730s or 1740s the decoration of these and other lacquer pieces began to show more European inspiration, and to draw less from the orient. Often they were painted with flowers in natural colours.

A Venetian room of the mid-eighteenth century, completely furnished in lacquer and sometimes also with lacquered doors and even panelling, must have been a marvellous sight, with its unique opulence and vibrancy of colour. Lacquer, no longer confined to *chinoiserie*, became increasingly popular for looking-glasses, toilet sets and all kinds of small items as well as furniture. In 1754 there were twenty-five lacquer-masters in Venice, all with thriving workshops; by 1773 there were forty-nine.

The grand salon of the Palazzo Ca' Rezzonico in Venice was re-created when the palace became a museum early this century. Although its own lacquer furniture and doors were removed, the contents of the salon of the Palazzo Calbo-Crotta were installed there, with matching silk wall-hangings and chair covers. The set of furniture, quite sober compared with some Venetian pieces, is decorated in dark green and gilt. Some items are more richly carved than others, but all are covered with *chinoiserie* figures and temples. One of the original doors from the salon was returned by the Accademia gallery. (The other was divided, and the two halves are both in America.) It is decorated with *chinoiserie* figures surrounded by garlands of flowers on a mustard yellow ground, probably the overall colour-scheme of the room in the mid-eighteenth century.

A rumour persists that the Ca' Rezzonico doors were painted by Tiepolo, who did in fact paint some of the ceilings in the palace, but they bear no relation to any of his known work. The decoration of Venetian furniture has in fact often been attributed to contemporary Venetian painters such as Tiepolo or Pittoni, but it is extremely unlikely that these members of the *Collegio dei pittori* would have collaborated with the lacquer *depentores*.

Members of noble Venetian families maintained small suites of rooms in or around the Piazza San Marco, which they used when they came to the city for official functions or festivities. They retired to them in quieter moments, to change or rest, or to entertain friends. The rooms were brightly and fashionably equipped, nearly always with suites of lacquer furniture, with chairs and small tables and stands predominating.

Many of these *casini*, often mentioned by Casanova in his memoirs, were kept under surveillance by the authorities, who felt that the opportunities they provided for private meetings might give birth to political conspiracies. Few of these apartments exist today and their furnishings and accoutrements have been scattered far and wide. One that does remain, without its furnishings, belonged to Donna Elena Priuli, wife of Federico Venier, one of the highest dignitaries in the Republic of Venice during the late eighteenth century. The room is intact, with its original plasterwork, a secret exit through a built-in cupboard, and a spy-hole in the wall. It was restored for the *Settecento Italiano* exhibition in 1929, and furnished with many lacquer pieces.

The Palazzo Querini-Stampaglia, now a museum, still has intact some small rooms furnished in lacquer, which give an impression of what these apartments must have been like when lacquerwork was fashionable.

Many small lacquer items were made in Venice in the middle and late eighteenth century for sale not only to Venetians but also to the many visitors who came to the Republic. These items included pincushions and all sorts of boxes and trays, sometimes as part of complete toilet sets including brushes, toilet-glass and candlesticks. Games-

Below: Chest of drawers; 18th century. The set of furniture to which it belongs came from the Palazzo Calbo-Crotta in Venice; silk wall-hangings matched the chair covers. See page 175 for detail.

boards were also popular, as were cases for musical instruments.

By 1785 the straighter lines of the Louis XVI style, nurtured in France, had come to Venice, to the chagrin of the lacquer-workers whose inspiration had thrived on the fantastic shapes and bright colours which had been so fashionable. Lacquer became unpopular and was not really revived until the latter part of the nineteenth century.

Other centres of lacquer manufacture

Turin was the most important centre of production in Italy, after Venice, and one of the most impressive lacquer rooms of the early eighteenth century is in its royal palace. Based on a design by the architect Filippo Juvarra, it is one of the most successful schemes incorporating lacquer panels ever devised. The shaped panels, some from the East and others copied from these by a local lacquer-master, Pietro Massa, were grouped together between the windows and doors and contained in an elaborate gilt framework. The result is grand and opulent without being fussy. A smaller, somewhat earlier, lacquer room in the same palace still retains the set of six lacquered stools that was made for it. With caned seats and vigorous cabriole legs, they are decorated with a *chinoiserie* motif.

Inspired by their king's example, the Savoy aristocracy also began to build rich palaces, and, though ivory-inlaid furniture was in vogue, quite a few lacquer pieces were also produced. Lacquer furniture made in Turin seems to draw heavily on Venetian styles for inspiration.

A lacquer room constructed in the Villa Vacchetti at Gerbido has sober panels, closely modelled on oriental screens, richly decorated with *chinoiserie* scenes in gilt on a scarlet ground.

A later example is in the palace of Stupinigi, an enormous and splendid royal hunting lodge outside Turin. The walls of a room in the king's apartments were covered with wonderful painted-silk wall-hangings, and Francesco Servorcelli decorated some lacquer furniture with flowers and arabesques on a brilliant yellow ground. The effect is ravishing.

During the eighteenth century Genoese craftsmen produced some lacquer furniture, but with none of the quality or charm of Venetian pieces. The lacquer was not nearly so well produced as in other parts of Italy, sometimes being applied directly onto the wood with little, if any, sizing underneath. The technique most often used in Genoa was known as *vernice della Madalena*. The designs were often simple, pastoral vignettes within a rococo framework on a pale blue, ivory or yellow ground.

A commode in the Palazzo Spinola provides a good example of the contrast with Venetian work: it is decorated with flower motifs and

Above: Detail from private theatre in the Italian Embassy, Paris. The exuberant style is characteristic of Palermo, while the gilt framework of the panels is reminiscent of the more restrained style of the lacquer room in the royal palace in Turin. See also page 174.

rocaille in gold and red on a black background, and on the sides there are figures from the *Commedia dell' Arte*. The surface is less refined and smooth than that of Venetian pieces because of the many layers of lacquer covering the pictorial decoration.

The smaller princely cities such as Modena and Ferrara produced little lacquer, and what they did produce slavishly copied the products made in Turin or Venice.

In 1748 Parma became the residence of Duke Philippe de Bourbon Parma and his wife Louise-Elisabeth of France, the favourite daughter of Louis XV. Her fond father sent coachloads of fine French furniture to fill the ducal palace at Parma, and French influence was very strong.

In Rome, lacquer was never as popular as in the more northern cities, though some was certainly produced. Father Filippo Bonnani, a contemporary authority on Chinese and European lacquer, records a lacquer-master in the Via dei Coronari around 1720 who made caskets, tables, desks and other small items, decorated in gilt arabesques and foliage, but nothing in a *chinoiserie* style.

A very handsome bureau, dating from about 1714, is probably of Roman origin and has fine mythological and waterside scenes, attributed to Sebastiano Conca, painted on its carcase. Tradition has it that the bureau was part of the dowry of Elizabeth Farnese when she married the future Philip V of Spain. More solid in shape than Venetian bureaux, the cabinet is typical of pieces produced in Rome.

One interesting example of Roman lacquering is a microscope belonging to Principe Urbano Barberini and made by a Jesuit father, Paulus Maria Petrini (1704–73), in the eighteenth century. It is decorated with *chinoiserie* in gilt on a black ground. Several lacquer-decorated commodes, typically Roman in shape with high cabriole legs, serpentine fronts and thick marble tops, are ornamented in gilt on blue and grey respectively. They are more sober than Venetian pieces in both shape and decoration.

The rigid rule of the Bourbon kings in Naples did not encourage the arts. Very little, if any, lacquer seems to have been produced there, with the possible exception of some flower-decorated commodes with brightly coloured grounds, close in style to pieces produced in Sicily. Palermo was an altogether livelier place, and the more exuberant trends of the eighteenth century found favour there. Fragments from two lacquer rooms survive, while pieces from a third have been used to construct a private theatre in the Italian Embassy in Paris. The use of gilt framework to contain the lacquer panels in these rooms is reminiscent of the more stately lacquer room in the Palazzo Reale of Turin, but the colours and the gusto of the carving are altogether more exuberant.

At the beginning of the nineteenth century the

decorative arts in Italy were influenced by the Napoleonic style emanating from France, and after this they followed the various styles that found favour in Europe. Very little lacquer furniture or smaller objects seem to have been produced, with the notable exception of Venetian blackamoor figures, which always seem to have been popular.

Towards the end of the century and into the beginning of the 1900s much eighteenth century Venetian lacquered furniture was copied.

England and Scotland

The widespread taste for oriental ware in England originated in the sixteenth century. The story begins with the licensed piratical activities of sailors under Queen Elizabeth I. Spoils from the plundered Portuguese carracks were rich and copious; they fired the imagination of the English, who began to dream of eastern lands overflowing with silks, spices, porcelain and carpets of fairy-tale splendour.

Until the end of the century, however, trading with the East remained in the hands of the Spanish and Portuguese, who by this time were uneasily united. But the setting up of the great trading companies by the English (East India Company, 1600) and the Dutch (Dutch East Indies Company, 1602) broke this monopoly and opened the way to a fuller exchange between Europe and

Asia, not only of goods but also of knowledge and ideas.

Along with the fine silks, spices and curiosities came some pieces of lacquerware – chests, screens and boxes. An English ship, the Clove, returned from Japan in 1614 with a cargo of 'Japanese wares, as ritch Scritoires, Trunckes, Beoubes [from the Japanese word, *byobu*, for 'screen'], Cupps and Dishes of all sortes, and of a most excellent varnish . . .' These items were auctioned by the East India Company, the 'small trunckes' fetching £4.5s and £5, and a 'small cabanet with drawers guilded and inlaid and sett with mother of pearle' going for £6.15s. In the previous year Princess Elizabeth, daughter of James I, received as a wedding present a 'cabinet of China worke' of which the value was said to be £10,000: it must have been a most remarkable piece.

An inventory of the possessions of the first Earl of Northampton at the time of his death in 1614 included a 'small table of China worke in gold and colours with flies and wormes upon a table . . .' and a 'Field bedstead of China worke black and silver branches . . . with the Armes of the Earl of Northampton upon the head piece'. It is not known whether this latter piece had been ordered from the East or was made in Europe.

At this time and for many years afterwards, decorative styles and terminology were confused: in the seventeenth and eighteenth centuries most Chinese and Indian goods were exported to Europe from ports in India and Java, and items were described haphazardly as 'Indian', 'Chinese' or 'Japanese' with no regard to their actual place of origin.

Early examples of English work are provided by one small group of objects: a ballot-box bearing the date 1619, two cabinets, and a box containing twelve trenchers. All have silver and gilt decoration on a black varnished ground, and on some of the pieces there is a curious mixture of Eastern and Western decorative motifs. Little more work of this type was produced in England over the next few decades, although lacquer imports continued to arrive from the orient.

During the second half of the seventeenth century there was an expansion in the East India trade, and lacquer was imported in greater quantity. It was highly admired for its hard, brilliant, mirror-like finish and exotic ornamentation. England was eager to embrace the curious foreign styles, and dealers hastily ordered as many pieces as they could for their fashion-conscious clientele. The variety of pieces was still more or less restricted to screens, cabinets and chests, and did not altogether satisfy some Western customers, who would probably have purchased whole suites of furniture in order to fill a room entirely 'in the Chinese style', had such suites been available. Nevertheless, a room could be panelled with

Below: Cabinet; 1688. Probably made in England, the cabinet, on an exotic stand, is decorated with gold and black lacquer.

Right: Clocks; 18th century. The grandmother (*left*) is by Samuel Short, the grandfather (*right*) by Edward East. Both are decorated with gilt *chinoiserie*. See page 180 for details.

Below: Bureau; *c.* 1690. Furniture of this kind was popular towards the end of the 17th century.

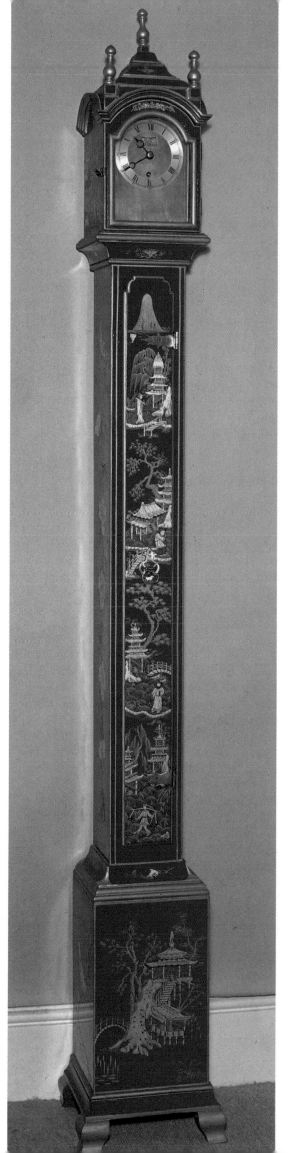

of japanned pieces, including a handsome day-bed which has a ground of clear red, with gilt *chinoiserie* decoration of figures, flowers and birds. Although dating from about 1730, this piece is of a style fashionable about twenty years earlier. Grendey produced a large amount of furniture for the export market: seventy of his pieces were bought for the palace of Lazcano in Spain. Another cabinet-maker was John Belchier, who made a red japanned bureau-bookcase for Erthig, in Denbighshire, in the early 1720s.

Over the next few years japanned furniture continued to be made, with floral and foliate designs enjoying some popularity in place of the pseudo-oriental figures. *Chinoiserie* was temporarily out of fashion, and the demand for japanning consequently lessened.

Then in the middle of the eighteenth century *chinoiserie* reappeared. A great many books of designs were being published: William Halfpenny's *New Designs for Chinese Temples* (1750), Lock and Copland's *A New Book of Ornaments* (1752), Edwards and Darly's *New Book of Chinese Designs* (1754), Thomas Chippendale's *The Gentleman and Cabinet-maker's Director* (1754) and Robert Sayer's *The Ladies Amusement, or the whole art of Japanning made easy* (1762) were only some of the publications that helped to foster a new interest in the Chinese style. The Frenchman Jean Pillement produced some notable designs of Chinese subjects which were engraved in London from 1757 to 1764 and subsequently served as inspiration for oriental decoration of all kinds.

Other influences from France were felt around this time. The most notable was the introduction into England of the commode; with its graceful, curving lines it was a very different piece of furniture from the more prosaic English chest of drawers and bureau. Commodes were sometimes imported from France made up with panels of oriental lacquer, and the admiration they aroused set the japanners to work once more.

The English conception of the East had become firmly established: a mélange of mandarins, monkeys, ho-ho birds and dragons rubbed shoulders in a landscape filled with willow trees, fretted bridges and curious pavilions hung about with pennants and bells, beneath little puffy clouds. Ornament became more three-dimensional, and all kinds of furniture – particularly such items as mirrors, candlestands and display cabinets – were embellished with carved and gilt *chinoiserie*.

Many japanned articles were made for bedrooms. Whole matching suites of furniture were designed, and were intended to be complemented by the use of Chinese wallpaper and Indian silk hangings. Thomas Chippendale of St Martin's Lane, William and John Linnell of Berkeley Square and others supplied between them quantities of high-quality japanned furniture.

A famous bed made for the Duke of Beaufort's Chinese bedroom at Badminton is now confidently attributed to John Linnell. (For many years it was thought to have been the work of Chippendale.) It is japanned red and blue, with Chinese motifs and a magnificent pagoda-shaped tester, at the four corners of which crouch four carved and gilt dragons. In the 1770s Chippendale did, however, supply a fine suite of green japanned furniture and the 'India paper' for the Chinese State Bed and Dressing-rooms at Nostell Priory, seat of Lord St Oswald. The superb bed and dressing-table, commode, press and chairs remain in the same rooms today. Chippendale is also known to have made green and white japanned furniture for the actor David Garrick's villa at Hampton in 1772–73, and various other commissioned pieces for great houses elsewhere.

Another producer of japanned ware in the mid- to late eighteenth century is Daniel Mills. We learn from his trade card that Mills, of Vine Street, Holborn, japanned and sold cabinets and other items, including copper, brass, tin and lead 'to ye utmost perfection' for the export, wholesale and retail trades. His card carries an engraving of a two-doored cabinet-on-stand that is typical of the period.

Soon after this the fashion for japanned furniture died away again. After the introduction of satinwood the finish provided by japan was no longer so much admired, and Robert Adam's neo-classical designs ousted the oriental motifs. It is true that in the 1790s the designs of both Sheraton and Hepplewhite included suggestions for japanning such articles as bed-cornices, candlestands, small screens and single chairs, but for larger items the demand had disappeared. There was a short revival when the Prince of Wales equipped his Pavilion at Brighton with imported bamboo and vast red and gold japanned panels, but this had little effect on public taste. Apart from a few pieces, such as 'fancy' chairs made of beech and japanned in the 1830s, and *papier mâché* articles which were already being manufactured (see below), there was little further production of English japanned furniture.

Japanned metalware

Concurrently with the production of japanned furniture, a japanned metalware industry had been growing up at Pontypool, in Monmouthshire. The original process invented by Thomas Algood in 1680 was improved by his son, Edward, who founded the Pontypool Japan Works in about 1725. There was a wide market for its products, which in the early days comprised a variety of boxes, usually with a black ground and with gold or coloured decoration. A crimson ground was developed in about 1740 and a tortoiseshell one in 1756; later decoration frequently included floral

Above: Lady's cabinet and two covered *papier mâché* vases; mid-19th century. The cabinet is decorated in the 'Moresque' style with gold leaf picked out with painted colours. All the pieces were made by Walton & Co. in Wolverhampton.

Right: Lady's cabinet; mid-19th century. Richly decorated with mother-of-pearl and gold leaf, it contains drawers for needlework, jewellery and writing materials.

Above: Japanned tray; early 19th century. Decoration of such pieces included many different subjects; this, from the Pontypool Japan Works founded in 1725, shows the capture of Fort Detroit. Note that the design has lost all pretence at being Chinese or even oriental.

designs, country scenes and sporting subjects, and in the 1770s a range of brighter colours was introduced. The work was hand-painted and therefore it was costly.

At first, japanning on metal had proved difficult: the surface tended to peel off after a while, and a really stable finish was hard to achieve. But in the early 1730s a technique was developed whereby iron plate could be dipped in tin which penetrated completely, rather than just coating the surface.

This innovation helped Edward Algood to perfect his japanning process – which, like that used for furniture, involved numerous coatings of varnish, separately fired on and hand-smoothed. Copper was also used for the base of the range of objects, which by the mid-century had extended to include a vast number of household articles. Bishop Pococke, after a visit to Pontypool in 1756, described the decoration as 'Chinese landscapes and figures in gold ...' The Pontypool factory closed in 1822, after a decline in quality.

In 1763 two of Edward Algood's sons, who had been working in the factory at Pontypool, left to start a similar factory at Usk, less than ten miles away. The products of this separate establishment were at first almost identical to those of Pontypool; later wares were decorated with military scenes and flower sprays, and in the early nineteenth century items were made to special order, painted, for example, with customers' coats of arms. The Usk factory closed in 1860.

Although imitations were made in and around Birmingham, 'Pontypool' became the word generally used to describe all japanned tin articles, whether produced by the Pontypool factory itself, or at Usk, or by any of the other factories. But the standards of workmanship reached by the Algood family were probably unmatched elsewhere.

From 1738 John Taylor (1711–75) of Birmingham produced, among other things, japanned snuff-boxes after the manner of Pontypool ware, which were of good quality. John Baskerville (1706–75), also of Birmingham and perhaps better known, in the printing world, for the type style he invented, went into production of japanned iron- and tinware in the early 1740s. In 1742 he invented a mechanical process of rolling and grinding iron to achieve a smooth, level finish, after which he devised methods of japanning the sheet iron to imitate mahogany or tortoiseshell. Baskerville carried on a flourishing trade in screens, picture-frames, cutlery-boxes, trays, panels to be used in cabinets, wainscoting and coachwork.

He also decorated his goods in polychromatic oil-paints – the new tea-urns, trays, bellows, tea-canisters and snuff-boxes would all carry highly coloured floral designs, landscapes or portraits. Some items of furniture were also made of metal with japanned decoration; these include an upholstered rocking-chair.

Bilston, home of enamelled wares, also produced some japanned tin pieces, possibly as a sideline. The chief products appear to have been coal-scuttles, tea-caddies, trays and boxes. Japanned snuff-boxes with enamelled lids were made in the 1740s, but apparently in no great number.

The Old Hall Works at Wolverhampton, and other firms in the town, produced japanned ironware in quantity for both the home market and the export trade, from the middle of the eighteenth century. The quality of finish was good, and prices were accordingly high. Some factories doubled up on the production of metal and *papier mâché* (see below). London also had its small share of metal-workers who japanned their products, among them Daniel Mills.

Japanning in Scotland

A separate, small japanning industry grew up in Scotland, beginning at Laurencekirk in Kincardineshire. From very small beginnings in 1765, the local landowner, Lord Gardenstone, an eccentric lawyer and philanthropist, built up a flourishing little town there. He financed the setting up of a library, a museum and an inn, and offered land on easy terms to encourage people to settle in the place. In 1787 on a visit to Spa in Belgium for his health he engaged a lacquer-master, Vincent Brixhe, to move to Laurencekirk 'on a plan to introduce and establish his art of painting on wood' after the manner of the Spa craftsmen. A Laurencekirk man, Charles Stiven (1753–1820), who excelled in the making of finely finished sycamore snuff-boxes and tea-caddies, lined with metal foil and with an integral wooden hinge, joined Brixhe in the workshop. Together they built up a successful small business which in time

Above: Japanned tin tray; late 19th or early 20th century. Gothic style in shape, it has a gold border and the stencilled and painted design is multicoloured. Made by the Japan Star Company, Bilston.

cats, local views, fruit, flowers, vine decoration, and so on. From the 1820s clan tartans were used as all-over patterns. At first these were applied by hand, but then William Smith II devised a mechanical method of printing onto the wood; later, machine-printed paper was glued onto the ware and then varnished. In about 1875 fern patterns were introduced, originally made by laying down ferns on the boxes in the manner of a stencil, but soon also produced by the quicker method of printed paper, glued on.

The products made from the 1830s included every imaginable kind of box and case for writing- and sewing-implements, money-boxes, trinket-boxes, pincushions, cosmetic-holders, string-boxes, little toys on wheels, tea-caddies and even brooches. But snuff was going out of favour by the 1830s, and as a result snuff-boxes went out of production.

The Smith factory continued well into the twentieth century, closing in 1937. Until that time they maintained their production of tartan and other wares, though there was a decline in quality.

Japanned papier mâché

The last material to which the japanners turned their hands in the eighteenth century was *papier mâché*. Another Birmingham figure, Henry Clay, collaborated with John Baskerville, to whom he was apprenticed, on the production of an extremely strong *papier mâché*, and, by the late 1770s, was able to make large pieces of furniture of *paper mâché* boards, which could be treated exactly like wood. These were subsequently japanned and decorated in bright colours with landscapes or even copies of paintings by the greater or lesser masters. Smaller pieces, such as trays and boxes, frequently bore *chinoiserie* decoration. Clay's work led to his appointment as Japanner-in-Ordinary to the Crown. In 1802 he

gained the royal warrant. The firm of Stiven and Sons continued until about 1868.

The industry spread, and in the early years of the nineteenth century snuff-boxes and other small wooden objects were being made in Mauchline, Cumnock, Auchinleck and Catrine, all in Ayrshire. The Smith family of Mauchline are the best known makers in this area, and indeed a commonly used generic name for all these small wooden objects, whatever their place of origin, is 'Mauchline ware'. The Smiths' japanned boxes were given up to thirty coats of varnish and polished with ground flint. Sycamore was the wood still generally used, but in the records was confusingly referred to as 'plane'.

Many different kinds of ornament were used on the boxes, including landscapes, sporting scenes, portraits of royalty or other personalities, dogs,

Right: Japanned snuff-box; 1830. Japanned wooden ware was made in Scotland in the early 19th century; a line from a poem by Robert Burns is on the box.

Above: Workbox; 19th century. The box was made by Jennens and Bettridge, well known for their *papier mâché* wares which included many household articles, japanned and decorated with a variety of metallic finishes.

Opposite page: Inkstand; mid-18th century. Made of oak veneered with panels of Japanese and French lacquer, the inkstand has gilt-bronze mounts.

moved to King Street, Covent Garden, in London, and worked there until his death ten years later.

In 1815 the firm of Jennens and Bettridge took over Clay's Birmingham works, and his royal appointment. The firm was lively and innovative, and enjoyed great success, particularly for its varied styles of decoration. These included oriental themes, often painted by Joseph Booth, who was in their employ from the early 1820s, and a kind of mother-of-pearl work introduced by George Souter in 1825. In this process the shell was stuck onto the piece to be decorated, and a pattern was made by varnishing the parts that were to remain and cutting away the rest with acid. Lustre ornamentation was also popular. The Birmingham Exhibition of 1849 included *paper mâché* exhibits japanned and decorated with overlaid gold leaf, gold dust or other metallic finishes including silver, copper, zinc and brass.

At the Great Exhibition in London in 1851, Jennens and Bettridge introduced to the public a most comfortable *papier mâché* chair, moulded to the shape of the human body. Also shown were beds, dressing-tables, sofas and a number of other

articles, including a baby's cot, a music stool and a case for a pianoforte – for which the firm received an award. However, it was found that this last item was unsuitable for its purpose, having no resonance. Jennens and Bettridge made some furniture with a wooden or metal base for greater strength and durability, and set in panels of japanned *papier mâché* for decoration: beds and chairs were among these pieces. In 1851 the company opened an office in New York to help with the administration of their thriving export trade; English *papier mâché* ware was in demand in America, Spain and Portugal, and production of an enormous range of household articles was in full swing.

Trays and boxes were always especially popular at home, and new designs were made as souvenirs of special occasions. When Queen Victoria came to the throne in 1837, a tray was designed at the Old Hall Works, Wolverhampton, in her honour, and another was produced to celebrate her marriage. After the death of the Prince Consort, articles were japanned for a while in sombre greys and mauves, and mourning jewellery in imitation of jet was made of black japanned paper.

Below: Cabinet of Japanese lacquer; late 17th century. Oriental imports became fashionable in France as a result of the influence of Cardinal Mazarin. The feet of this cabinet were probably added after shipping.

In the 1860s, however, a decline set in. Demand subsided, and in 1864 Jennens and Bettridge were forced to close their American branch. Smaller firms went out of business; the larger ones maintained their dwindling stocks for a while, selling out gradually to their straggling customers until the end of the century. *Papier mâché*, and with it japanned decoration generally, was no longer fashionable.

France

Oriental curiosities entered France through the port of Venice, and after the mid-sixteenth century by way of Portugal and Spain. The Dutch and the British then forged their own firm trading links with the East; the French followed suit, founding the *Compagnie des Indes* in 1664, and regular commerce was established.

Panels, cabinets and boxes were the usual forms in which lacquer became familiar. These were marketed in France from the Portuguese stalls at the annual Foire de Saint Germain, and were described by Paul Scarron in 1640 as '*beaux ouvrages de vernis*'. In 1644 John Evelyn noted oriental cabinets and other curiosities being unloaded from a trading ship at Dieppe. The inventory of Cardinal Mazarin's possessions, drawn up in 1653, includes several imported oriental lacquer cabinets, and no doubt the prestige of the cardinal, a well-known collector of Eastern treasures, did much to foster the taste for such wares among his acquaintances.

Little information is available on any imitation lacquer made in the early years. We know that Marie de Médici, who married Henri IV in 1600, became an admirer of the exotic substance, for she employed Etienne Sager to execute 'with lacquer, gum and gold decoration in the manner of [China], cabinets, chests, boxes, panelling, ornaments for churches, chaplets, and other small articles ...' But other than this, until later in the century when Louis XIV began to bring Versailles to its full glory, there is no evidence of any imitation of Chinese or other lacquer in France.

aventuriné, that is, powdered with gold, brass or copper in imitation of aventurine, a spangled Venetian glass. But some of the finest *vernis Martin* panels were simply left unornamented; their lustrous reflective surfaces needed no adornment. Almost any object at this time might be completed by the addition of ormolu mounts. These elegant, decorative gilt bronze trimmings became important elements in furniture design, particularly on the superlatively fine commodes produced in Paris at the height of the rococo era.

In 1772 Jean Felix Watin wrote a work entitled *L'art de faire et d'employer des vernis, ou l'art du vernisseur*, which includes information about the making and use of French varnish. The author, himself a craftsman in the field, is considered the foremost authority on the technical aspects of *vernis*. He describes the use of garlic, absinthe, salt and vinegar as part of the process, and frequently refers to the work of the Martin brothers.

The Martins had royal patronage for lacquer panels and furnishings from early in their career. In or before 1741 they were appointed to decorate some of the *Petits Appartements* at Versailles, in their special green and gold, for Louis XV's queen, Marie Leszczynska; and in 1784 their factory (which consisted of three separate workshops) was given the title of *Manufacture royale*. In

Below: Inkstand by René Dubois; 18th century. Lacquered with green *vernis Martin*, it was probably made for Louis XV, together with a matching table and *cartonnier*.

Right: Chest of drawers; 18th century. Made of oak veneered in ebony, with panels of Japanese and European lacquer, it is one of a pair given by Louis XV to his wife Marie Leszczynska for her bedchamber at Fontainebleau.

this year Etienne-Simon Martin began a further programme of decoration at Versailles and completed several rooms over the next few years. Some of this work survives, the colours ranging from pale yellow to deep Prussian blue. In 1752 Madame de Pompadour spent over 58,000 *livres* on having her château of Bellevue refurbished by the Martins, and also employed them to restore lacquered objects she owned.

The reputation of *vernis Martin* was not confined to France. In 1747 Frederick the Great requested that one of the Martin family should go to work for him in Berlin. Jean Alexandre, son of Robert, took up the position and remained some years, lacquering several of the rooms in Frederick's palaces. In 1765 another Frenchman, Sebastien Chevalier, was summoned to work as lacquer-master to Frederick, presumably to replace Jean Alexandre, who returned to Paris at around this time.

Apart from satisfying their royal and aristocratic patrons' wishes in the matters of doing up châteaux and supplying costly items of furniture in the most up-to-date styles, the Martin brothers provided more modest households with articles ranging from cupboards and tables to inkstands, boxes of varying sizes for every imaginable purpose, cups, goblets, barbers' bowls and accessories for the top of a dressing-table. Some of

the small objects, including pill-boxes and snuff-boxes, were made of moulded *papier mâché*. Decorative elements consisted of *chinoiserie* motifs, rustic scenes after one of the masters – a Watteauesque *fête champêtre*, for example – or floral designs, birds, and the like. There were many imitators, who produced similar wares of poorer quality and marketed them much more cheaply, having skimped on the production process. These inferior pieces cracked, chipped and deteriorated rapidly; even so, they were dangerous competition. Today the genuine work of the Martin brothers remains an example of superb quality in European lacquer varnishes.

In the last decades of the eighteenth century, the Martins' business gradually declined. The demand for lacquer in France had waned, and in later years was confined chiefly to the carriage-building trade – that very trade from which the brothers' business had sprung. By the end of the century, however, this too no longer required the use of the Martins' fine lacquer, and we hear no more of the family.

French cabinet-makers of the mid- to late eighteenth century

The strict regulations of the medieval guild system, which were in force with some variations

until the French Revolution in 1789, precisely delineated the functional areas of each craft guild, and also stringently supervised the quality of all work produced by its members. A mid-eighteenth century commode, for example, might have been produced by four craftsmen: a lacquerer, who made the lacquer panels; a cabinet-maker, who constructed the carcase and shaped all the wooden components; a bronze caster and chiseller, who produced the mounts; and a gilder, who applied the gold to these mounts. The cabinet-maker joined the wood, fixed the lacquer panels and attached the ormolu mounts, and it was he who stamped the carcase of the piece with his registered mark. Lacquer panels, therefore, are anonymous, and we have no means of identifying the lacquer-masters by their work. The Martin brothers' reputation was such that it is safe to assume that the work coming from their factory was of the finest quality and was probably used on most of the best lacquer pieces of the time.

Not every craftsman belonged to the guilds: a few highly privileged cabinet-makers of outstanding quality were above the regulations. There were also many outlaws who set themselves up in 'free' areas – sanctuaries left over from medieval

rights of protection. Without the stringent supervision of the guilds, many – though not all – of these workers were guilty of shoddy craftsmanship and considerably undercut the guild members' prices. Imitations of the Martins' work would undoubtedly have been produced by men such as these.

Oriental lacquer, as well as the superb French imitations of it by the Martins, was very popular at the court of Louis XV at this time. The asymmetrical quality of Eastern design perfectly complemented the graceful curves of the rococo style, and this was the era of the greatest appreciation and use of lacquer panels imported from China and Japan. Cabinet-makers often combined these with European lacquer in the same piece of furniture.

In 1755 Louis XV gave his wife Marie Leszczynska a pair of small chests of drawers for her bedchamber in Fontainebleau, to match a pair in his own room; the curved fronts and sides were veneered with panels of black and gold lacquer – European on the front, Japanese on the sides. One of the pair bears the stamp of the cabinet-maker Nicolas Jean Marchand (*c.* 1697–after 1757) who also made other commodes in this way.

Another cabinet-maker who worked with both Japanese and European lacquer was Bernard van Risenburgh (d. 1767), who was known until the late 1950s only by the initials BVRB with which he stamped his work. Van Risenburgh, one of the greatest masters of the rococo period, made furniture of outstanding quality, using various decorative techniques. He specialized in making commodes and smaller boudoir pieces for ladies, including little writing-desks, bedside tables and chiffoniers. The lacquer on his earlier pieces is French; on later ones it is Japanese. But whatever he used, he had an eye to the pictorial content – unlike some of his contemporaries who allowed lacquer panels to be cut about, regardless of how the decoration would finally be positioned.

Jacques Dubois (c. 1693–1763) produced many pieces of lacquered furniture, as did his son, René (1737–99). A Dubois commode known as the Marriage Coffer of Queen Marie Antoinette – though this name has no firm foundation – incorporates panels of both European and Japanese lacquer, and is thought to be by the younger Dubois (who certainly made other pieces for the queen). It was he who made the much celebrated

writing-table in the latter years of Louis XV's reign, which came into the possession of Catherine II of Russia, and on which the Treaty of Tilsit was said to have been signed in 1807. This table has *vernis Martin* in green and gold, and is of extremely fine decorative quality. René Dubois was one of the most notable of the Parisian cabinet-makers of his day. Both Jacques and René Dubois exported their furniture, much of which went to Russia.

Other cabinet-makers known for their use of both French and oriental lacquer include Pierre II Migeon, patronized by Madame de Pompadour, and Jean Demoulin (1715–98), whose work included a polychrome commode for the Duc de Choiseul at the château of Chanteloup; Pierre Garnier (c. 1720–c.1800); Roger Vandercruse, called Lacroix (1728–99); Martin Carlin (d. 1785); and Adam Weisweiler (c.1750–1809), who made intricate and beautiful pieces of furniture for Marie Antoinette and her contemporaries.

After the mid-century the rococo style declined. Shapes once again became formal and classical in inspiration, though the interpretation could be either delicate or more severe. French furniture was now at its most excellent in terms of both technique and decorative finish. Lacquer as an ornamental veneer for the body of the piece was still popular – and occasionally a lacquered metal plaque, ornamented with flowers or fruit, was applied to a piece of furniture as part of the overall design. But there was strong competition from other decorative materials. Marquetry, both geometric and pictorial, in many different kinds of wood, had become exceptionally fine. Plain mahogany and other precious veneers were also used, while panels of *pietre dure*, an inlay of hard and semi-precious stones, or Sèvres porcelain medallions were sometimes incorporated in a design.

The upheaval of the French Revolution brought

Right: Black lacquer commode with ornate gilt decoration; 1767.

Below: Black lacquer cabinet made by Adam Weisweiler; *c.* 1784. Made for Louis XVI's study at Versailles, it combines intricate ornamentation with elegant design.

about a general decline in craftsmanship. The guild system was discontinued, and although the tradition of fine workmanship naturally lingered on for a while, the new régime did not encourage the luxury hitherto in demand.

Tôle ware

In the mid-eighteenth century, advances were made throughout Europe in the production of japanning on metal. Tea- and coffee-pots, vases, candlesticks, bowls, boxes and other items – known as *tôle peinte* or *tôle vernis* – were all made prolifically in tin, or occasionally copper, and japanned. They were decorated with oriental designs, flowers, landscapes and, later, portraits, and sometimes embellished with decorative bronze fittings.

In 1767 a workshop was set up by François Samousat for the production of japanned goods, using a lacquer said to be 'hard, brilliant, tough and of a brilliant black'. He evidently purveyed his wares to the king, for his factory was designated *Manufacture royale de vernis façon de Chine*.

Samousat's work was no doubt of good quality; however, a great deal of cheap japanned ware on the market was definitely not. There was a brisk trade between France and England at this period. Among other things, large quantities of English Pontypool products were imported during the 1770s and eagerly snapped up. By this time imitations of Pontypool wares were already being made in France; one Sieur Clément started to make lacquered tin articles in the English style from the end of the 1760s. Among his products were plaques intended for mounting on furniture; but these were presumably not in the English style. After a few years Clément's work was pronounced to be of inferior quality and his business declined; his workshop was revived by Sieur Framéry, who produced objects with an *aventuriné* ground and relief decoration.

Tôle continued to be made into the nineteenth century, but there was a general drop in standards of workmanship, and the craft became no longer worthy of the name.

Germany

The fashion for oriental lacquer was stimulated, in Europe, by wares that had either been imported directly from the East or else had been acquired by piracy on the Eastern trade routes. However, until the nineteenth century Germany was part of the Holy Roman Empire and consisted of a number of small, mostly landlocked member states with no Eastern trade. Furthermore, until 1648 most of these states were involved in the chaos and destruction of the Thirty Years War. It is not surprising, therefore, that lacquer was late in gaining favour in Germany.

There is, however, some isolated evidence that

Right: Clavichord; 1732. Made at the workshop of the Hass family in Hamburg, then a famous music centre, it has red and gilt lacquer on the exterior of the case and a *chinoiserie* scene of figures in a landscape inside.

a handful of men may have been working in lacquer in Nürnberg and Augsburg in the early seventeenth century. A certain Paul Kick, possibly a relation of the Dutch William Kick who was working in the Netherlands in 1609, is known to have been active in Nürnberg during the 1630s and is cited as a 'painter of Indian lacquer' in 1648, while a lacquer panel, dated 1628 and depicting a battle scene with a stylized floral border, is attributed to an anonymous follower of the Augsburg painter Johann König.

Two other Augsburg pieces are fir-wood boxes ordered by the curio dealer Philipp Hainhofer in 1632 for display in a cabinet he was preparing for the city. From their decoration it looks as if they were crude copies by a local craftsman of some plates from Goa already in Hainhofer's possession. Perhaps the Goan source was also responsible for the mention of 'Indian' lacquer (above) rather than Chinese or Japanese.

Augsburg and Nürnberg were, however, the foremost centres of printing in Germany, and later, throughout the eighteenth century, were major suppliers of the engraved patterns which were used as sources for painted designs, particularly by lacquer-masters working in small principalities who did not have access to a collection of oriental porcelain, let alone to original Eastern lacquer. Many *chinoiserie* designs by such artists as Martin Engelbrecht, Elias Baeck, the more skilful Paul Decker who published a series of designs for lacquerwork, and Johann Esaisas Nilson came from these cities.

Late seventeenth century developments

It was only towards the end of the seventeenth century that Germany became the important lacquer-making centre she was to remain for over 150 years. There are early indications of local manufacture in the seaports of Bremen and Hamburg. An inventory of 1689 for the Electress Dorothea, wife of Frederick William of Brandenburg, includes 'Hamburg lacquer trays on stands with turned columns'. It is also known that two lacquer craftsmen, Evert Sachsenhausen and Marcus Albrecht, had worked in the city considerably earlier in the century.

During this period Hamburg was becoming increasingly famous as a musical centre: the composer Georg Philipp Telemann lived there, and Carl Philipp Emanuel Bach was a notable keyboard musician and the director of music in the five leading churches in the city, as well as a prolific composer. At the turn of the century there were some fifteen families of stringed-instrument makers, of whom the best known were Fleischer, Zell and Hass. The cases of their clavichords were generally decorated with red, green and gilt lacquer on the outside, with a genre scene, often depicting a musical gathering, on the inside, in

Above: Clavichord, shown in colour on page 194; 1732.

lighter colours. The instruments from the Hass workshops display *chinoiserie* in various styles, indicating that a number of different people worked on them. The decoration of one instrument of about 1723 incorporates European figures dressed in Chinese robes against a naively drawn landscape background, and contrasts strongly with another piece executed around 1732–55 by an artist who is not only more skilful but also evidently has a knowledge of Far Eastern patterns. The style of this second artist is distinctive; and, although like most lacquer-masters of his day he is anonymous, there are three clavichords and a double-domed desk with decoration characteristic of his work.

A clavichord of 1728, decorated by yet another master for the Fleischer family workshops, incorporates monkeys among its Chinese figures. Monkey scenes or *singeries* were to become a popular element in rococo ornamentation, and originated from the work of the French court designer Jean Bérain.

In Bremen there was no such incentive for lacquer decoration. However, one lacquer-master is known: in 1688 Nicolaus Woltmann applied for permission to work 'pruning flowers as well as lacquerwork'. Woltmann had learned both arts during a ten-year stay in England, which is significant since it demonstrates the extent to which the lacquer trade in northern Europe looked to England for its example.

Another known lacquer-master worked in Brunswick, where again English influence was much in evidence, probably because of the link established by George I of England, who came from the ducal family of Brunswick-Lüneburg. Johann Christoph Lesieur was born in Hanover and became a citizen of Brunswick in 1717; two surviving chests of drawers by him are decorated with elements taken from Stalker and Parker's 1688 *Treatise on Japaning*. But even though his work was competent, his business failed; in common with most provincial German lacquer-workers he lacked the patronage of a central court or rich nobleman, and he did not have the resources to compete with the plentiful supply of English imports. On the whole, wealthy patrons who wished to furnish their palaces and country estates in the latest fashion looked to Berlin, Holland and England.

Royal patrons

In 1717–19 Maximilian II Emanuel, Elector of Bavaria, who had lived in Brussels and France, conceived the idea for a pavilion at his palace in Nymphenburg. This 'Pagodenburg' was executed by his architect Joseph Effner. The lower storey was decorated with tiles, while upstairs there were two lacquer rooms, one in red and one in blue, decorated with 'Indian figures and birds'.

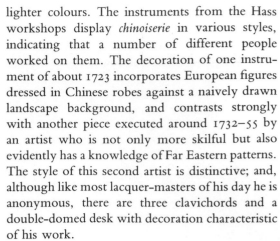

Above: Black and gold lacquer cabinet-on-stand, attributed to Gérard Dagly; *c.* 1700. Dagly was a renowned lacquer-master in Berlin whose work was so fine it could not be distinguished from oriental originals.

tals, partly in raised lacquer. Slender pilasters separated the panels, which were framed in dark red and brown with an elaborate gilt stucco cresting. The room owes its success to the combination of rococo *chinoiserie* landscapes and restrained architectural frames; *chinoiserie* frames would have produced a more oriental, but possibly overwhelming effect.

Surviving examples of lacquerwork executed for royal patrons are also in the palace of Count Wenzel Adalbert von Sternberg in Prague; at Augustenberg, the home of Princess Augusta Dorothea of Schwarzburg-Arnstadt in Thuringia; at the manor of Weikersheim owned by Count Carl Ludwig of Hohenloe, and in the Neue Residenz at Bamberg.

Craftsmen in Berlin: the Dagly family
Except in the important cities lacquer production in Germany was sparse, and because of the number of states into which the country was divided there was no specifically national style. The German contribution to European lacquer owes much to a single outstanding lacquer-master and his disciples. That man is Gérard Dagly (1657–1726), a native of Spa in Belgium who worked for the Prussian court, mainly in Berlin, where he established a shop in 1686. He came from a family of lacquer-masters who had worked since the seventeenth century at Spa, a fashionable watering-place. Because of the secrecy with which most lacquer-masters guarded their methods and recipes, little is known about them generally. However, there was a great deal of information about Dagly in the Berlin archives, and although much of it was destroyed during World War II, Hans Huth was able to use it in his article 'Lacquerwork by Gérard Dagly' published in *The Connoisseur* in 1935, and to expand on it in his later books.

Dagly learned his trade from his father, spent a brief spell in France and came to Berlin when he was 21. He may have been a member of the Reformed Church, seeking asylum with the Elector Frederick II after the revocation of the Edict of Nantes by Louis XIV in 1685; or perhaps he was invited to Berlin by the Elector at the recommendation of the Prince of Orange, who was acquainted with the Dagly family.

On 12 June 1687, Dagly became an official court artist and received a diploma in recognition of his 'special knowledge in gilding and doing lacquerwork'. His duties were to varnish, lacquer and maintain such items as tables, cabinets, trays and candlestands. When Frederick II died in 1688, his successor confirmed the contract and made Dagly Master of the Curio Room. To have achieved such recognition within two years of his arrival in Berlin, Dagly must already have been held in high regard.

The Pagodenburg still contains its original furnishings, including two Japanese chests mounted with good Parisian gilt mounts.

The Margrave of Baden-Baden, Ludwig Wilhelm, known as Turken-Louis on account of his distinguished service in the war against the Turks, shared with his wife a passion for things Eastern, including lacquer. An inventory made after his death even mentions a set of nightgowns which repeated the pattern of a lacquer dressing-set in his bedroom. After his death his widow, Sibylla Augusta, built a well-known summer residence near Baden-Baden, known as Schloss Favorite. Despite some changes, the original decor and furnishings still exude the spirit of frivolity that is characteristic of rococo *chinoiserie*, at its height in German domestic architecture.

But perhaps the finest lacquer room in Germany was the *Lack-kabinett* at Schloss Ludwigsburg, executed between 1714 and 1722 by Johann Jacob Sänger. The panels were lacquered in black and decorated with landscapes incorporating birds, dragons and even classical vases on pedes-

Below: Harpsichord made by the Dagly workshop; 1710. It has *chinoiserie* figures on a white lacquer background, and delicate floral sprays. The only white European lacquerwork to have survived without yellowing comes from the workshops of Dagly and Schnell.

His position as Master of the Curio Room undoubtedly stimulated his own output. Frederick III continued to add to the collection, which included Chinese and Japanese porcelain and soapstone carvings, and four of Dagly's lacquer cabinets were made to house such objects. They are depicted in an engraving of the Curio Room, dated 1696.

By this time Dagly's workshop was under the direction of his brother Jacques (who later went to the Gobelins factory in Paris). Specialized groups of workmen were employed in the production of lacquer, stucco figures, and in gilding and painting ornaments. The men were of various nationalities: many would have been French Huguenots, renowned for their skill in a variety of trades, and forced to seek refuge abroad from religious persecution.

In 1696 Dagly applied to the Elector for a monopoly in making and selling lacquerwork in Berlin, complaining that much of this extremely inferior lacquer was being sold under his name. The Elector granted him the privilege he sought and renewed the agreement in 1702, when it was more precisely defined in Dagly's interests.

Although he was given permission to mark and number every piece made in his shop, none of these have been found. However, he certainly worked to private commission as well as for the court and was known throughout Germany for his skill. A traveller from Frankfurt, Zacharias Conrad Uffenbach, saw him in Berlin in 1702 and described him as being 'incomparable in matters of lacquer'. When Frederick III died in 1713 he was succeeded by Frederick William I, who wished to save money for his wars and had little interest in the arts. He dismissed most of the court artists, including Jacques and Gérard Dagly.

Jacques went to Paris, while Gérard continued as consultant to various German courts: in 1715 he was working for the Elector palatine, Jan Wilhelm, on a hunting lodge at Bensberg that was to be modelled on Versailles. It was at Bensberg that Dagly died in the same year.

Certain features are characteristic of Dagly's work. One is a border of stylized, scrolling foliage resembling the endive or seaweed marquetry that was used in Italy and that was popular in England in the late seventeenth century; it is punctuated at regular intervals by chrysanthemum-like flower heads. Another feature is the groups of figures he frequently used: two dancers with flying sleeves, and a group of two or three musicians, are both motifs copied from vases in the Charlottenburg Chinese room; while that of a seated dignitary with two servants standing behind him holding fans derives from an engraving by Peter Schenk the Elder printed in Amsterdam in 1702. This group appears within a pagoda-like palace on the doors of a blue and white cabinet that is known to be by Dagly.

Another cabinet bearing many of Dagly's hallmarks is decorated in white, with fine raised lacquer on the doors. It repeats a motif from a Japanese chest in the court collection, and is of such high quality that it might be an authentic oriental piece but for the manner in which some birds are depicted. The standard of workmanship suggests that it was made by Dagly himself; he claimed he could imitate any oriental piece, and certainly this is substantiated by another cabinet whose doors are authentically oriental, while the sides and stand are known to originate from the Dagly workshop and are decorated with oriental-style patterns.

Notable among other products of the Dagly workshop is a harpsichord decorated in white of about 1710. Pieces by even the best lacquer-masters such as van Risenburgh and the Martin brothers in France turned yellow with age; the only ones to have remained white come from the workshops of Dagly or his one-time apprentice, Schnell, and so it can be assumed that Dagly's recipe for his lacquer included some special ingredient or process.

Further evidence of Dagly's craftsmanship is provided by an inventory of 1704 which mentions lacquered tin sugar-containers and a matching bottle by Dagly: this implies that he was able to lacquer tin more or less contemporaneously with the production of the first Pontypool ware in England, and many years before *tôle* was produced in France in the 1740s.

After Dagly: the eighteenth century in Berlin
After the closure of Dagly's shop in 1713, the lacquer trade in Berlin flourished without the restrictions imposed by his monopoly. Andreas Völkert was a lacquer-master of this period who is known to have worked for Queen Sophia Dorothea. One of his pieces was a cabinet-on-stand intended to contain a collection of watches. It was described as being 'blue inside and decorated in black and gold on the outside', and it was surmounted in the English manner with a carved coat of arms by William King, a sculptor who worked in the style of Grinling Gibbons. Völkert probably also made a lacquered fire-screen in Schloss Charlottenburg bearing the cypher of the queen inside and decorated outside with stylized Chinese flowers and foliage. The execution of the borders, with a seated mandarin at the top, closely resembles that of some domed cupboards lacquered on the outside in blue and inside in red, and decorated with caricatured Chinese scenes.

Another identifiable lacquer-worker is David Pennewitz, who was the manager of a stoneware shop at Plaue, near Berlin. As well as decorating pottery he executed a lacquer room for the manor of Plaue. Although his work includes some *chinoiserie* motifs from Stalker and Parker, it is otherwise composed of European elements derived from the designs of Bérain and possibly from the prints used as patterns by the Dresden leather-workers, which Pennewitz would have seen when he worked at Meissen.

After 1740 there was little lacquerwork in Berlin. One of the Martin brothers, Jean Alexandre, was there between 1747 and 1767 and decorated the 'flower' room at the palace of Sans Souci in natural colours on a yellow ground, as well as the king's study in the New Palace. An oval room in the same palace was later lacquered by another Frenchman, Sebastian Chevalier; he established a lacquer workshop in Berlin where he made many small items of furniture. These were decorated with delicate floral sprigs such as those painted on contemporary French and German porcelain. After the death of Frederick William II in 1797, he lost his royal patronage; the last that is recorded of him is an application to work in Russia, which was rejected.

Dresden
Second to Berlin as a lacquer-making centre was Dresden. Augustus the Strong, who became Elector of Saxony in 1694, was a well-known patron of the arts and he may have been inspired to start a lacquer workshop there by the Dagly cabinet he inherited from his father. In the early part of his reign he was preoccupied with his struggles to become King of Poland (he was deposed for the five years 1704–9). In 1710, however, Martin Schnell, who had worked under Dagly from 1703 to 1709, was hired by Augustus as 'court lacquer-master' for a salary of 3,000 talers. A major part of Schnell's work would have consisted of providing

Above: Pilgrim bottle, probably by Martin Schnell; 1715. Red stoneware is lacquered in polychrome.

Below: Papier mâché box with portrait of George IV, by Stobwasser; early 19th century. Johann Stobwasser's large library of books and prints provided decorative subjects for his work.

lacquered furnishings for three palaces, an Indian, a Japanese and a Turkish one, built or redecorated by Augustus between 1716 and 1723. In 1717 Schnell made 'Cabinets, Clavicembaloes and screens' worth 1,145 talers. He also worked to private commission up to his death in 1740, and between 1712 and 1716 he was employed by the porcelain factory at Meissen to lacquer and decorate their wares. In this way a much broader range of colours could be achieved than had been possible in enamels, but with use the lacquer wore off: lacquered ceramics are very rare today. There is, however, a pilgrim bottle of about 1715 that is probably by Schnell. It is lacquered in polychrome with a *chinoiserie* landscape and a lambrequin border around the lower half, in imitation of embossed designs to be found on Dutch silver of the late seventeenth and early eighteenth centuries. The pieces for which Schnell is perhaps most renowned are trays on which the decorative motifs are flowers and Chinese genre scenes.

Raised lacquerwork by Schnell is almost indistinguishable from that of his master, Dagly; but certain variations in shape indicate the provenance of pieces of lacquered furniture. In Berlin the legs of tables and cabinet-stands were usually scrolling and connected by flat, inwardly curving stretchers, whereas in Dresden they were often tapering and square, and joined by straight stretchers. A pediment composed of half-round segments was also a distinctive feature of furniture that was made in Dresden.

Before many of the originals were destroyed in World War II, Rudolf van Arps-Aubert made a thorough study of Dresden furniture which shows that local craftsmen were obviously much influenced by English furniture; a bureau still exists, generally considered to be English, which probably served as a model for many contemporary pieces. Certainly Dresden lacquerwork was of a very high standard.

Schnell lacquered leather and linen as well as furniture, and between 1731 and 1735 it is recorded that he lacquered six leather screens and decorated linen hangings with oriental figures for the king's Japanese palace. None of these survives, but a leather screen painted in oil by Johann George Näcke suggests what they would have looked like: it is decorated with Italian *Commedia dell' Arte* figures in polychrome framed by Bérainesque rococo scrolls and ornaments, and there are monochrome panels of *chinoiserie* at the base of each leaf of the screen.

The last two pieces known to have been made in Saxony are bureau book-cases, each with a broken pediment in the English style, and possibly dating from around 1740. They are lacquered in gold and red on the outside, and blue and gold inside, with *chinoiserie* framed by borders of diaper work reminiscent of contemporary Sèvres porcelain. Both bureaux are fitted with fine French ormolu mounts.

Later German ware: Stobwasser lacquer and japanning

The production of fine lacquer for the courts of Berlin and Dresden, as well as smaller German states, came to an end during the second half of the eighteenth century. However, it was then that the seeds of commercial lacquer-making were being sown in Brunswick by Johann Heinrich Stobwasser, who settled there in 1763. Although Brunswick was one of the few places in which lacquer had been made continuously since the early eighteenth century, the quality of this ware was inferior to that of Dresden or Berlin, and trade had not flourished.

Stobwasser was born in Saxony, the son of a pedlar, and while travelling with his father he became familiar with Ansbach lacquer. This consisted chiefly of objects such as sticks, belts and munitions-cases made for the military. The decoration was often primitive, but the lacquer was well known for its durability. Recognizing its commercial potential, Stobwasser persuaded a member of the principal lacquer-making family of the town, the Eberlains, to give him the secret formula, which he then improved on. He used the result of his work on *papier mâché* and decorated this in the style of English japanned ware. He later

decorated tinware as well, taking his designs of figures and landscapes from prints. The products sold so well that Stobwasser's whole family was employed in the business, each person specializing in one of the manufacturing processes.

In 1765, encouraged by the favourable terms that the Duke of Brunswick was offering to artisans who settled in his town, Stobwasser, his father Georg Siegmund, and his three sisters moved to Brunswick. They set up a shop which soon began to produce a mass of small items including pipes, boxes, mugs, trays and tabletops. An occasional piece of furniture was made to order, but Stobwasser recognized that volume of output was more important for his business and he rarely accepted private commissions.

In 1769 he was granted the exclusive right to produce 'Brunswick lacquerware' and, in recognition of the industrial nature of his establishment, permission to erect a sign above his premises reading 'Georg Siegmund Stobwasser und Sohn'. Significantly, he was also permitted to employ specialist turners and cabinet-makers, both masters and apprentices: until now the guild system would have obliged him to employ only soldiers working in their free time as assistants. One of the soldiers he employed was a cabinet-maker by trade, a French Huguenot named Jean Guérin. Guérin started lacquering cardboard table-tops which were labelled under his own name although

Above: Japanned tobacco-jar with bronze handles, from the Stobwasser workshop, Brunswick; *c.* 1800. The floral decoration is in red and gold. Erotic pictures were often painted on the undersides of these jars for the 'gentlemanly' pleasures of the smoking-room.

Right: Table with japanned inset by Stobwasser; 1800. It shows the Queen Dowager of Edward IV of England entreating protection for her sons, Edward and Richard.

they had been made in the Stobwasser workshop. He later married one of Stobwasser's sisters and in 1772 moved to Berlin in response to Frederick the Great's search for craftsmen in Prussia. The couple set up a shop there which gave the Stobwasser enterprise an extra foothold in Prussia: by 1774 they had outlets in Hamburg, Berlin, Halberstadt, Leipzig and Silesia. During the next twenty years the workforce at the Brunswick shop increased from twenty-four to eighty.

In the early days of production objects were made of *papier mâché* or wood. By 1778 a tinsmith is mentioned on the payroll. The tin was imported from England and, despite heavy duties, much of the tinware was exported to Russia. Other wares went to Hungary and Turkey.

In 1810 Johann Heinrich Stobwasser retired and married the widow of the cabinet-maker David Röntgen. The Brunswick business continued under new management as Meyer und Ried, and as late as 1842 their wares were praised at an industrial exhibition held at Mainz. Stobwasser's son, Christian Heinrich, established a branch of the family enterprise in Berlin, where he manufactured metal lamps.

Some craftsmen left the Stobwasser firm to set up their own businesses in other parts of Germany, Austria and Bohemia. The lacquer industry, as it became, flourished until the mid-nineteenth century when transfer-printing, another cheap means of decorating objects, supplanted it.

Stobwasser products are distinguished less for their originality than for their good design and decoration, which was often taken from English prints. One of Guérin's table-tops, for example, is decorated with a careful copy of a picture of *The Sons of Edward IV in the Tower of London*. Among the most recognizable objects made by the firm are snuff-boxes with waisted or inward-curving sides. These were moulded, turned and given five or more coats of lacquer, with a baking between each one, to give a high gloss. The outlines of the design were then inscribed on a ground of whiting, and when the pattern had been painted in oils, the whole was given a further coat of lacquer and air-dried.

In order to ensure that his products were painted to a consistently high standard, Stobwasser amassed a large library of illustrated books and prints of works by Rembrandt, Gérard Dou, Poussin and Fragonard, as well as contemporary artists. He also established an art school in Brunswick from which he selected the most talented pupils.

While his tin boxes were often gilded inside, his *papier mâché* ware was usually brown or later black, with a mottled outside achieved by overlaying black or green on red. Although he was allowed to mark his ware after 1775 with a horse over the letters 'St', he rarely did so: many of his

papier mâché pieces are inscribed 'Stobwasser's Fabrik', with the name of the painting. In addition to famous pictures, subjects for decoration included portraits, topographical material and, inside the lids of many of his snuff-boxes, 'equivoca' or erotic subjects. (The practice of furnishing the insides of lids, or the undersides of tobacco-boxes, with titillating subjects had been adopted by Dutch silversmiths in the middle of the previous century.) In quality Stobwasser's tinware is the equal of English Pontypool and French *tôle*, and it is often decorated similarly with flowers or neo-classical landscapes within borders, on a coloured ground.

Within ten years of setting up his firm in Brunswick, Stobwasser's products were known throughout Europe. By the beginning of the nineteenth century there were some thirty lacquer firms in production in German-speaking parts of Europe, all probably founded by craftsmen from the original enterprise.

The Netherlands

During the seventeenth century the Dutch Republic (or Northern Provinces, as distinct from the Spanish Netherlands) became a world maritime power. The Dutch East India Company (Vereenigde Oostindische Compagnie) was founded in 1602. Throughout this period the arts flourished – notably those of the silversmith, the weaver and the cabinet-maker. It is perhaps surprising, therefore, that so little is known about lacquer-making in the first part of the seventeenth century, when the Dutch cabinet-makers, who were generally so quick to follow foreign styles such as boulle, must have been making pieces in imitation of the quantities of fashionable oriental lacquer that was being imported.

Although we know that a guild of lacquer-workers was formed in Amsterdam in 1610, and that William Kick, a prominent lacquer-master, made chests, trays and so on, and invented a process for lacquering tin, no pieces by Kick or his contemporaries survive. One popular item at this time would have been a type of lacquered table decorated with mother-of-pearl inlay and floral *chinoiserie*: an example survives, which was made in Venice but copied from a Dutch original.

In Antwerp, however, in what was then the Spanish Netherlands, a new piece of furniture was being manufactured. A cabinet, on a stand, it consisted of a number of small drawers and sometimes a cupboard designed to contain a collection of jewels, shells or other precious objects. Such cabinets were often decorated with exotic veneers (a novel decorative style of the seventeenth century), with inlays of mother-of-pearl, brass, semi-precious stones, tortoiseshell or stained ivory or bone – or with lacquer. A late

Opposite page: Cabinet; 1700. Cabinets-on-stands, of this type, were made in the Netherlands to house collections of curios. The insides had little drawers and shelves, sometimes lined with velvet or plush, and the cabinets were often decorated with exotic veneers, an innovation of the 17th century. Lacquered examples like this one were probably cheaper to make.

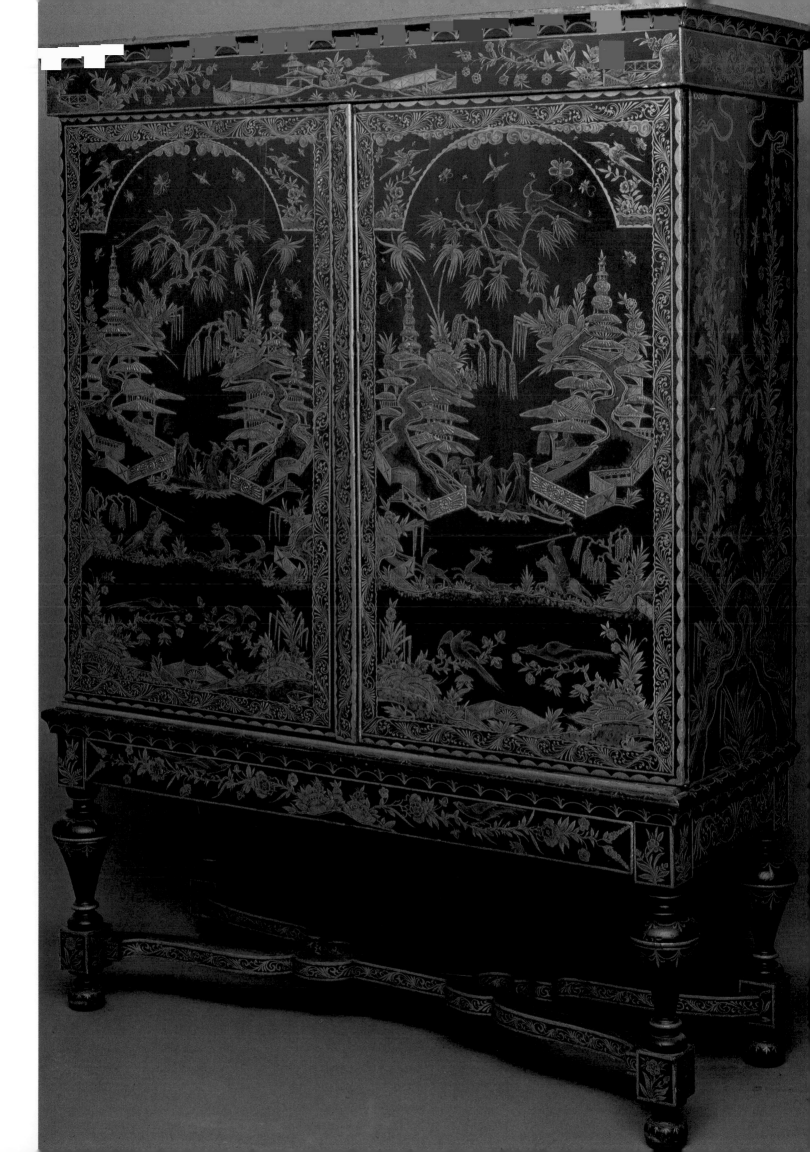

seventeenth century desk exists that, on grounds of shape, may be attributed to Antwerp; it is decorated in raised lacquer on a white ground, and the *chinoiserie* is executed in a conspicuously European style in a manner that closely resembles the blue decoration seen on contemporary Dutch Delftware.

Other pieces may be ascribed to the Netherlands because their decoration incorporates European flowers in oriental vase – probably copied from contemporary flower paintings. (The Dutch at this time were becoming interested in gardening and botany. Engravings illustrating plant specimens were frequently copied in paintings and on veneered or lacquered furniture.

Below: Folding table from doll's house; *c.* 1740. A rare surviving piece of furniture designed and lacquered in Holland, with an ornate floral border. Folding breakfast tables were popular at the time, and dolls' houses often contained exact replicas.

It is almost impossible to distinguish Dutch cabinets made at the end of the seventeenth century from contemporary English ones as their stands are often identical. Close trading links between the two countries meant that many Dutch pieces found their way into English homes. However, from the evidence of one early eighteenth century cabinet still owned by the Dutch family for whom it was made, certain other cabinets can in fact be identified as originating in the Netherlands. The piece has a stepped top, resembling the stepped gables of Dutch houses, on which pottery can be displayed. Both the cabinet and its stand are decorated in raised lacquer in gold on red, in a much more oriental design than the early Antwerp pieces. By this time many kinds of furniture were being lacquered, including display cabinets, corner cupboards and the popular tip-up tables of which miniature examples can be seen in Christof van Brant's doll's house of 1700.

Another kind of cabinet, with glass-fronted doors for the display of precious objects, appeared about 1730–40. These were usually lacquered mahogany pieces, and today they are rare, though many fakes exist. A genuine example of about 1740 with high cabriole legs and an ornately gilded, carved apron demonstrates the skill with which contemporary Dutch lacquer-workers were able to imitate oriental designs.

There are no longer any completely lacquered rooms in the Netherlands dating from either the seventeenth or early eighteenth centuries. A panelled room at Rosenborg, once thought to have been lacquered by Samuel Clauszon in 1615, was in fact probably decorated in the late seventeenth century, with designs from Stalker and Parker's *Treatise* and the engravings in John Nieuhoff's book on China published in 1665. There are, however, high-quality examples of mid-eighteenth century lacquer in the Chinese and Japanese rooms at Huis ten Bosch, the summer palace near the Hague. These were decorated in stages from about 1734 to 1785 in black and gold, and the later decorations of the Japanese room illustrate the disciplined use to which lacquer was put shortly before its popularity waned.

Belgium

One of the oldest centres of European lacquer production still in existence today is Spa in the bishopric of Liège, the home town of Gérard Dagly who was to become famous as the court lacquer-master in Berlin. The health-giving properties of Spa waters were discovered in the fourteenth century and it became a fashionable resort for the unhealthy rich from many countries in the centuries that followed, earning the appellation of 'Café de l'Europe'.

It seems likely that the tradition of lacquer-

making in Spa may have been initiated by the manufacturers of walking-sticks, for which there was a constant demand. It was not long before these characteristic long staffs or *bourdons*, usually with a knob on the end, became fashionable accessories for the healthy as well as the infirm, of both sexes. Important visitors to Spa were traditionally presented with a *bourdon*: the earliest recorded instance of this was in 1600. Soon, other objects and trinkets, including bowls, brushes, bellows (to blow away hair-powder) and, by the end of the century, mirror-frames and toilet-boxes, were being made for visitors. (This stimulus to trade was comparable to that at English watering-places where enamel boxes inscribed 'A Trifle From ———' were being sold.) Lacquer pieces were decorated variously with genre scenes from paintings by artists such as Teniers, landscapes taken from Dutch paintings, 'nymphs' in the manner of Coysevaux and Coustou, and *chinoiserie*.

In 1689 the physician Edmond Nessel published a pamphlet in which he praised the 'thousands of niceties made in lacquer in the Indian fashion'. He mentions flat and raised lacquer gilding, inlays of mother-of-pearl, brass and other metals in the manner of boulle – and marvels at the large range of colours that were used.

In 1729 Baron Pöllnitz wrote that the lacquer-masters of Spa 'mimick Japan so exactly that it is difficult to find the difference'. By this time sets of small toilet-boxes were among the most lavish of the items available. *Bourdons* were still popular:

Pöllnitz writes of a varnished cane decorated with 'a little cupid who was spitting a heart near a fire', with the inscription 'I make roast meat of them'. One lacquer-master working at this time was Vincent Rousseau; his signed boxes are decorated with pastoral scenes.

Articles for the toilette, including tweezer- and scissor-cases, were among the most common lacquered objects being produced, although by the early eighteenth century small pieces of furniture were decorated as well. Two specialities of Spa were containers called 'bergamottes', for anise or fennel seeds, which were taken to counteract 'the savage effect of the water', and a similar box known as an 'orangette' for orange blossoms.

The lacquer trade required many associated craftsmen: turners, cabinet-makers, makers of toilet-boxes and knick-knacks, and others. During the season five hundred to six hundred workmen were employed at Spa. Their products became so famous throughout Europe that many lacquer-workers were summoned to foreign courts. Renier Roidkin worked for some time between 1722 and 1741 for the Elector of Cologne; and a member of the Xhrouet family went to work at the residence of the Margrave of Bayreuth in 1763, while Vincent Brixhe was persuaded by Lord Gardenstone to set up a lacquer workshop in Kincardineshire in Scotland.

The wood used for lacquered furniture at Spa was plane, alder or linden. After the piece had been shaped, it was soaked in the water of the Pouhon spring said to be rich in tannin, which both dyed the wood brown and protected it from woodworm. No undercoat was used, but the ground colours were applied in a solution of glue. After the decoration had been painted on in gouache, the object was coated with sandarac, then polished and repolished several times.

Trade was severely damaged by the French Revolution at the end of the eighteenth century. Although there was a certain revival after 1815 when Spa again became a fashionable watering-place, by the time of the Great Exhibition in London in 1851 interest in Spa lacquer had declined. Recently there has been renewed interest, and boxes are once more manufactured and sold in the town.

Scandinavia

Throughout the seventeenth century and in the first part of the eighteenth, Scandinavian art was greatly influenced by the Dutch. From about 1660 to the early 1800s English influence was important and craftsmen modelled much of their work on lacquer imported from England. One of the earliest known Scandinavian pieces is a Swedish corner cupboard from the first half of the eighteenth century. It is decorated with tall trees and fruit in a style that makes no attempt to imitate oriental art, and inside there is a genre picture of a man counting his money, probably added later. Another simple, early eighteenth century table

Below: Desk; *c.* 1750. Polychromed over mottled brown lacquer, it is decorated with *chinoiserie* genre paintings of charm but no great technical skill. The desk was made in Spa.

cabinet has *lacca povera* additions incorporating mid-eighteenth century Augsberg prints. Both pieces are plainly decorated in comparison with the ebullient rococo lacquer being produced farther south at this period.

A skilful lacquer-worker active around the middle of the century was the Norwegian Niels Lochstoer, by whom there are various signed pieces including two long-case clocks decorated in the English style. Lochstoer, who had been apprenticed in London, worked in Braggernes, and in 1780 he was awarded a medal by the government for his researches into methods of japanning wood, *papier mâché* and tin.

Various lacquer-workers are known to have

been active in Copenhagen, while further proof of the popularity of the art in Denmark is provided by a room in Rosenborg Castle executed by Dutch artists. This is decorated with lacquer panels in dark green, framed in imitation tortoiseshell. The designs, drawing on both oriental and European motifs, are finely picked out in gold. A lacquer desk and some chairs at the castle were imported from the East. Both of Frederick IV's wives, Queen Louise (*d.*1721) and Queen Anna Sophia (*d.*1741), are known to have practised *lacca povera*; an inventory of 1743 lists sixty-two pieces of lacquer furniture belonging to Anna Sophia, and there are lacquered vases at Rosenborg said to have been decorated by one of the two queens.

At the Swedish court of the late eighteenth century some lacquer furniture was produced of considerably greater sophistication than elsewhere in Scandinavia.

Niels Dahlin, a cabinet-maker known to have been working from 1761 to 1787, was probably trained in Paris. A desk by him, of about 1765–70, shows no amateurism either in its structure or in its decoration: panels of Japanese lacquer are skilfully incorporated into the design, which is further enhanced by fine gilt mounts.

Spain and Portugal

Little lacquered furniture of note was manufactured in either of these countries despite the opportunities to copy oriental art that their Far Eastern trade must have provided. What eighteenth century lacquered furniture exists is heavily indebted to the design of English pieces, and the lacquer decoration is often applied haphazardly, without much attempt to adapt the *chinoiseries* to the contours of the furniture.

Portuguese painters, however, developed a fine technique for lacquer which was used to decorate furniture and rooms, and even shrines and organcases. The most important example of Iberian lacquerwork is the interior of the library at the University of Coimbra, in Portugal, which was executed between 1716 and 1723 by Manuel de Silva. There are three rooms panelled with lacquer, one in red, another in blue and the third in green, with gilt *chinoiserie*. A profusion of baroque elements such as garlands of flowers, trophies, armorial devices and putti give an impression of sumptuous richness to the rooms, and even the shelf-fronts of the vast bookcases have been decorated. The light rococo *chinoiserie* almost escapes notice in the midst of the baroque splendour of the overall design.

Left: Bracket clock; 1750. The Norwegian lacquer-worker Niels Lochstoer served his apprenticeship in England, and this clock by him shows the influence of the English style.

Russia

The Russian court and aristocracy of the eighteenth and nineteenth centuries looked to Western Europe for direction in taste and fashion. Although during the eighteenth century Russia's closest political links were with Sweden, in cultural matters Dutch influence was predominant. Peter the Great had spent some time in the Netherlands, where he would have seen both Dutch and English lacquer; and it is known that in 1717 he visited the workshops of Jacques Dagly at the Gobelins in Paris. So possibly it was he who introduced the craft of lacquer-making to Russia.

When *Mon Plaisir*, the czar's summer residence, was built at Peterhof between 1715 and 1725, it included a Chinese hall containing more than ninety lacquer panels executed by two Russian lacquer-masters, Ivan Tikhanov and Perfil Fjodorov, and twelve other workers. The panels, which were decorated with gold *chinoiserie* on a black ground and framed in red, were further embellished by a profusion of ornamental stucco borders, and brackets for the display of porcelain. They were so well executed that in later years it was thought they were authentic oriental work. During World War II the room was extensively damaged by bombs, but four panels survived and lacquer-workers from Palekh were therefore able to restore the rest.

When the Great Palace at Tsarskoje Tselo was refurbished for Empress Elizabeth in the 1740s, a lacquer-master called Neumeier is recorded as having provided lacquer wall-hangings for the great hall. The succeeding reign of Catherine the Great (1762–96) was one of major importance for Russia both politically and in the arts. In 1762 the landed gentry were released from compulsory military service, giving them the leisure to build palaces, great houses and country villas. Traditional lacquer-making, to decorate furniture and rooms for the court and nobility, flourished until the second half of the eighteenth century. A small table-top desk lacquered in red and black, and a cabinet decorated in red, both embellished with gilt *chinoiserie*, are examples of pieces produced during this period. The desk could not have been made before 1705 since the motifs on it derive from a book published that year.

It was perhaps at this time that some of the nobility set up lacquer workshops using serf labour. According to a report by a German scientist, Peter Pallas, who studied the remote provinces of Russia, at least two successful industrial works were in operation by 1769. At Nizhni Tagil and Nevianskoi, iron mills owned by the Demidov family produced sheet-iron, cannons, and other heavy metalwork; in addition there was a flourishing trade in copper and iron kettles, and lacquered tinware and treen (turned-wood) items. The Demidovs' principal lacquer-master was a certain Khudejarof. A lacquered tin box decorated with the Demidov arms bears his signature. Trays decorated with landscapes and historical scenes in a Western style were a typical product of Nizhni Tagil, where there was a school to train craftsmen. The lacquerware was said to be as durable as oriental work, and production continued at both places until well into the nineteenth century.

Another, much smaller lacquer workshop was established by Prince Scheremetjev in Kuskovo near Moscow, for which he freed some of his own serfs. The Vishniakov family worked here and were obviously successful since by 1876 they had 246 employees. A marked box from this period is decorated in typical fashion: 'A Family at Tea' shows three people sitting at a table on which there is a large samovar; each one is drinking from a *kovsch* (boat-shaped drinking vessel) – or perhaps out of the saucer.

Towards the end of the eighteenth century a number of lacquer-making centres were established throughout Russia. A. I. Austin, who may have been an Englishman, set up a workshop near Moscow, while in another one, belonging to A. Laboutin, trays decorated in the Pontypool manner were made. These usually had a shaped outline and were painted with scattered flower-sprigs in polychrome, and rococo cartouches and diaper-work panels in gilt, all interspersed with miscellaneous insects and exotic birds. Production figures from a workshop run by a Captain Ternberg indicate the popularity of such items: in 1809 1,447 lacquered objects were sold for a total of 11,723 roubles.

Folk art

Uniquely in Russia, lacquer is also a form of folk art. Traditional lacquer of this kind was mostly applied to domestic treen items such as cups, bowls and salvers, and had been produced since the early eighteenth century. These objects are usually decorated with bold, unsophisticated floral designs in red and black on a silver ground. The name for such ware was 'Khokloma', after a village in the province of Gorki to the east of the Volga river, where it was made in the settlements of the religious group known as the Old Believers, who had left the official church. Khokloma ware was sold at fairs and even the poorest households possessed some. Today it is still produced, with government encouragement.

Piotr Lukutin

In 1798 Pavel Ivanovitch Korobov set up a lacquer workshop, still in production, at Danilkovo (now Fedoskino) twenty-two miles from Moscow. Korobov had visited Stobwasser's shop in Brunswick and persuaded some of his craftsmen to come to Russia. Korobov made visors for soldiers' caps as well as snuff-boxes. In 1824 the shop

Above: Detail from a box made at Palekh; *c.* 1929. The tradition of Russian lacquerwork was revived at Palekh, originally a centre of icon-painting, after the Revolution. Egg tempera was used for decoration.

was taken over by his son-in-law, Piotr Vasielievich Lukutin, who made such a success of the business that the very name Lukutin came to mean 'lacquered snuff-box'. The reputation of his lacquer, which was as great in Russia as that of the Martin brothers' work in France, rested chiefly on the fact that it was long-lasting and did not chip. Lukutin achieved this by a meticulous process which he developed himself and which is probably still in use at the present workshop. The box was first shaped by pressing cardboard sheets around a wooden block, the base and the lid being made separately. The two halves were then dried naturally, and after being soaked in heated vegetable oil they were baked for several days at about 93°C (200°F). The resulting material was as hard as wood. After the lid had been fixed to the back with hinges, the box was lacquered and painted in the usual way, with the ground often executed in black and red to produce a tortoiseshell effect; finally it was covered in three or four coats of oil, which gave both the painted colours and the ground an extraordinary brilliance.

Initially the boxes were decorated in the English or German manner, with designs taken from prints; but gradually a distinct Russian style evolved, often depicting Russian scenes. Lukutin bought up a number of smaller workshops in the area, and by the end of the nineteenth century the

firm had a virtual monopoly of lacquer production in Russia. The Lukutin family continued to own the firm until 1904, when it was finally forced to close.

Lukutin ware was signed in various ways. From 1828 objects were marked with the imperial eagle painted in gold. Another mark at this time was FPL, standing for 'Factory Piotr Lukutin'; these initials subsequently changed according to whichever member of the family was in charge. After 1881 four eagles were added to indicate the four czars under whom the Lukutins had worked, and the words 'Factory Lukutin Moscow' also appeared.

The aim of the firm was to produce a range of items that would be attractive to all social classes in Russia, at a wide range of prices. Merchandise was exported to the United States, and Lukutin succeeded in broadening the reputation of his lacquer by exhibiting it at the international trade fairs which were a feature of the nineteenth century.

Modern lacquer

At the beginning of the twentieth century the demand for lacquer gradually diminished, and after the Revolution the industry would probably have collapsed completely without the encouragement of certain individuals such as the writer Maxim Gorki, who had worked as an icon-painter. Eventually it was the icon-painters who saved the Russian lacquer industry; after the Revolution they were trained to decorate lacquer instead, and at the old icon-painting centres of Palekh, Mstera, Koluy and Zestovo the art was revived, with egg tempera for the decoration. At Fedoskino, where the industry was based on the Lukutin tradition, oils were used. Subjects for illustration were usually taken from Russian folklore or the fairy tales and stories of Pushkin and other native writers. Some three hundred craftsmen work at Fedoskino today, producing about four thousand boxes a month.

The industry still flourishes: the government has imposed heavy duties on imported lacquer, and provides subsidies when necessary.

8

The United States

The great vogue for *chinoiserie* which swept England during the second half of the seventeenth century spread to the American colonies around 1700. Highly decorated painted furniture was much admired by the European colonists, and the first encyclopedia published in America contains a section on 'Oeconomical Painting' which defines the purpose of painting furniture as twofold: 'to preserve and embellish'. The art of lacquering, and the technique of adding heavy varnish to a surface painted in oils to produce a highly polished effect, fulfil such aims perfectly.

Above: Chair with decoration painted to resemble japanning; *c.* 1796. Made in Philadelphia. See page 215 for detail.

Opposite: Highboy of maple and pine with japanned decoration; *c.* 1700. Made in Boston.

Japanned furniture had been imported to Massachusetts as early as the 1690s, and Boston quickly became the main centre for both import and manufacture. Although this may seem a strange role for a traditional Puritan stronghold, where anything remotely frivolous usually met with stern disapproval, it undoubtedly reflects the city's vigorous commercial expansion at the time, and the tendency of leading citizens and successful merchants to copy English fads and fashions.

American craftsmen and artists, like their European counterparts, were unable to match the exquisite lacquerwork of the East because they lacked both the proper materials and an understanding of the complex techniques involved.

American japanners simplified the process used by English japanners. Maple and pine were the preferred woods, and because these are denser than oak or deal the need for a gesso base was eliminated. The painted – often black or tortoiseshell – ground was decorated with shallow relief ornaments modelled in gesso, smoothed with sharkskin, and varnished. If a tortoiseshell effect was called for a reddish-brown ground colour was applied, and the artist would then add splotches of lampblack mixed with oil resin. Silver or gold leaf, or metallic powders, were applied to the raised gesso areas, and details were drawn with a fine brush dipped in lampblack. Finally, a few coats of clear varnish were applied. This method eliminated the tedious and expensive mixing of seed-lac with ground colours, but unfortunately the distortions that were caused by the various drying times required by the underlying ingredients and the varnished top layer makes japanned furniture the most fragile example of early American art.

Creating suitable patterns presented a problem for American craftsmen, who lacked the wide range of examples that had flooded the European market during the craze for all things oriental.

The American colonists, their imaginations fired by such exotic suggestions of Eastern splendour, freely adapted the designs they found to produce some of the liveliest and most pleasing examples of New World art. One of the earliest surviving examples of an American japanned piece is a Boston-made high chest of drawers in the William and Mary style, where the drawer fronts are covered with rather crudely executed but charming animals, flowers, birds, oriental figures, and even a large camel! Two chairs, also in the William and Mary style, are thought to have been made in New England at the same time. These are decorated with gilt oriental motifs and red lacquer, which suggests that lacquering had become a fairly common method of decorating furniture. In addition to chairs and chests of drawers, highboys and accompanying lowboys were often japanned, and japanning was some-

times even used as wall decoration. Painted panels have been found that are unlacquered, but covered in *chinoiserie* designs.

The eighteenth century

In the years between 1712 and 1771 more than a dozen craftsmen were active in the japanning business in Boston. One of the most skilled, Thomas Johnston Sr., was born in England in 1708 and worked in Boston for the years between 1732 and 1767.

Johnston was a highly versatile craftsman who also engraved copper plates for prints, painted coats of arms and built organs, and the card which he engraved himself is decorated with two cherub heads. These may provide a clue to the japanner of the famous Boston 'Pimm Highboy', so-called because the name of the cabinet-maker, John Pimm, is chalked on its drawers. Although there is no supporting documentation, the two gilded cherub heads which form part of the chest's magnificent ornamentation, and which also appear on two companion pieces, suggest that Pimm left these works in Johnston's Ann Street workshop to be decorated, probably adding his name to them to avoid having his work confused with someone else's.

Thomas Johnston's sons, Thomas Jr. and Benjamin, also became japanners; the family name is sometimes spelled Johnson. Other Boston craftsmen included John Gore, Nehemiah Partridge, Daniel Rea II and III, and Stephen Whiting, but the popularity of the technique was not confined to named masters: a print and map seller called William Price advertised japanned furniture for sale in 1726 'by one late from London'.

Most American japanned furniture is unsigned and undated, but one important exception is a high chest of drawers which bears the initials 'W. R.', as well as the signature Robert Davis. The initials are almost certainly those of William Randall or Randle, one of the earliest Boston artists and cabinet-makers whose works survive. Randall's work dates from 1715 to 1739, but he originally went into partnership with Robert Davis to make looking-glasses and frames for shipment to coastal towns.

The only two japanners known to advertise in New York also represented a family enterprise. Gerardus Duyckinck, Senior and Junior, were active between 1735 and 1772, and advertised in city newspapers that they also stocked materials for amateur japanners, including 'prints of sundry sorts, readily colored'. However, several high-quality examples of New York japanning exist, made by unknown artists, and suggesting *lacca povera*.

Lacquered furniture was also produced in Connecticut. 'Country cousins' of the sleek

Above: Detail from the long-case clock by Bartholomew Barwell on page 214; *c.* 1755. Many American makers used japanned dials to resemble brass, although imported workings also found their way on to the market.

Massachusetts examples follow the Boston tradition of simulating tortoiseshell japanning by painting a black pigment over a red ground, although the fantastic decorative figures are painted in a cream oil-paint rather than being built up in gesso. The figures have a unique vitality and seem to have been applied according to the artist's whim, rather than to follow any coherent pattern. The liveliest images include a sea-horse, a kneeling falconer, and an American Indian shooting a bird with a bow and arrow: the splendid array also depicts a crowned lion, giraffes, gazelles and exotic flora and fauna. It has been suggested that the designer may have turned for inspiration to crewel work, lacking oriental patterns.

Japanning never caught on in staid Philadelphia, although a Sebastiano Martini placed advertisements in the late 1700s to offer japanned trays and his services in painting and lacquering, and the delightfully named Plunket Fleeson is known to have offered 'a neat japan'd chest of drawers to be sold cheap' in 1742.

The common use of black and red paint, which together with white lead were the pigments easiest to obtain and best suited for furniture, lends a japanned appearance to much eighteenth century decorated furniture. This is especially true of a small group of chests, where the distinctive sampler-like decoration reinforces the oriental air of the pieces. They were probably made between 1710 and 1735, in rural eastern Massachusetts: some of the most charming examples are those identified and described by Esther Stevens Fraser Brazer in her 1933 study, 'The Tantalizing Chests of Taunton'. Of the group she studied – all made in Taunton, Massachusetts – one small chest bears the inscription 'Taunton/RC/1729', a reference which experts believe is to a local drum-maker called Robert Crossman, who lived from 1707 to

1799. The chests are simple in form, with white pine sideboards continuing to the floor, where they are cut out to form feet. The great delicacy of the tree, vine and bird designs, and the colour scheme of vermilion and white against a rusty brownish-black ground, give the pieces a distinctly oriental appearance, although no overtly Eastern references appear in the decoration.

Clocks were an important fixture in any prosperous Colonial household. Tall long-case clocks were the most popular, and there was a bustling trade in japanned clocks imported from renowned English clockmakers such as Thomas Wagstaffe, James Atkinson and Edward Faulkner. The fine quality of much of this japanning set the American craftsmen high standards, and provided them with greatly needed models. In New York japanned clock-cases were often prepared in the English style, with whiting applied to fill in the wide-grained oak that was generally used. Raised figures, decorated in gold, red and dark ochre, were then applied against backgrounds of tortoiseshell, black or olive-green – the only background colours used in New York, except for looking-glasses with dark blue or pomegranate frames.

Two excellent clockmakers who emigrated from England in 1749 probably brought a fondness for japanned clock-cases with them. Gawen Brown, 'lately from London', that year advertised his shop 'at Mr. Johnston's, Japanner, in Brattle-Street, Boston, near Mr. Cooper's Meeting House, where he makes and sells all sorts of plain, repeating and astronomical Clocks, with Cases plain, black walnut, mahogany or Japann'd'. This advertisement suggests that Brown's fine tall pine clock was decorated by Thomas Johnston. Its gilt *chinoiserie*, with richly developed motifs and sophisticated composition, shows a more mature

Above: Detail of chair on page 211; *c.* 1796. This fine example of a painted or 'fancy' chair used the japan colours in delicate designs inspired by Hepplewhite and Sheraton.

Above right: Side-chair; *c.* 1817. The Empire style soon reached American furniture-makers; the Baltimore firm of John and Hugh Finlay was one of the most fashionable.

Opposite, left: Secretaire in the Empire style, possibly by Joseph Meeks; *c.* 1825.

Opposite, far left: Clock by Bartholomew Barwell; *c.* 1755. See page 213 for detail.

These two pieces illustrate the change in the use of japanning over 75 years. The classical *chinoiserie* decoration on the clock is restrained and elegant, while the secretaire is ebonized and gilded, carved and stencilled, with yellow silk backing.

style than the earlier ornamentation of the Randall-Davis variety. Another Brown clock, signed and dated 1766, is in a domed Queen Anne case which has been lacquered by a master.

By 1730 japanning had become a popular amateur pastime in the Colonies, as in Europe, where the practice of using motifs cut from specially designed prints for lacquering was called *lacca povera* or *découpure*. The hobbyist pasted the motif on to a piece of furniture, painted it, and covered it with several coats of lacquer. A Mrs Hiller taught japanning to young Boston ladies from 1725 to 1748, and in 1739 a Mr John Waghorne advertised in the same city that he would teach ladies 'to japan in the newest method'. Waghorne later added that he had 'lately received a fresh parcel of materials for the new method of japanning which was invented in France, for the amusement and benefit of the ladies, and is now practiced by most of the Quality gentry in Great Britain with the greatest satisfaction'.

Despite the popularity of *lacca povera* techniques in Boston and New York, no known pieces have survived. Newspaper advertisements were placed in New York papers by japanners as late as the mid-1770s, but by then interest in fine lacquering of furniture had waned.

The Federal period

The popularity of elaborately painted and decorated japanned-look furniture dominates this period, which dates from 1788 until the 1820s. Decorative devices commonly included wreaths, urns, tablets and busts, floral sprays and gilt scrolls against a white ground.

The favourite subject of japanners around the turn of the century was 'fancy chairs', and the huge popularity of these until the end of the 1830s finally led to mass production, and a subsequent decline in style. Among the best-known examples of lacquered chairs are six walnut Queen Anne side-chairs which bear the arms of Samuel Pickering Gardner, a prosperous Boston merchant. They were made in Boston between 1730 and 1760, but the gilt japanning on a black background was added after 1790. Gardner's grandniece Eliza Blanchard married Robert C. Winthrop in 1832, and according to a Winthrop-Blanchard family tradition the chairs were sent to China for decoration around 1795. Later examination, however, has revealed that the work is not true Chinese but rather nineteenth century *chinoiserie*, with tightly detailed, small-scale leafage in the neo-classical manner which had become fashionable, while the scrolls and grape-leaves on the stiles and legs are reminiscent of the border designs on Chinese porcelains.

Fancy chairs were available quite early in New York. American Windsor chairs, one of the most exciting forms of native furniture, were often painted, and John De Witt and Company of New York City advertised 'Windsor Chairs japann'd and neatly flowered' from 1795 to 1799. In 1797 William Challen, 'Fancy Chairmaker from London', advertised 'all sorts of dyed, japanned, wangee and bamboo chairs, settees, etc. and every article in the fancy chair line'. Hepplewhite and Sheraton were instrumental in popularizing painted furniture, and it quickly became a stylish and sophisticated feature in the fashionable parlours of the young nation. *The Cabinet Dictionary* of 1803 includes a section on the techniques and

Above: Chair, shown in colour on page 215; *c.* 1817. Painted maple with black decoration was a natural extension of the painted and japanned furniture of the 18th century.

Below: Secretaire, shown in colour on page 214; *c.* 1825. The early 19th century was one of the last periods when the grandiose use of gold and black was fashionable.

designs of painted furniture, in which Sheraton advocates japanning because 'varnish colours' were greatly preferable to the cheaper and less complicated 'common oil painting' usually used to decorate furniture. (Fancy furniture is sometimes called 'Fancy Sheraton', in honour of the designer who did so much to popularize it, although it was actually produced both before and after the years in which he was so influential.) By the early nineteenth century a wide range of colours and finishes were being manufactured in America to meet demand: Herman Vosburgh and Company of New York advertised in 1804 that they were offering 'the following Hard Varnishes, of their own manufacture, warranted equal to any ever imported, and 50 per cent cheaper: – Copal Varnishes, Japan Varnishes, Shellaca, Gold and Silver Sizes, Black Japan Varnishes for horsemens's caps, holsters, &c., Do. of any color for printing on leather, paper, &c. Gold Lacker for Metals'.

Baltimore soon led the cities and towns producing fancy furniture, most of it painted and varnished, and enthusiasm lasted well into the nineteenth century. At the turn of the century fifty makers and painters of fancy furniture were based there, with two of the best known being John and Hugh Finlay, Irish brothers who worked in Baltimore from 1803 to 1838, and who also advertised in New York. When the architect Benjamin Latrobe joined forces with President James Madison and his wife Dolly in 1804 to supervise the furnishing of the White House, he drew up furniture designs and sent them off to the Finlay brothers with a note that said, 'I hope you will be able to bend your whole force to them immediately.' Hallmarks of their style include delicate leafy borders and columns in gold, with painted seat rails. The exceptionally fine execution of these pieces verifies a Finlay advertisement listing '... all colors, gilt ornamented and varnished in a stile not equalled on the continent – with real Views, Fancy Landscapes, Flowers, Trophies of Music, War, Husbandry, Love, &c. &c ... Painted, Japanned and real Marble Top Sideboards.' The Finlays and other American fancy painters of the time often refer to japanned finishes. They mean transparent varnish colours, usually black and gold, as opposed to the transparent colours applied over whiting or size by English fancy chair decorators.

The later nineteenth century

In contrast to fancy furniture other furniture of the period combines several elements, and japanning appears in some of these as well. A fine example is an oak and mahogany centre table made in New York around 1830. This combines outstanding black japanning with Gothic elements

on a basic Empire form, and the gold motifs show detailed oriental scenes crowded together on the densely decorated table-top.

The French influence with its interpretations of Greek and Roman form and decoration was also felt in America, and the 'Greek Revival' style – with liberal dashes of Egyptian motifs – had a strong impact, especially in New York. Japanning was used effectively on chairs based on the Greek *klismos*, with classical lines and flared legs.

Custom-made furniture ultimately proved less profitable than that made in quantity, and a number of New York firms were the first to recognize the possibilities of this method of production at the beginning of the nineteenth century. The chairs made in this way, however, were painted and decorated to simulate lacquering. As the population expanded westwards manufacturers shipped chairs on steamboats and packets to satisfy the great demand; they were sometimes called 'steamboat fancies'. Lambert Hitchcock made a major impact on both the production and marketing of chairs, and popularized the chairs named after him. He was the first to make knockdown chairs, which could easily be shipped in pieces to their destination for later assembly. The success of this design enabled him to build a large factory at Barkhamstead, Connecticut, in 1818 (later re-named Hitchcocksville, now Riverton). Here he was soon producing fifty well-made and decorated chairs a day: the famous Hitchcock chairs, with turned fronts and rungs, and decorative stencilling. These stylish yet inexpensive chairs sold for $1.50 each, less than half the cost of a fancy chair, and innumerable competitors from Massachusetts, Rhode Island, New York and Ohio soon followed suit.

Hitchcock-style furniture was characterized by the way in which it imitated the effect of japanning at a low cost. A dark paint was first applied, and the wood was then coated with a binding medium such as varnish and turpentine. When that was nearly dry a paper stencil was laid on the surfaces to be decorated; several stencils were generally used for a single design, which gave a high degree of fine detail. Then a metallic powder was brushed on to the stencils: bronze, being cheapest, was the most common, but gold, silver, brass and zinc were also used. When the stencils were combined with freehand work and a variety of paint colours applied, the results show a rich variety and individual flair. The most popular stencils combined fruit, flowers and leaves, with an occasional lyre, cornucopia or building. Stencilling until about 1830 was inventive and excitingly varied – even the women and children who worked in the industry sometimes added individual touches – but it later declined, and some pieces carry only a single stencil and very little shading. The only chair signed by Hitchcock himself dates from his earliest period. Made between 1825 and 1829, it is painted black, with delicate bronze-gilded stencilling.

Hitchcock and his imitators, for whom business was booming in the mid-1800s, had progressed far from the Colonial japanners, who in turn had imitated European versions of oriental lacquer. There was, however, an underlying common aim: to cover the basic material of an article with decoration. A dark background was still used to simulate a lacquered surface, and the colourful decorations were covered with varnish to give a high finish to the chairs. But the few japanners left found themselves without work when carved or veneered woods replaced the fashion for Hitch-cock chairs in the late 1860s; some turned to decorating household items such as sewing-machines with lithographed decals.

Pieces of nineteenth century furniture which have been signed or dated by their makers are as rare as in earlier Colonial days.

Great fortunes were made during the 1830s in trade with China, and an octagonal pedestal table which is ornamented to simulate oriental lacquer seems a fitting symbol of its time. Unusually, it is both signed and dated, and is the work of Elisha Anthony of Albany, New York, made in 1830. The table is a strange and rather grotesque combination of Eastern and Western styles, with heavy carved animal feet, and classical carving topped by Chinese figures and landscapes.

Tinware and *papier mâché*

Around 1740 two Irish partners had set up a tinsmith shop in Berlin, Connecticut, introducing a major industry to America, and providing ideal material for japanners. They imported small sheets of tin from Wales and shaped them into household articles such as pots, tea-caddies, sugar-boxes and trinket-holders. To make large trays they joined the sheets together and hammered them into shape over moulds. The tinware was then coated with varnish, dried, decorated with oil-paints (or later with stencils), and varnished again. The earliest japanners of tinware include Zacharias Stevens, Oliver Buckley, Eliza and Elijah North, and Oliver Filley. Stevens moved to Stevens Plains, Maine, in 1789, and as others followed the place became a major japan-ning centre: at the height of its prosperity in 1852, Stevens Plains produced merchandise worth $27,000 in one year. Oliver Filley, working in Connecticut, became so successful he opened shops in Pennsylvania and New York.

The creation of the turnpikes in 1791 and the opening of the Erie canal gave the burgeoning lacquered tinware industry a big boost, since products could now be shipped as far west as Ohio. In Ohio itself, the Zoar community began producing its own lacquered tin household articles, with the addition of distinctive Pennsylvania Dutch patterns.

In Pennsylvania itself the Dutch community was especially attracted to decorated tinware, because its bright designs were so like their own characteristic motifs.

Tinware was generally decorated with bright but unimaginative designs, and japanners simply copied the best-selling patterns of flowers, fruit and leaves in bright blue, yellow, vermilion and green paints, often set against a white back-ground. There was competition however, from Bilston, in the English Midlands. Their wares are known to have been exported as far afield as America, presumably because they were made so cheaply: indeed, according to a report of the day, Americans were considered an ideal market be-cause of their 'lack of wealth and education'! Some experts believe that the Bilston exports are oc-casionally mis-identified as 'homemade' Ameri-can wares.

Jennens and Bettridge, English manufacturers of *papier mâché* wares, opened a New York branch in 1851, a year after *papier mâché* furniture was first produced in America by the Litchfield Company in Connecticut. Some of the latter's employees were English immigrants from the Midlands, who had failed to establish their own successful lacquerwork business in the 1830s. Although *papier mâché* lacquerware never really captured the public fancy in America, the Litchfield Company enjoyed an initial success with the manufacture of daguerreotype cases and small trinkets, and then moved into the production of *papier mâché* clock-cases. This involved the importation of clock-works to Connecticut, which were fitted into elegant lacquer cases decorated with mother-of-pearl inlay and gilt borders. Sometimes the lac-quer wasn't perfectly smooth, but the clocks were fine pieces of work, and so accurate that they were used on railways and steamboats.

The technique involved gluing together sheets of paper to form a board that could be cut, scrolled, and finally varnished. The surface was then gilded and inlaid with mother-of-pearl. Two of the finest examples of the company's wares are an ornate clock, and a shapely, frilled-edge candle-stand with a white pine base and a *papier mâché* top. But despite its flourishing trade – production was up to fifty-five clocks a day in 1852 – the company closed in 1854, when it was sold. The famous and flamboyant P. T. Barnum was a Litchfield company director, and some assessments ascribe the company's end to his ebullient methods. The fashion for *papier-mâché*, in any case, was to be a short-lived one. In 1864 Jennens and Bettridge closed their New York branch, and this move coincided with a general decline in the popularity of lacquerware.

Above: Cupboard with *découpâge* decoration; c. 1940. In spite of its popularity in England and France, *papier mâché* never reached the same level of acceptance in America. However, similar effects were achieved with paint, and the technique of *découpâge*. Called *lacca povera* in Europe, *découpâge* is popular with artists interested in easily achieving the decorative effects of lacquer and *papier mâché*.

9

The Twentieth Century

There have been two major developments affecting the craft of lacquer during the twentieth century: the vogue for Japanese art, which had so much influence on European taste around the turn of the century, and, later, the invention of high-gloss lacquer-look finishes, which made possible the new coloured decorations of Art Deco and later styles.

Designers like Eileen Gray and Jean Dunand in Paris, and interior decorators like Syrie Maugham, were in the forefront of those who recognized the potential of lacquer and adapted this classical medium to the needs of contemporary living.

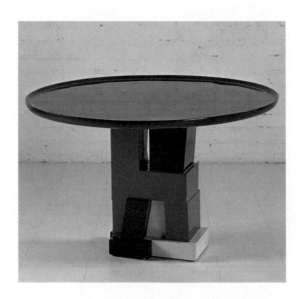

Above: Cubist table by Eyre de Lanux; *c.* 1928.

Opposite: La Destin screen by Eileen Gray;
c. 1923. The deep red lacquer screen features
two nude figures, and has an abstract pattern on the back.

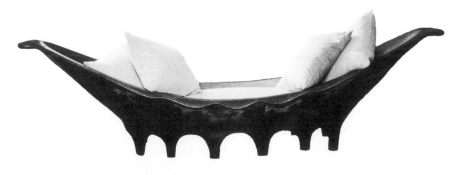

The world of art had become fascinated with Japanese prints and paintings as early as the 1870s, but the popular high point of the Art Nouveau style they inspired was the great Paris Exhibition of 1900. Earlier exhibitions had been held in Paris in 1855, when curious imitations of London's Crystal Palace disfigured the Champs Élysées, in 1867 and in 1889 (to commemorate the centenary of the start of the French Revolution), when the Eiffel Tower was built as a symbol of the new science of engineering – the engineers were the stars of the show – and electric lighting was used for the first time to illuminate an exhibition. There were also a few hints, in 1889, of the changing taste in art; the English exhibited works by painters such as Edward Burne-Jones and Sir Lawrence Alma Tadema.

In 1900 the whole world joined in what was later called 'The Great Bazaar', *Paris Universelle*. The site covered more than 1,500 acres and required a whole transport system – *le Metro*, the start of today's underground railway system. A new bridge was built over the Seine, and in the gardens of the Trôcodero an incredible collection of national pavilions appeared. Domes, minarets, igloos, castles and palazzos jostled with tents and folk art churches, Russian 'villages' and Swiss 'alpine meadows'.

There were also many representatives of the exotic East. At Loie Fuller's theatre, a Japanese actress thrilled the public and horrified her traditional and chauvinist compatriots. In the Japanese pavilion itself there were paper lanterns, gardens and cascades – an unexpected breath of tranquillity. The main hall contained 'an exhibition of priceless lacquer'.

The Bing pavilion was one of the major attractions for a public interested in the decorative arts; George de Feure exhibited a group of interiors in the most sophisticated Art Nouveau style, with gold finishes 'soft and subdued as the finest lacquer'. De Feure used oriental motifs as well as colours – carved lotus buds, sinuous curves and swirling lines.

One result of the exhibition was to reinforce fashionable interest in Japanese crafts, with the ensured and continuing success of at least two lacquer workshops in Paris. These were concerned mainly with the restoration of antiques, and panels for reproduction pieces. Genuine lacquer was imported at great cost, and its use required incredible skill and physical courage – the fumes from heated pots of lacquer can be noxious and even dangerous in an enclosed space.

In 1898 Eileen Gray (1878–1977) was a young Irish student at the Slade School of Art in London. She became fascinated by the work of lacquer restorers in an English studio, and worked there until she was able to go to Paris and establish herself with a Japanese lacquer-master, Sugawara.

Opposite page, top:
Chaise-longue by Eileen
Gray; *c.* 1920. Made for
Suzanne Talbot, it is in
brown mottled lacquer.

Opposite page, centre:
Black lacquered
commode; *c.* 1920. The
doors, by Jean Dunand,
were made in 1923, and
are interchangeable with
an earlier pair. The
commode is by Jacques-
Emile Ruhlmann.

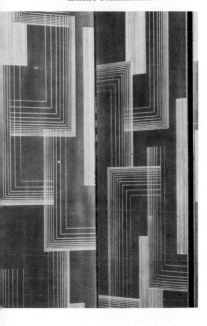

Above: Detail from the
lacquer screen by Jean
Dunand shown on page
222; *c.* 1922.

Opposite page, bottom:
Leather chair with
lacquered frame by
Eileen Gray; *c.* 1930.
This may have been
among the last individual
pieces she designed, and
is remarkable for its re-
semblance to modern
furniture.

Here she finished the apprenticeship begun in London. By 1913 she was exhibiting pieces she had designed and lacquered herself, in the *Salon des Artistes Decorateurs.*

The fashion designer Jacques Doucet had been one of the great collectors of the period. In 1912 he sold his collection, which included some of the greatest works of the eighteenth century *ebénistes,* bought a new apartment and commissioned contemporary work by many craftspeople, including Eileen Gray. She made tables and at least one signed and dated piece, a magnificent screen in deep red lacquer with two nude figures on one side and a totally abstract pattern on the back.

During World War I Eileen Gray returned to London with Sugawara and his Japanese workers, but by 1919 they had resettled in Paris and she started work on one of the most exciting and extensive commissions of her career: the design and execution of furniture, carpets, lighting fixtures and entire walls for Suzanne Talbot, a well-known fashion designer. While some of the pieces were intensely theatrical and decorative, many were expressions of interest in a more severe architectural approach, and in abstract patterns; a corridor was lined entirely with rectangular 'bricks' of lacquer textured with powdered stone. By now she was doing relatively little lacquering herself – this was handled by Sugawara and other Japanese lacquerers in Paris.

It should be stressed that although Eileen Gray's designs were uncompromisingly her own, the techniques she used were very traditional. No short cuts were taken and the pieces were by their very nature enormously expensive.

She sold much of her output through a gallery she called Jean Desert – no one knows why she chose this particular name – and in one year sold twenty-one carpets and only three pieces of lacquered furniture.

In 1923, when she exhibited an entire room with divan, two pierced lacquer screens, lacquer doors in dark brown and gold, and panels lacquered in red and white, it was too much for the French establishment; the critics damned the entire exhibition. Only architects, and in particular the Dutch architects of the new de Stijl movement, appreciated her work. Gradually she turned away from individual pieces of decoration and furniture, closed Jean Desert in 1930, and concentrated on houses and entire rebuilding schemes. She never really returned to lacquering, but what she had done was enough to spark off one of the great influences in European and American interior design – the use of glossy lacquered finishes throughout a house.

Jean Dunand (1877–1942) worked at the same time as Eileen Gray and, like her, was fascinated by the effect of lacquer, especially lacquer inlaid with other materials. He was originally a sculptor, and so was perhaps naturally conscious of the surface texture of all his pieces. Although he began working in lacquer fairly early, the majority of his best pieces date from the 1920s and 1930s. One of his favourite techniques, traditional inlay using crushed egg-shell to create an uneven and highly tactile surface, has remained a *tour de force* for modern lacquerers. In Japan, a modern lacquer-master, Taro Maruyama, has continued to adapt and refine this ancient technique, using it especially for all-over decoration. Dunand himself also used the egg-shell to make pictures; a black lacquered table of *c.*1925 has drifts of egg-shell that simulate falling snow, while a nest of tables uses egg-shells in a chequerboard pattern. However, many furniture tops were inlaid with a random mosaic of egg-shells to create a crackled effect, similar to that on porcelain or glass. Dunand also worked on the *Normandie,* the great French liner built in the early 1930s. Most of his work is stamped 'Jean Dunand Lacquer' and the best pieces are highly prized.

In 1924 Katsku Hamanaka came from Japan to advise Eileen Gray and Dunand on some of the more unusual classical Japanese lacquer techniques, especially the use of aventurine. While in Paris, he decorated various pieces for other designers interested in lacquer, including at least one table by Jacques-Emile Ruhlmann (1879–1933), using *maki-e* to create a scene with birds and flowers. Ruhlmann was the most successful designer and maker of luxury furniture in Paris; his workshops used only the finest woods and the most exotic inlays and he commissioned the most famous decorators. However, in spite of a reputation as a fashionable parvenu, his pieces are beautifully and elegantly simple, and his lacquerware is of supreme quality.

Although Eileen Gray, together with Jean Dunand, was the major influence on modern lacquer design, they were not alone. At the turn of the century, members of the Arts and Craft Movement in England and the Scottish creators of the Glasgow Style – Charles Rennie Mackintosh (1868–1928), Herbert MacNair (1868–1955) and Margaret (1865–1933) and Frances (1874–1921) Macdonald – were conscious of the debt they owed to the formal simplicity of Japanese art. Mackintosh's black painted furniture has a great similarity to many Japanese pieces.

Sometimes the debt is even more obvious. A cabinet by Ernest Gimson (1864–1914), made *c.*1910, is set on a black lacquered stand of modern design, with carved gesso ornamentation taken directly from gold lacquer pieces.

Some painted furniture and small pieces by Arthur and Lucia Mathews, American artists and decorators working in San Francisco from *c.*1908 to 1920, resemble lacquer to a remarkable degree, although they were painted and varnished; one

222   *The Twentieth Century*

Above: Elco linear system desk and caddy; modern. Hard lacquer finishes are popular and practical.

Left: Lacquer screen by Jean Dunand; *c.* 1922. See page 221 for detail.

Below: Modern lacquer by Japanese master Suzuku.

small box has a design of flower-heads, an adaptation of a well-known lacquer screen design dating from the 1880s.

In the 1930s, the Haywood-Wakefield Company in Gardner, Massachusetts, made a number of pieces covered in black lacquer with red lacquer handles, using maple-wood as a base. A more unusual piece, designed by Norman Bel Geddes for the Simmons furniture company in America, was lacquered in yellow and black on steel. This foreshadows the development of the commercial lacquer finishes that are now so typical of the modern period.

While traditional lacquer was one of the most practical surfaces of its time, it was not entirely suitable for twentieth century homes. The surface could be chipped, and damaged by alcohol, while central heating affected the wood base and caused cracks in the surface layers which eventually led to flaking off. During the 1930s the craze for pale colours inspired the scientific development of lacquer paints which could be sprayed or painted on under industrial conditions, and which provided a near-perfect surface for the white and cream furniture that was fashionable. For a while, every photograph in *Vogue* or *House and Garden* was focused on white – Syrie Maugham was only one trend-setter who lacquered everything in sight to match white or cream walls – furniture, cupboards, even a grand piano. The plain, glossy surfaces made this new style perfect for mass production.

Kitchens and bathrooms were part of the 1930s life-style, and remained glossy and hygienic even when wood, chrome and leather became popular for living-rooms once more. The plastic sheetings which became fashionable in the 1950s are tougher versions of lacquer and have been used in homes and factories for many years.

The 1980s have seen a new vogue for lacquer that shows little sign of disappearing. Brilliantly coloured chairs and tables from Italy and America are lacquered in primary reds, whites and yellows as well as pastel shades. These make use of spray lacquering, which creates a smooth impenetrable surface even more durable and glossy than classic lacquer. The paints are applied in layers much as the traditional materials were. The best-quality furniture may have seven or eight layers.

Kitchen cabinets also now have lacquer-painted finishes, as plastic loses its appeal. This allows for more decorative finishes on mouldings and handles in keeping with today's definition of the kitchen as the heart of the home, a living-room for all the family, as well as a working space for the cook.

Ornament and decoration are becoming popular again, with chintzes and stripes for chairs, braids and festoons for curtains, patterns and pictures everywhere. Lacquer boxes are imported from India and Thailand, lacquer ornaments from the East. Japanese dolls come complete with whole households of tiny lacquer furniture, and lacquer trays in simple, austere shapes and new colours are imported by Liberty's in London and Bloomingdale's in New York. The finest examples of modern oriental lacquer are exhibited with all the reverence and care which is their due. It is safe to assume that both the popular market and the art world will be able to enjoy the pleasures of lacquer for many years to come.

Glossary

The entries and cross-references are in **bold** type for quick reference.
In the Chinese entries, the Pinyin spelling has been given first, the traditional spelling, which you may still find in reference books, second.

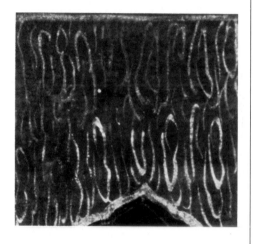

abri
Oily or marbled pattern in Persian lacquer.

akikusa
Autumn leaves and grasses, especially as used in **Kōdai-ji** lacquers of Japan.

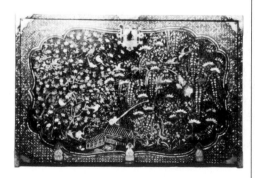

aogai
Japanese term for blue-green iridescent haliotis shell used for inlay, of finer quality than pieces used in **raden**. See also **mother-of-pearl inlay**.

applied gold leaf
One of several techniques originally from the Han dynasty (206 BC–221 AD). The gold leaf to which silver powder was added was stuck to a black lacquer ground, and then decorated with oil-based paints. The paint had a tendency to peel off.

appliqué
Pieces of material attached to a surface to form a design; the term is not confined to lacquer.

Ardebil carpet
Famous Persian carpet dating to 500 BC, already of sophisticated design and manufacture – 350 knots to the square inch. Many Persian lacquer designs are similar to traditional carpet patterns.

armour
Both metal and leather pieces of armour were lacquered for protection as well as for decoration.

atelier
French term for studio, also used for a group of artists who work together.

aventuriné
Decorative finish on lacquer achieved by powdering surface with bronze, gold, or copper. Named for a spangled quartz, it was perfected by the Martin workshops in Paris in the early eighteenth century. See also **vernis Martin**.

Bantam work
The English had established a pepper industry in Bantam, a port of western Java, but were expelled by the Dutch in 1682. The port nonetheless gave its name to lacquer transhipped from China, and to imitations made in England late in the seventeenth century. Similar to **Coromandel lacquer**.

basketry
Lacquer, being lightweight, was often used with basketwork for portable carriers.

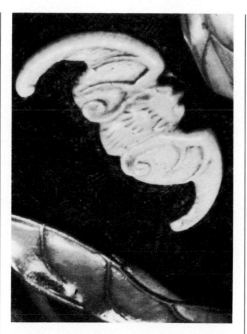

bats
Motif, common in Chinese lacquer, signifying long life.

bon
Japanese term for tray, almost always made of lacquer.

bourdon
Staff or walking-stick, traditionally presented to important visitors to the Belgian watering-place of Spa. Spa became an important centre of lacquer trifles for the gift trade, which were produced in large quantities.

Buddhism
Shrines and figures were often lacquered in gold. See also **Zen** and **sutra box**.

bunkō
Japanese document-box.

calligraphy
The art of writing; calligraphic inscriptions are an important part of many Eastern designs.

cartouche
An ornamental tablet in a frame or scroll, usually oval or lozenged shaped.

carved marble lacquer
Known as *tixi* or *xipi* in Chinese, *guri* in Japanese. The Chinese term means 'rhinoceros skin' or 'western skin'. Most Europeans use *guri*, 'crooked ring', which refers to the spiral of the decoration. Layers of contrasting lacquer colours are applied to the object; early Chinese wares were red, black and yellow, with black used for the top layer. Japanese versions made in the late eighteenth and early nineteenth centuries often have red top layers. The design is cut with a sharp instrument producing slanted V- or U-shaped grooves that show off the layered effect. The motifs are spiral scrolls and cloud-like shapes.

ch'iang-chin see **qiangjin**

ch'iang-yin see **qiangyin**

chi'lin
Chinese term for mythical beast depicted on carvings and paintings.

chinkin-bori
Japanese term, 'sunken-gold carving', for **qiangjin**.

chinoiserie
French term applied to all decorative Western designs influenced by Chinese art. The major feature is pseudo-Chinese figures in very European interpretations of Chinese landscapes taken from imported porcelain and pottery. The craze reached its height during the eighteenth century, extending even to dresses and textile patterns: 'Almost everywhere, all is Chinese . . . every chair . . . the frames of glasses . . . the tables, the walls, all covered with Chinese figures which resemble nothing in God's creation!' (*Letters on the English Nation*, 1756)

chiri-e
Japanese term for recessed rim, typical of Heian period (794–1185) boxes.

chōnin
Japanese term for the well-to-do middle class which developed in the towns; its members became patrons of the arts, and encouraged the production of lacquered everyday objects.

cloisonné
Decorative technique in which delicate ribbons of metal are set on edge and attached to a base; the spaces are filled with coloured enamels. Some lacquer designs resemble *cloisonné*, with metal inlay ribbons dividing gold or coloured lacquers.

Coccus lacca
Insect indigenous to India which excretes a protective resin from which **shellac** is derived. See also **Coccus nige**, **lac**.

Coccus nige
Insect similar to *C. lacca*, but indigenous to Central America. See also **nij**.

Coromandel lacquer
Lacquerware characterized by intricate incised designs cut out of several layers of lacquer to the hardwood base; the spaces are filled with bright-coloured lacquer or pieces of **hardstone**, ivory, etc. It was produced in large quantities for the export market, so much is of inferior quality. The name comes from the English East India Company's trading post on the Coromandel coast of southeast India where the wares were transhipped from China to Europe. Coromandel lacquer is similar to **Bantam work**.

crewel work
Type of wool embroidery, often couched on the surface giving strong brightly coloured designs.

découpure
French term for a type of *découpâge* usually called by its Italian name, **lacca povera**.

dei-e
Japanese term for painting with gold and silver powders mixed with glue. See also **kingin-e, yūshoku**.

diamyō
Local feudal landlords in Japan who provided military support for the **shōgunate**.

diaper
An all-over repeating pattern, usually geometric but sometimes floral, which covers the surface or the background of a design. The term, originally used of a white linen or cotton cloth with a square or diamond weave, derives from the Greek '*diaspros*'. Chinese official and Imperial wares often used standardized forms: a humped wave for water, lines or stars for air, squares or zigzags for earth.

diwǎn
Arabic word for collection of poems; such books were often decorated with lacquer bindings.

Dīwānī
Arabic 'poetic' style of calligraphy favoured by Turkish scribes.

dou
Chinese term for lidded bowl, a favourite form for Japanese and Chinese lacquerers.

dry lacquer
A sophisticated method for making pure lacquer objects. Layers of fibre cloth were dipped in lacquer and pressed to the entire surface of a wood or clay mould. When dry, the inner mould was removed leaving a perfect shell which could be lacquered again until it was as thick as required, and then polished. From the

sixth century this technique was used for sculpture, especially Buddhist statues which were carried in processions. Dry lacquer was used well into the thirteenth and fourteenth centuries.

dui hong see **zhao hong**

ebéniste
French term for cabinet-makers of fine furniture.

e-nashiji
Japanese technique, 'picture **nashiji**', in which fine particles of gold and silver are

sprinkled within a definite design to make a picture rather than a background. First used around 1600.

famille-jaune, famille-noir, famille-rose, famille-verte
Terms for Chinese enamelled polychrome porcelains developed from Wanli five-colour wares. They were, respectively, predominantly yellow, black, rose or green.

fan
A favourite design motif. Lacquered fans were also popular: flat fans are oriental, folded ones were made for export to European markets.

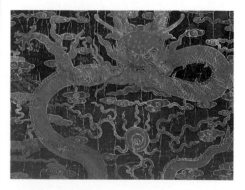

flaming pearl
Common Chinese motif, often with a dragon chasing the pearl in an intertwined pattern.

fu cai see **fu hong**

fu hong
Chinese technique of lacquer decoration ('covered red') with semi-transparent pieces of tortoiseshell applied over red pigment. The term *fu cai*, 'covered colours', is used when the pigment is some other colour such as green.

galamdān-e bozorg
Persian word for pen-boxes, one of the most common objects used by Islamic lacquer-workers.

gamboge
General name for trees of the East Asian *Garcinia* species, and also for the yellow gum resin of these trees, used to make a yellow lacquer.

games boxes
Often lacquered, these boxes can sometimes be found complete with ivory fittings.

gesso
Coating material made by mixing chalk or whiting with glue; it can be sandpapered to give a flawlessly smooth surface, and is used as a ground preparation on wood for painting, gilding, and European lacquering.

gul va bulbul
Islamic design motif of a bird and flowers.

guri
Japanese term meaning 'crooked ring'. See also **carved marble lacquer**.

haku-e
Japanese technique of painted gold lacquer.

hardstone
Common in **Coromandel lacquer**; carved pieces were inlaid in lacquer bases, usually in floral or landscape designs.

harigaki
Japanese term for 'needle-drawing'; fine lines of even width were incised or scratched into a wet, gold-sprinkled surface.

hatayi
Persian term for palmette flowers.

Hatsune see **monogatari**

heidatsu
Japanese technique, originally from China; thin sheets of gold, silver or pewter were cut into shapes and applied to a lacquer base.

helmet see **armour**

Higashiyama lacquer
Group or style of wares owned by the shōgun Yoshimasa (1435–96). The name is taken from a mountain near Kyōto, where he lived. Higashiyama pieces are characterized by the influence of literary subjects and allusions, as well as by their very high quality.

highboy
American term for tall chest of drawers on legs.

high relief
Carving in which figures stand away from the background, or are almost detached from the surface.

hiramaki-e
Japanese technique ('flat sprinkled picture'); a type of **maki-e** in very **low relief**.

hirame-fun
Japanese term ('flat-eye dust'); flakes of metal used for **maki-e**.

incising
Engraving technique which cuts through a top layer of lacquer, often to be filled with a contrasting colour.

Indianish werk
German term for lacquerwork. Most early lacquer pieces were imported through ports in India and Java, and items were described haphazardly as Indian, Chinese or Japanese, regardless of where they were made.

inrō
A box or nest of boxes, originally used as a portable seal box (hence the word which means 'seal basket' in Japanese), and also for herbs, medicines and any small articles. The boxes are connected by a cord running along each side and controlled by an *ojime*, or bead, to open or close the box. The top of the cord runs through a netsuke, a small toggle which slips through the sash of the kimono and hangs on top, keeping the *inrō* safe. Many of the greatest lacquer masterpieces are *inrō*, in spite of their small size, and there are complete sets of *inrō*, *ojime* and netsuke, decorated and carved with a single theme. The **chōnin** were proud of these personal possessions; one nineteenth century Japanese merchant had over a hundred sets in his wardrobe. When Western dress became the norm, the *inrō* lost its usefulness, and became an object for collectors.

japanning, Japan work
English and American term for imitations of genuine Chinese and Japanese lacquerwork. *A Treatise on Japaning and Varnishing* published in England in 1688 by John Stalker and George Parker was the main source of information on everything to do with the subject; it contained both lacquer recipes and designs for decoration. Japanning is used today to mean every kind of lacquer 'lookalike' – wood or metal painted and varnished to simulate the gloss and finish of lacquer, even when the designs are thoroughly Western rather than oriental.

Jogahana-nuri

Painted lacquer, from the town of Jogahana in Japan. Pigments were bound with plain oil or a mixture of oil and lacquer, but without the addition of a drying agent. The technique is said to have been brought from China by workers at Nagasaki. **Mitsuda-e** is similar but uses an agent, lead monoxide, to help the lacquer dry quickly.

Kaga-maki-e

Lacquerware of exceptional quality, produced during the early Edo period (1615–86) in Kanazawa, Japan. Its distinctive feature is the contrast and balance between complex designs and undecorated areas, usually of black lacquer, which sometimes take up more than half of the surface area.

kamabokogata

Japanese term ('box in fish or sausage shape') for the European coffer with a domed lid which was copied so much in export wares, particularly **Namban lacquers**.

Kamakura-bori

Decorative Japanese technique taking its name from the town of Kamakura, the most important place of its manufacture. Like **zhao hong**, it was a way of simulating carved lacquer; a wooden base was carved then covered with a thin layer of lacquer. See also **tsuishu**.

kanshitsu

Japanese term for **dry lacquer**, used most often for shrines or roof decorations; also statues.

khashab madhūna

Arabic term for varnished wood, also used for lacquered surfaces.

Kimma

Technique from which **Zōkoku-nuri** was adapted in the nineteenth century. A black lacquer ground is covered with a rubber solution and the design is engraved through the rubber to the lacquer beneath. The whole surface is then covered with red lacquer which is left to dry. The piece is washed down, removing the layer of red and the rubber underneath, and leaving only the red lacquer in the engraved lines. The technique became very popular in the early twentieth century, although most of the designs executed in Kimma are unusually stiff and geometric for Japanese art.

kingin-e

Japanese technique; gold and silver powders are bound with glue and applied with a brush to an already lacquered and dried surface. It was seldom used after the Heian period (794–1185) since **maki-e** gave a similar effect but was much more durable.

Kin-maki-e

Japanese term, 'gold gold work', for a type of lacquer remarkable for its lustre.

kinrande

Japanese technique, popularly known as 'gold brocade'; gold foil is applied and then incised to create elaborate designs. First used on porcelain.

kirigane

Japanese term for tiny squared gold flakes used in **maki-e**.

Kōami

School of lacquerers in the Edo period (1615–1868). Members of this family, who worked for the emperor as well as the Tokugawa shōgunate, were responsible for some of the finest wares of the time.

Kōdai-ji lacquers
Japanese lacquerware that derives its name from the Kōdai-ji temple, built in Kyōto in 1605 or 1606. More than thirty lacquer items survive in its collection. The term also refers to the style based on these pieces. It features the naturalistic representation of autumn plants and grasses (see also **akikusa**) and the surface area is often divided by a diagonal line, sometimes incorporating a zigzag separating contrasting designs.

lac
Resin formed by insects on several species of acacia trees in India. Secreted around the bodies of *Coccus lacca*, the *lac* acts as a protective coat, and remains on the twigs and also in the bodies of dead insects. The resin and insect shells are processed in several stages to produce **shellac**. The first step involves a granulated substance called seed *lac*, which is refined until orange shellac is produced. Alcohol solutions of shellac are used as varnish. The wood '*lac*', which derives from the Sanskrit *laksa*, was adapted in the West to describe the oriental finish as well as European imitations, causing a great deal of confusion.

lac burgauté, laque burgauté
Used by the authors of *Histoire de la Porcelaine*, published in 1862, to refer to porcelain covered with mother-of-pearl lacquer, and sometimes subsequently used by writers to describe all lacquer decorated with mother-of-pearl inlay. The word comes from 'Burgau', a type of bright-coloured mother-of-pearl.

lacca povera
Using designs cut from prints for lacquering. It was popular with amateurs in seventeenth and eighteenth century Europe and America, who pasted motifs on an object, painted them and covered the surface with varnish.

lacquer
There are two distinct types of lacquer. 'True' lacquer, in the opinion of most authorities, is the grey-white sap of the *Rhus verniciflua*, a tree indigenous to central and southern China, or the sap of other trees of the *Rhus* genus. It becomes highly resistant to heat, damp and chemicals after being dried in a humid atmosphere (one tradition has it that the best lacquer is dried on a boat in the middle of a lake). This is the Far Eastern type. The second kind is processed from **lac**, and is used for Indian and Middle Eastern lacquerware.

lacquer painting
A Chinese technique in which true coloured lacquer is used as the medium. Techniques in which the design is painted on a background of tinted varnish or lacquer with oil- or water-based paints, then covered by a colourless varnish, should properly be called 'painted lacquer'. See also **urushi-e**.

lai rot nam
Thai term meaning 'designs washed with water'; a special type of gilded lacquer decoration. A protective fluid is painted over that part of the lacquer which is not to be gilded, and is rinsed away in running water when the gold has been applied.

lāk, laki
Persian words denoting both a coating material for protecting objects, and a red pigment used by painters.

lampblack
Permanent oil pigment often used to increase the density of black paint in japanning.

lien
Chinese term for toilet-boxes.

lo-tian
Chinese term for lacquer with **mother-of-pearl inlay**.

lowboy
American term for chest of drawers on legs.

low relief
Carving in which figures project only slightly above the surface, and no part is detached from the background.

maki-e
General term for all Japanese decorative techniques in which a design is painted on to a lacquer ground, and gold and silver (or other metal) powders and flakes are sprinkled on while the lacquer is still wet. Highly diverse colour and pictorial effects can be achieved, and it is far more durable than the older technique of **kingin-e**. There are three main types. In *togidashi* the design is dried then covered with more layers of lacquer the same colour as the background; this is finally polished down until the design

reappears, flush with the surface. A final layer of transparent lacquer is added. In *hiramaki-e* the finished design is covered with layers of transparent lacquer thinned with camphor, and polished down so that the design area projects slightly from the surface. In *takamaki-e* the design is built up with lacquer and charcoal powder so that even after covering and polishing it stands out in relief.

marbled lacquer see **abri**, **carved marbled lacquer**

marchand merciers
French term for furniture dealers and auctioneers.

marqash
General Persian term for gold dust techniques.

mitsuda-e
Japanese oil-painting on lacquer that makes use of a vegetable oil as the medium with the addition of lead monoxide, or litharge, to dry the oil more quickly. Used instead of **urushi-e**, pure lacquer-painting, it provided artists with a much wider range of colours, particularly for flesh tones and other pastels.

mokume-nuri
Japanese inlay technique which simulates the texture of wood.

monogatari
Japanese 'tales' such as the *Taketori monogatari*, 'The bamboo cutter's tale', and *Genji monogatari*, 'Tale of Genji'. Classics of early Japanese literature, they are often used by lacquer-workers to decorate boxes and *inrō*. The Hatsune story in the *Genji* was used by Nagashige, a member of the **Kōami** school, on the Hatsune wedding-set made in the nineteenth century.

mother-of-pearl inlay
Lo-tian is the most common Chinese name for lacquer inlaid with mother-of-pearl. Originally fairly thick pieces of shell were used to create ornate, floral-based patterns with incised details. The best examples incorporate copper wire. Later on the technique changed and artists began creating pictorial designs based on the landscape paintings of the Song (960–1279) and Yuan (1280–1368) dynasties. Instead of incising, minute pieces of iridescent haliotis shells were used skilfully to provide the details. Mother-of-pearl did not appeal to the Japanese taste as much as to the Europeans, so was not used to make complete designs until it was developed mainly for export in the seventeenth century. See also **aogai**, **raden**.

moulded lacquer see **zhao hong**

naggāsh bashi
Arabic term for the equivalent of Painter Laureate or Academician.

najŏn
Korean term for the technique of inlaying fragments of various shells and other materials in a lacquer ground to form a design. The technique is derived from the Chinese **ping-tuo**, to which it is similar.

Namban lacquers
Group of Japanese lacquers of the Momoyama (1568–1615) period. 'Namban' means 'southern barbarian', and the term was used for both men and the objects which were imported into Japan from the south. In lacquer it refers to Japanese work produced for, and influenced by, European traders. Wares for the home market depict Europeans in minute detail; export wares were often European carcasses decorated in Japanese style.

nashiji
Japanese lacquer technique simulating the look of aventurine, a quartz incorporating shimmering spangles or flakes of mica. Gold, silver, or metal powders were used; *nashiji* is most often used as an overall background to a design, especially on inner lids or drawers.

nashiji-fun
The grains used in making *nashiji*.

Negoro-nuri
Japanese lacquerware that takes its name from the Negoro temple. The original pieces were used by priests from the end of the thirteenth century until the destruction of the temple in 1585. The first wares had monochrome red surfaces, which became worn through centuries of handling so that the black was revealed in places; this effect was later deliberately imitated.

netsuke see **inrō**

nij, nije, ajin
Local Indian name used in Central America, especially Guatemala and El Salvador, for a waxy material extracted from the *Coccus nige* insect and used to make a kind of lacquer finish for decorated gourds. The gourds are cut into baskets, containers, bowls, etc, then dried, rubbed with *nij* until they gleam, decorated and finally coated with thinned *nij* to make a shellac finish.

nuri
Japanese term meaning 'wares', as in **Negoro-nuri**.

oil-painting
Painting used on lacquer pieces to extend the range of colours, especially for flesh tones and pastels. See also **painted lacquer**.

oily pattern see **abri**

ojime see **inrō**

ōyoroi
Type of Japanese armour made of individual leather or metal plates, usually decorated and protected with lacquer.

painted lacquer

A technique which covers many individual recipes for mixing pigments with oil instead of lacquer. Colouring materials also included malachite or cinnabar (giving the famous red colour of much Chinese carved lacquer) and tong oil, made from the seeds of *Aleurites cordata*. Today artists use oil-paints of the finest quality.

palanquin

Chair or bed carried by porters, made for women and high officials of the government, as well as for wealthy leaders. Lacquer finishes are the most common decoration, with embroidered curtains and metal mountings.

panelling

In eighteenth century Europe, lacquer panels were mounted on walls to create 'Chinese' or 'Japanese' rooms. Panels were gradually replaced by decorative but less expensive wallpaper, although panels of lacquer were revived by Eileen Gray in the 1920s in Paris.

papier mâché

French term meaning mashed or chewed paper. The paper was pulped or torn into strips, and mixed with glue, chalk and sometimes sawdust to be shaped, baked, and carved into any shape that was required, before being decorated and polished to a glossy finish. It was known in ancient Persia, and became popular in eighteenth and nineteenth century Europe for making articles such as picture frames, tables, chairs, boxes, screens, trays, etc. Henry Clay patented a particularly strong and glossy form called Clay-ware in the eighteenth century. Designs were made to order and decorations ranged from *chinoiserie* to the rich floral jumbles of Victorian painting, often inlaid with mother-of-pearl.

ping-tuo

Chinese term for inlaid metal-foil decoration.

Pontypool

Japanned metalware manufactured by a process invented in 1680 by Thomas Algood. It was improved by his son Edward and made at the Pontypool Japan Works from *c.*1725. The name was also used of similar wares made at nearby Usk or in Birmingham from the 1760s.

qiangjin; ch'iang-chin

Literally 'etched gold'; *qiangjin* wares were probably first made in China early in the fourteenth century. An adhesive of lacquer and orpiment (yellow arsenic trisulphide) is applied over an incised design, and gold leaf is pressed into the grooves. Surplus gold is removed with cotton-wool. *Qiangjin* was an important influence on the fifteenth century lacquers of the Ryukyu Islands.

qiangyin; ch'iang-yin

The same technique as above except that silver was used instead of gold, with an adhesive of lacquer and lead carbonate powder. However, silver tarnished too quickly and the technique was never popular.

quatrefoil
Ornamental form divided into four lobes. During the Han dynasty (206 BC–221 AD), quatrefoil inlays of precious metals were popular on lacquer boxes.

raden
Japanese term for mother-of-pearl inlay using thick, large pieces.

repoussé
Relief designs on metal which are hammered out from the reverse. The technique has been practised since very early times.

Rhus verniciflua (R. vernicifera)
Indigenous to China and probably transplanted to Korea and Japan, this is the most important source of lacquer for the Eastern world. However, the sap from three other trees of the same genus has also been used: *R. ambigua*, which grows in Japan, Formosa and the Ryukyu Islands; *R. succedanea*, in Japan, the Ryukyu Islands and South East Asia (where it is the primary source); and *R. trichocarpa* in China, Korea and Japan.

rococo
An exuberant style of decoration rich with S-shaped curves and shells, flowers, foliage and fruits. These were often disposed around *chinoiserie* landscapes and figures; the finest examples date from 1740 to 1760 in France and from 1745 to 1765 in England.

ru-yi
Mythical animal heads often used as motifs in Chinese art.

sabi-ji
Japanese lacquer technique simulating rusty metal.

sai-e
Japanese term for painting on lacquer using pigments dissolved in glue. See also **yūshoku**.

sake
Japanese rice wine; the small bottles and cups in which it was served were favourite objects with lacquerers.

samurai
Warriors of traditional Japanese society, military men whose great period was in the fifteenth and sixteenth centuries.

se
Chinese zither, often lacquered with appropriate designs.

seed-lac see **lac**

senmurv
Persian word for mythical animal depicted on paintings.

setār
Long-necked lute, depicted in many Persian lacquer-paintings.

sgraffiato
Italian term for scratched decoration, used for designs incised through a top layer or coating to show the body beneath, usually a contrasting colour.

shellac
A contraction of shell and **lac**; the *lac* itself is concentrated by evaporation, then stretched into thin sheets or plates. The pieces are dissolved in alcohol to make a varnish or lacquer finish. Shellac was an important ingredient of European imitations of true lacquer, and is used today in most lacquer-painted finishes.

shōgunate
Collective term for the military governments of Japan, from Yoritomo (*c.*1192) to the start of the Meiji period (1868). The shōgunate was the court of the ruling shōgun, and supported artists and craftsmen as well as the army. Some of the finest work in Japan was done for the shōgunate and includes personal possessions for the shōgun and his family as well as pieces for official use in rituals and religious ceremonies.

singeries
Scenes depicting monkeys instead of human beings, very popular in *chinoiserie* pieces.

son nhat, son nhi
Vietnamese term for the layers of filtered resin which are suitable for decorative work.

sumi-e togidashi
Japanese lacquer technique; a powder made from camellia-wood charcoal is sprinkled on to the design. Various shades of powder can be built up by adding more or less silver to the charcoal. After drying, the surface is covered with transparent lacquer and polished down (*togidashi*). The special effect of this technique is to simulate an ink-painting. See also **maki-e**.

sutra boxes
Boxes which contain Buddhist documents; used by Chinese and Japanese lacquer-workers.

suzuribako
Japanese writing-box, usually lacquered.

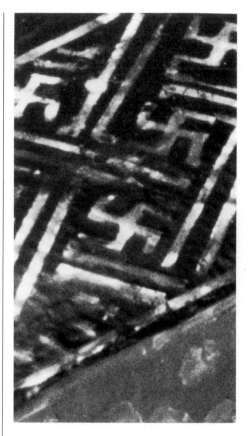

swastika
Motif used in many borders and diaper patterns, to mean good luck; since its adoption by the Nazis it has seldom been used for that particular symbolism.

Taihō-itsuryō
Japanese law of 701 AD which required every household to plant lacquer trees, and remit some of the lacquer sap as a tax.

takamaki-e
High relief **maki-e**.

tamamushi
Beetle with iridescent wing-cases which were used in ornamental filigree on the Tamamushi shrine (*c*.650 AD). The technique is thought to have come from Korea, for no other Japanese examples are known.

tempera
Traditional medium for painting, using egg instead of water as a binding agent. Tempera painted over a lacquer base and then varnished has a particularly rich and luminous effect, and was much favoured by Islamic artists.

tianqi; tian cai
Chinese lacquer technique similar to **Coromandel lacquer**. In dry *tianqi*, the most popular version, the background was allowed to harden completely before the design was cut out to a depth of about half a millimetre, and then filled in with lacquer of contrasting colours. In wet *tianqi*, the contrasting lacquer was applied while the base was still wet.

tixi
Chinese term for **carved marble lacquer**.

togidashi
A type of **maki-e**.

tôle, tôle peinte, tôle vernis
French term for japanned metalware, derived from *tôle*, sheet metal, from which the wares were cut. *Tôle* is also sometimes used in America to describe imported japanned metalware, whether or not it is French (see below).

Toleware, Tolerware
American term for japanned tinware, especially imported pieces. 'Philadelphia tinware' is also used to describe the American version of **Pontypool** ware.

Tosa
Province of Japan renowned for its fine painters.

trefoil
Three-lobed ornament much used on boxes of the Han dynasty (206 BC–221 AD). See also **quatrefoil**.

tsuba
Japanese sword guard, made of pierced metal. It was often lacquered, originally to protect the metal from rust but later more often for purely decorative purposes. *Tsubas* can be easily detached from the sword and are a favourite item for collectors; lacquered examples can be very elaborate and are highly prized.

Tsugaru-nuri
Distinctive lacquer manufactured during the seventeenth century in Tsugaru. It has a mottled surface of red, yellow, green, brown and black. The technique involved setting an uneven surface into the base lacquer by using eggshells, rice or simply dead leaves. Layers of different-coloured lacquers were applied, and then polished down to a smooth finish.

tsuikin
Ryukyuan technique meaning 'piled-up brocade'; the term is used to cover two related processes. The finest work uses inlays of hardstone, soapstone, woods and stained ivory to form a picture in **high relief**. The cheaper, more popular process used coloured lacquer mixed with burned earth or powdered whetstone to simulate the effect of the stones. The fine work was called *Zhou zhi* in China, after its Ming dynasty (1368–1644) inventor, probably fictional.

tsuishu, tsuikoko
Japanese techniques similar to **carved marble lacquer**. *Tsuikoko*, 'piled-up

black', consisted of layers of black lacquer carved into elaborate designs; *tsuishu*, or 'piled-up red', was more popular. Alternating layers gave additional contrast to designs.

Tsuishuyōsei
Japanese school of lacquerers specializing in carved lacquers (see above), and known since the fifteenth century.

tui hong see **zhao hong**

urishibe
General term for lacquer craftsmen in Japan, dating back to the Kofun period (*c*.250–252).

urushi-e
Japanese technique of true lacquer-painting, used especially during the Edo period (1615–1868). The coloured pigments were dissolved in lacquer, which limited the palette to yellow, red, green, brown and black. See also **mitsuda-e**.

uta-e
Poem picture, a general Japanese description of designs based on the words of a poem; the intention was to re-create the emotional effect of a scene, as well as illustrate it.

varnish
General term for any resinous solution that, on drying, provides a glossy coat, usually clear or tinted. Lacquer can be described as a kind of varnish, but only if the lacquer is transparent.

vernice della Madalena
Italian term for a lacquer formula. It was most often used in Genoa, where it had been developed by a lacquer-master living near the church of Santa Madalena.

vernis de Gobelins
Transparent varnish patented in 1713 by Jacques Dagly at the Gobelins factory.

vernis de la Chine
Generic French term for lacquer.

vernis Martin
One of the finest European lacquer finishes, created *c*.1730 by Guillaume Martin and his brother in Paris. It was the only European finish to reproduce the oriental decorative effect of a light sprinkling of metal powder set into the top layers of lacquer before it has dried.

Wajima-nuri
Seventeenth century Japanese technique similar to **chinkin-bori**. A clay from the town of Wajima was mixed with the lacquer, making an extremely smooth, strong surface for engraving.

Wakasa-nuri
Lacquer technique first used in Wakasa during the seventeenth century, a

variation of **Tsugaru-nuri**. Layers of coloured lacquer were applied to an uneven base, and silver or gold foil was pressed firmly into the hollows before the whole was smoothed down and given a coat of transparent lacquer. The effect was to add ripples of metal to the mottled surface.

walls see **panelling**

wan
Japanese term for bowls.

xipi
Chinese term for the **carved marble lacquer** technique.

Yun
Generic Vietnamese word for lacquer.

yūshoku
Japanese technique in which a transparent oil was applied over **sai-e** (painting with pigments blended with glue) and **dei-e** (painting with gold and silver powders blended with glue). The oil protected the painting and raised the ornamental effect. For obvious reasons the technique was seldom used on food containers, even on the outside.

Zen
The Zen Buddhist sect of China and Japan, noted for its reliance on meditation rather than the practice of any particular doctrine. Zen was founded in the late fifth century and has had a very strong influence on all aspects of Japanese culture; its simple, symbolic designs reveal great depths of meaning with minimal imagery.

zhao hong; dui hong; tui hong
Chinese imitation of **carved marble lacquer**. Raw lacquer was mixed with ashes and piled up to a 'carved' shape, then dried and coated with a final thin layer of lacquer. As an imitation this

moulded lacquer was more or less successful to the untutored eye, but wares were disparagingly refused by knowledgeable buyers.

Zhou zhi
Chinese term for **tsuikin**.

Zōkoku-nuri
Lacquerware created by Tamakaji Zokoku (1806–69), one of the great exponents of *Kimma-nuri*. His designs in **Kimma** and carved lacquer were a great influence on many modern lacquer-masters.

See illustration, *right* for examples of carved and painted modern lacquer.

Zonsei-nuri
A form of *Kimma-nuri*, a Japanese technique in which a lacquer-painting is laid on a lacquer ground. When dry the outlines of the painting are engraved to accentuate the design. The incisions that have been created are sometimes filled with gold dust.

How to Restore Lacquer

The instructions below apply equally to repairing and restoring an extensively damaged piece of old lacquerwork, and to giving a totally new lacquered finish to a piece of furniture or other object. However, the following points must be considered before starting either task.

If the damaged piece is old, it would be wise to take it to a museum or an antique expert for valuation. Restoration of really valuable pieces is best carried out by professionals.

If you decide to do the job yourself, check the extent of the damage. Small scratches and chips can easily be disguised by using matching shades of enamel paint, obtainable in small pots from art-and-craft or hobby shops. Larger repairs will need the full treatment described below, but remember that this requires both time and patience; consider, instead, using the services of a professional restorer.

Any object to which a lacquer surface is applied must be structurally sound. Wooden furniture must have stable joints, as any movement would put pressure on the lacquer coating, causing it to crack. Lacquering looks and works best on plain, bold, geometric shapes with no carving or moulding. (Genuine oriental lacquerwork has both carving and moulding, but because of the unique physical properties of genuine lacquer they are worked into the lacquer coating itself.)

Preparation

1. With repair work, the remaining details of any painted design or motif you may wish to restore must be recorded before applying the new lacquer base. Do this by tracing them. Use a sharp pencil and make careful notes on the tracing-paper of exact colours, thickness of paint, shading, etc. Work slowly, in a good light.

The tracing-paper should be covered in enough descriptive information to allow you to reproduce a reasonably accurate copy of the original decoration.

Where the original design is very badly worn, it would be better to select a new one. Consult books on the history of the decorative arts or, if you can find them, copies of old pattern books, to ensure you choose an historically authentic motif. Make sure it is the right size (it may have to be scaled up or down) and shape for the object to which it will be applied.

2. Once decorative detail has been decided upon – a newly lacquered piece may not need any – the surface to which the lacquer is to be applied must be prepared. So that the lacquer will adhere correctly, and to achieve an optimum finish, this needs to be clean, dry, smooth and non-porous.

Wood is the commonest base for both traditional and modern lacquerwork. Because a lacquer finish completely obscures any inherent qualities of the wood itself, cheap, open-grained wood has frequently been used. This tends to crack and move, and much of the damage to the lacquer finish, especially in Victorian pieces, is due to this. This does not mean to say that a high-quality wooden base is essential: the only requirement is that it should be structurally sound.

If restoring an old piece, check first for cracks and chips. These can easily be filled by using a proprietary wood-filler; as this will always shrink slightly on drying, slightly overfill a gap. Work from the underside or wrong side of the piece. Then the best way to achieve a good surface for a lacquered finish, whether on new or old wood, is to apply several coats of synthetic gesso.

First rub the piece with medium sandpaper, to obtain a smooth, even surface. Don't worry about removing any remaining decoration on an old piece – this will be covered by the new coat. Now wipe over with a cloth dipped in white spirit, to remove grease and dirt.

Mix powdered gesso with enough water to form a paint consistency. Follow the instructions on the packet and mix enough for applying four to five coats. Apply with broad strokes, using an old or cheap brush. Cover evenly and leave to dry for about an hour. Then rub down with medium sandpaper until smooth. Dust off with a soft cloth moistened with white spirit. Repeat until a

Above: Work from the underside of a wooden piece when repairing cracks or chips.

smooth, bone-hard finish is obtained: this will mean applying up to five coats.

In the eighteenth and nineteenth centuries gesso was used to imitate the intricate carving and moulding found in traditional oriental lacquer. (Only true lacquer has the right qualities for carving and shaping.) The gesso was mixed to a thick paste, applied to the wooden base and moulded to the required form (then covered with the thin imitation lacquer finish).

If restoring a piece constructed in this way, copy this method by applying the last coat of gesso as a mouldable paste. Always allow for the gesso to shrink slightly on drying. Be careful, when sanding down, not to destroy any moulded details.

Now apply a thin coat of shellac (mixed two parts shellac to one part methylated spirits) to the entire gessoed surface. Leave to dry. The surface is now ready for lacquering.

Tinware was commonly used as a base for imitation European lacquerwork (known as 'japanning'), especially during the late eighteenth and early nineteenth centuries. Good, authentic pieces from this period will be valuable now, and should be dealt with by a professional restorer. However, prepare a not-so-precious old piece, or a new piece, of tinware as follows:

First, make sure the surface is free from dents. Remove these by tapping lightly with the rounded end of a hammer, wrapped in a thin layer of tissue-paper or cotton-wool. Then rub the surface lightly with fine sandpaper and dust off. Now apply one coat of rust-preventive paint, and then leave it to dry completely.

Using fine, wet-and-dry sandpaper, lightly rub the surface under running water until smooth. Apply a further coat of rust-preventive paint and again, when dry, sand down lightly under running water. Finally, dry the surface with a cloth. It is now ready for the lacquer.

Papier mâché was another popular, cheap base for late eighteenth and early nineteenth century japanning. Not only small jewellery and snuff-boxes but large items of furniture were made from it and given a pseudo-oriental lacquer finish. Though not enjoying such popularity now, *papier mâché* still serves as a base for similar *chinoiserie* trinkets.

Always check the value of an old piece of lacquered *papier mâché* before attempting to repair it. It is a fairly delicate material. Preparing an old piece for re-lacquering consists mainly of filling in chips or larger missing chunks. The easiest and best way to do this is to use a proprietary wood-filler. Follow the instructions supplied by the manufacturer, remembering to slightly overfill, as the filler shrinks on drying.

When completely dry, rub lightly with fine sandpaper so that the surface of the filled area is smooth, and level with the surrounding area.

The repaired 'patch' must also match the surrounding surface in colour. Use artists' oil-paints applied on a fine artists' brush, mixing the paint with a small palette-knife and testing the shade several times on a piece of white card, to obtain a matching tone.

Finish by lightly rubbing the whole surface to be lacquered with some fine sandpaper.

Lacquering

Technique

The following hints apply to any of the lacquer recipes:

1. Always work in a well-lit space, so that all details of the piece you are lacquering are clearly visible. Daylight is the best light source.

2. Position the piece on a secure support that allows easy access to all parts to be lacquered. A few sheets of damp newspaper covering this support will attract dust away from the object.

3. When applying the lacquer, dip the brush into the mixture so that it comes halfway up the bristles. Do not load the brush too heavily. Use a soft, 1- to 1½-inch (2.5 to 3.5 cm) ox-hair brush. Press the bristles gently against the walls of the container to remove excess lacquer. (Wiping the brush vigorously against the rim causes bubbles in the lacquer.)

Start in the middle of the surface to be lacquered, moving the brush lightly in one direction. Load the brush with more lacquer and then, overlapping the initial starting point, work in the opposite direction. Work first in one plane across the entire surface, then at right angles to it, to ensure a good coating.

4. Apply as many coats as stated in the recipe, allowing each coat to dry thoroughly before applying the next. This can take up to two days. The room temperature should be around 21°C (70°F).

5. After every second coat and the final coat, wipe the surface with soapy luke-warm water, and rub lightly with fine

Left: High-quality tinware should be repaired by a professional.

wet-and-dry sandpaper. Then dust with a soft cloth, moistened with white spirit.

6. Finish with two thin coats of shellac (mixed one part shellac to one part pure methylated spirits). Use a soft, 1- to 1½-inch (2.5 to 3.5 cm) ox-hair brush, kept especially for this purpose. When the first coat is dry, rub gently with fine steel wool and dust off with a soft cloth moistened with white spirit – then apply the second coat.

Note: Japan paints are ideal for use in the lacquer recipes. Though readily available in the United States, they are extremely difficult to find in Britain: demand is not high enough for mass export. Basically, they consist of pigment suspended in an oil-free resin varnish, and a good approximation can be made by mixing artists' powdered pigment with clear gloss polyurethane varnish. This 'paint' can be thinned with white spirit.

Types of Lacquer

True oriental lacquer is made from the sap of the *lac* tree (*Rhus verniciflua*), thickened by standing in hot sunlight to allow evaporation, then strained and finally coloured with organic pigments.

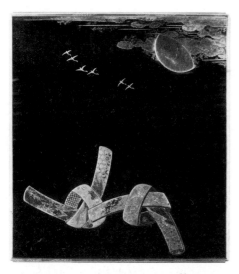

Above: Between 30 and 40 coats of lacquer are needed to produce the kind of sheen shown on this oriental piece.

Between thirty to forty coats of this are essential to produce a good-quality lacquer base. Each coat must be perfectly even and absolutely dry before the next is applied. Lacquer dries best in a damp atmosphere, so after each coating the object is placed in a special damp, dust-free chamber for several days. Each coat must be extremely fine, too – thirty

layers together should be little more than a few millimetres thick!

It takes little imagination to realize that even if it were possible to obtain adequate supplies of *Rhus verniciflua* sap, the skill and patience required for its correct application is beyond most of us. Many eighteenth and nineteenth century craftsmen thought the same: as the fashion for japanning grew, numerous artful imitations of oriental lacquer were invented, one of the most notable being *vernis Martin*, created in Paris around 1730 by the Martin brothers. Details of the exact recipe for *vernis Martin* are lost, but the following gives a good modern copy:

Vernis Martin

Materials

Japan paint, sufficient for five coats, of a slightly lighter tone than final finish

White spirit

Bowl of lukewarm water

Fine wet-and-dry sandpaper

Soft cloth

White shellac, sufficient for one coat, mixed 1 part shellac to 1 part pure methylated spirits. Do not mix until ready to use, as it dries very quickly.

Fine steel wool

Glazing medium, mixed from:
1 part soya-bean oil
1 part clear gloss varnish
1 part white spirit.
Mix enough for one coat when ready to use.

Artists' powdered pigment in final shade – use sufficient to colour the glazing medium to the required tone

Clear gloss polyurethane varnish, sufficient for two coats of entire lacquered surface

Gold metallic powder

Cardboard tube

Piece of fine cheesecloth, sufficient to cover the end of the cardboard tube and overlap by 5 cm (2 inches)

Elastic band, large enough to fit tightly around the end of the cardboard tube

Method

Mix the japan paint with white spirit to a thin, runny consistency. Using the general technique described above, apply five coats to the prepared surface. To finish off, apply only *one* coat of thinned, white shellac. When dry, rub this with fine steel wool.

Mix the glazing medium thoroughly and tint to the desired final shade, using

artists' powdered pigment. Apply with a soft, 1-inch (2.5 cm) ox-hair brush in broad strokes. Place the object in a warm (21°C/70°F), dust-free place and leave to dry for a week.

Thin the varnish to an easy-flowing consistency with white spirit. Apply one coat, then leave until completely dry (about eight hours). Apply a second coat of varnish.

Wrap the piece of cheesecloth tightly over one end of the cardboard tube, holding it in place with the elastic band. This device will act as a 'sieve'. While the second coat of varnish is still tacky, fill the cardboard 'sieve' with a little metallic gold powder. Tapping the side of the tube lightly, sprinkle the gold powder, as desired, over the tacky surface. Now leave for the varnish to dry completely.

When dry, rub lightly with soapy water and fine wet-and-dry sandpaper, until smooth. Apply three further coats of varnish, sanding lightly with soapy water and wet-and-dry paper between each coating.

When the final coat is completely dry, and if no further decoration of this finish is required, rub the surface lightly with a little bees-wax polish applied on a soft cloth. This gives a rich lustre.

In all the recipes the rich 'lacquer' sheen is reproduced by means of various varnishes that include shellac. Shellac is produced by processing a substance secreted by an insect native to India. The result, known as 'lac', is frequently confused with true oriental lacquer. In fact it has only a few of the properties of true lacquer – mainly a tough and glossy finish – but these were enough to satisfy the booming European market for *chinoiserie* in the eighteenth and early nineteenth centuries. Large, multi-panelled Coromandel screens were especially popular. This recipe reproduces the type of lacquer finish found on these:

Coromandel Lacquer

Materials

Base coat, mixed from the following hues of japan paint:
4 parts purple-red
2 parts burnt sienna
1 part orange-red
Thinned with 1 part white spirit. Mix enough for five coats.

Bowl of soapy lukewarm water

Fine wet-and-dry sandpaper

Soft cloth

Orange shellac, sufficient for two coats, mixed 2 parts shellac to 1 part pure methylated spirits. Do not mix until ready to use, as it dries very quickly.

Fine steel wool

Glazing medium, mixed from:
1 part soya-bean oil
1 part clear, gloss varnish
1 part white spirit
Mix enough for one coat, when ready to use.

Artists' powdered pigment, mixed 4 parts raw umber to 1 part lampblack, sufficient to colour glazing medium to required tone

Method

Mix the base coat, then strain through a fine mesh (such as an old pair of tights) into a clean container. Apply five coats according to the technique described for *vernis Martin*. The final coat should be rubbed with sandpaper, using soapy water as a lubricant, until it is satin-smooth. Then seal with two coats of the orange shellac mix. Leave the final shellac coat to dry for at least an hour, before rubbing lightly with fine steel wool.

Coromandel panels (*left*) and screens (*above*) were popular imports; hardstone pieces can be replaced with comparative ease.

Now, using broad strokes, apply one streaky coating of the tinted glazing medium. Leave in a warm place (21°C/ 70°F) until completely dry. This lacquer base is now ready for decorating.

The classical black, vermilion and yellow oriental lacquers were also frequently copied in Europe; the following recipes are good modern approximations to the formulae used.

English Black Lacquer

Materials

Base coat, sufficient for four coats, made from:

  10 parts flat black oil-based paint (from hardware or DIY store)

  3 parts burnt umber japan paint

  1 part clear gloss varnish

  Mixed with enough white spirit to give a thin, runny consistency.

Bowl of lukewarm, soapy water

Fine wet-and-dry sandpaper

Soft cloth

Top coat, sufficient for one coat, mixed from:

  3 parts raw umber japan paint

  1 part lampblack japan paint

  4 parts spar varnish

  4 parts white spirit

  8 parts asphaltum

  Do not mix the top coat until ready for use.

Rottenstone

White shellac, sufficient for one coat, mixed 1 part shellac to 1 part pure methylated spirits. Do not mix until ready to use, as it dries very quickly.

Fine steel wool

Method

Mix the base coat, then strain through a fine mesh into a clean container. Apply four coats, using the technique described for *vernis Martin*. After smoothing the final coat and wiping over with a soft cloth moistened with white spirit, mix the top coat.

Strain the top coat through a fine mesh into a heat-proof container, then place this over a very low heat and stir gently until the temperature of the mixture is 21°C (70°F). Keep the mixture at approximately this heat while applying. Using broad, even strokes apply one coating of top coat. Allow to dry for at least three days: the surface should be completely hard. Rub gently with rottenstone, and leave for a further two days.

Then wipe with soapy, lukewarm water and rub gently, until smooth, with fine wet-and-dry sandpaper. Wipe with a soft cloth moistened with white spirit. Mix the shellac and apply one coat. When completely dry, rub the surface lightly with fine steel wool. The surface is now ready for decorating.

Vermilion or Yellow Lacquers

Materials

Black undercoat, sufficient for four coats, made from:

  20 parts flat black oil-based paint (from hardware or DIY store)

  2 parts burnt umber japan paint

  1 part spar varnish

  Mixed with white spirit to a runny consistency.

Bowl of lukewarm soapy water

Fine wet-and-dry sandpaper

Soft cloth

Top coat, sufficient for two coats, mixed from either:

(a) For vermilion

  4 parts purple-red japan paint

  2 parts orange-red japan paint

  1 part flake white artists' oil-paint

  2 parts white spirit

or

(b) For yellow

  4 parts chrome yellow japan paint

  1 part raw sienna japan paint

  2 parts white spirit

White shellac, sufficient for one coat, mixed from 1 part shellac to 1 part pure methylated spirits. Do not mix until ready to use, as it dries very quickly.

Fine steel wool

Method

Mix the undercoat and strain through a fine mesh into a clean container. Apply four coats using the technique described for *vernis Martin*.

After smoothing the final coat and wiping with a soft cloth moistened with white spirit, mix the top coat in the desired finishing colour. Strain the top coat through a fine mesh into a clean container.

Apply one coat of the top coat. Allow to dry completely, then sand lightly with fine wet-and-dry sandpaper using soapy water as a lubricant. Apply a second coat of the top coat. Again, when dry, sand lightly using fine wet-and-dry paper and soapy water, until satin-smooth.

Mix the shellac and apply one coat. Leave until completely dry, then rub the surface lightly with fine steel wool. The

new lacquer finish is now ready for decorating.

Decorating

If there is to be any decoration it will have been chosen before applying the lacquer base. All design details should have been recorded on a tracing.

1. To transfer the traced design to the lacquered surface, rub the back of the tracing with either a soft pencil (if transferring to a light-coloured surface) or with white chalk-dust (if applying to a dark-coloured surface). Place the traced design, the right way up and in the correct position, over the lacquer base. Use masking-tape to secure the tracing.

With a sharp, hard pencil, and working slowly and carefully, draw over all the design details on the tracing so that they transfer clearly to the lacquered surface. When the drawing is complete, check that no details have been forgotten. Then gently peel off the masking-tape and lift away the tracing-paper. Be careful not to smudge the transferred design.

2. Details of hue and shading should also have been recorded on the tracing. Follow these carefully, when painting in the decoration. Artists' oil-paints are recommended for this, applied with an artists' fine sable brush.

Mix paints to the desired tone on a paper palette, using a small palette-knife. (Tear-off paper-palette pads are available from art-and-craft supply shops.) Use *pure* turpentine and spar varnish to thin and mix the paint. A ready supply of small pieces of cotton rag is useful for wiping brushes and fingers.

3. The hues which are most useful when decorating lacquerwork in an authentic manner are:

Titanium white	Alizarin crimson
Chrome yellow	Prussian blue
Yellow lake	Burnt sienna
Yellow ochre	Raw umber
Vermilion	Burnt umber

Arrange these – one generous 'blob' of each – around the edge of your palette.

Take two small pots or jars (egg-cups will do), filling one with pure turpentine and the other with spar varnish. Mix the paint to the desired tone in the centre of the palette, using a palette-knife. Add equal amounts of pure turpentine and spar varnish, drop by drop, until a fluid consistency is obtained. Wipe the palette-knife clean before using it to mix another shade.

4. Work slowly and carefully, following the information you have recorded, and using a brush of a suitable size for the area you are working on. Before starting, practise on scrap paper until brush-strokes are smooth and even.

5. To paint a straight line, use a special striping-brush: this is very fine, with exceptionally long bristles. Draw the line in lightly with a pencil first, to act as a guide. Load the brush well with paint and apply with one continuous, smooth gliding action, along the whole length of the line. Practise first! If you make a mistake, quickly wipe away the paint already applied with a piece of cotton-wool soaked in pure turpentine – then begin again.

6. Stencilled decoration in gold leaf was extremely popular on japanware. To imitate or restore this effect, follow these instructions (a tracing having first been made, in the usual manner, before you obscure the original design with a new lacquer base):

Materials
Tracing of design
White chalk-powder
Sheet of dark-coloured card, about 2mm
    thick, suitable for cutting the stencil
    from. It should cover the area of the
    design and give at least a 2.5 cm
    (1-inch) overlap.
Masking-tape
Sharp pencil
Sheet of glass, larger than the stencil
Fine cutting-knife, with replaceable
    blades (a small Stanley knife is ideal)
Powdered gold leaf
Sheet of cardboard
Piece of denim rag
Cotton-wool
Turpentine

Method
Coat the back of the traced design lightly with white chalk-powder. Tape this, right side up, onto the piece of stencil card. Using a sharp pencil, draw over the design shape, on the tracing. Work carefully and check that you have not missed any details. Then carefully remove the tape and the tracing.

Place the piece of stencil card, with the design now transferred on to it, on the glass sheet. Tape firmly in position with masking-tape. Cut the stencil in the card, with the fine knife: make clean, accurate cuts, and do not hurry. When you are satisfied that the stencil is complete, carefully peel away the masking-tape and remove the stencil. Place the stencil, in the correct position, on the newly lacquered base, and fix firmly with masking-tape.

Tap a little of the gold leaf powder onto the sheet of cardboard. Wrap a piece of denim rag around your index finger, and dab this in the gold powder to give a good coating.

Quickly, but taking care, dab the gold powder over the cut-away areas in the stencil.

Do not do this at random: work in one direction across the stencil, making sure no gold powder slips under the edge of the stencil.

When complete, carefully peel away the masking-tape, then the stencil. If any gold has slipped under the edge of the stencil, giving a 'fuzzy' edge, clean this now, using a swab of cotton-wool moistened with pure turpentine and leave the gold to dry for forty-eight hours.

Varnishing

When decoration is completely dry, a final protective 'barrier' of varnish must be applied. Purists insist on spar varnish, but modern clear gloss polyurethane varnish can be used.

Apply in broad strokes, in one direction, evenly across the entire lacquered surface. Use at least three coats, letting each coat dry thoroughly. Then sand lightly with fine wet-and-dry sandpaper, lubricated with lukewarm, soapy water. Wipe over with a soft cloth, then apply the next coat.

Sand the final coat lightly, in the usual way. Wipe with a soft cloth, then polish the surface with rottenstone. For an especially deep shine, now apply a little bees-wax polish, rubbed on gently with a soft cloth.

Modern lacquerwork

So far, recipes have been given that approximate to eighteenth and nineteenth century facsimiles of traditional oriental finishes. As lacquering originated in the orient it is not surprising that many modern pieces are still created in a *chinoiserie* style.

However, the deep sheen finish of lacquer also complements the sleek and often geometric forms of modern furniture and *bric-à-brac*. Lacquerwork that is thoroughly Western in design is now enjoying increasing popularity.

When lacquering a piece there is no need (unless it is restoration work) to create a pseudo-oriental object. Work the base using the recipe for English Black or for Vermilion or Yellow Lacquers (or colour it in any other hue). Design your own modern decorative motifs or adapt ideas from professional designers, by looking around shops, or in books and in magazines.

Increasingly, high-class furniture shops are stocking lacquer pieces worked by professional craftsmen. They do not, however, use the sap of the *Rhus verniciflua* tree.

The two most common lacquers used by modern professionals are of polyester and cellulose. Unlike the eighteenth century facsimiles of oriental lacquer (and the recipes given for home-made lacquer) these do share qualities, other than cosmetic ones, with true lacquer: they, too, are heat-resistant, waterproof and extremely durable.

Polyester and cellulose lacquers, once mixed, dry rock-hard within fifteen minutes of being exposed to the air. Each coat is usually sprayed on to ensure quick and even application. Once dry, the surface is sanded lightly to give a satin-smooth finish and dusted off, and then the next coat is applied. As with traditional lacquering, as many as thirty to forty coats may be given to achieve an extremely rich, deep sheen. Such work may not require the patience demanded of the traditional Chinese and Japanese craftsmen, but it does need a comparable degree of skill.

Hints on cleaning and caring for lacquer

1. All lacquer should be dusted regularly with a soft cloth to avoid fine scratches, caused by grit and dust, which can reduce the depth of sheen.

2. To clean and polish any lacquered object with a wooden base, rub lightly with bees-wax polish (or any non-silicone furniture polish) applied sparingly on a soft cloth.

3. To clean lacquered *papier mâché* or tinware, wipe away dirt using a soft sponge and soapy (non-detergent) warm water.

Dry with a clean, soft cloth. Then rub the lacquer surface lightly with a little bees-wax or non-silicone polish, applied on another clean, soft cloth.

Suppliers

Many of the materials required for lacquering are available from non-specialist stores.

Proprietary wood-filler; wet-and-dry sandpaper; white spirit; soft lint-free cloth; rust-preventive paint; 1-inch (and larger) ox-hair paint-brushes; fine steel wool; clear polyurethane gloss varnish; flat black oil-based paint; asphaltum; pure methylated spirits; masking-tape; pure turpentine; palette-knives; small Stanley knives	Most hardware stores and do-it-yourself shops

Art and craft shops, and some good stationers, supply the material listed below.

Tracing-paper; pencils; synthetic powder gesso; shellac – white and orange; artists' oil-colours; japan paints; artists' powdered pigments; pad of tear-off paper palettes; small palette-knives; pure turpentine; sheet of card *c.* 2mm thick for cutting stencil from; small Stanley knives; fine artists' sable brushes; striping-brush; gold metallic powder (powdered gold leaf); white chalk; masking-tape	Art and craft supply shops and some good stationers
Soya-bean oil	Health food shops; high-class grocers
Spar varnish	Marine supply stores
Bees-wax polish	Antique shops; high-class furniture stores; furniture-makers and restorers

Recommended Specialist Suppliers

Most of the materials are available in any high street store of the type suggested. However, if you have difficulties try one of the specialists listed below:

BRITAIN

Flat paint; varnishes; metal leaf	**Colourways**, 70 Alderman's Hill, London N13.
	Simpsons Paints Ltd, 122–124 Broadley Street, London NW8.
Flat paint; bees-wax polish; varnishes; shellac	**John T. Keep and Sons Ltd**, 15 Theobalds Road, London WC1.
Flat paint; varnishes; metal leaf; lacquers (to the trade); bees-wax polish	**John Myland Ltd**, 80 Norwood High Street, London SE27.
Flat paint; specialist paint-brushes; metal leaf	**J.H. Ratcliffe and Co Ltd**, 135A Linaker Street, Southport, Lancashire.
Specialist paint-brushes	**F.A. Heffer and Co Ltd**, 24 The Pavement, London SW4.
Artists' oil-colours; artists' powdered pigments; synthetic powdered gesso; fine sable brushes; striping-brushes; metal leaf and powder; pads of tear-off paper palettes; small palette-knives; pencils; tracing-paper; card for stencil-cutting; pure turpentine; shellac in small quantities	**George Rowney and Co Ltd**, 12 Percy Street, London W1.
	Winsor and Newton, 51–52 Rathbone Place, London W1.
	C. Roberson and Co Ltd, 77 Parkway, London NW1.
	L. Cornelissen and Son, 22 Great Queen Street, London WC2.
	E. Ploton (Sundries) Ltd, 273 Archway Road, London N6 (also has a mail-order service).

Lacquer Workshops

Furniture conservation materials, including polishes; also, advice on restoration and conservation

Weaves and Waxes, 53 Church Street, Bloxham, Banbury, Oxfordshire.

Rottenstone

Gedge and Co (Clerkenwell) Ltd, 88 St John Street, London EC1.

THE UNITED STATES

In a country the size of the United States it is virtually impossible to list every supplier. The ones below are well-known specialists; alternatively, contact your local museum if you want to find a specific material. Japan paints are readily available.

Gold leaf, metallic and gilding materials

M. Swift and Sons, 10 Love Lane, Hartford, Connecticut.

Tinware, stencils

Craft House, 1542 Main Road, Tiverton, Rhode Island.

Japan paints, art supplies

Painted Finishes, 6795 Michigan Avenue, Chicago, Illinois.

Kembal & Sons, 1335 Tremont Avenue, Newton Corner, Boston, Massachusetts.

Paper and Paint Suppliers (local shops in Cambridge, Massachusetts, area).

Sam Flax Inc. (major suppliers; mail order catalogue available).

Britain

Beco Antiques Ltd, 169 Bermondsey Street, London SE1.
Restoration and new work, mainly in 'period' style, including lacquering, japanning and decoration.

Guy Bedford, The English Lacquer Shop, 82 Marchmont Street, London WC1.
New work, using cellulose lacquer. Decorates in the traditional Japanese fashion. Work is always on display in the shop, but also takes commissions.

James Bourlet & Sons Ltd, 263 Fulham Road, London SW3.
Restoration work – lacquer and gilding.

Guy Burn, Arch 18, Valentia Place, London SW9.
New work, using spray-on polyester lacquer. Works to commission.

George Ciancimino, 307 King's Road, London SW3.
New work, designed and made to commission. Furniture only.

Diane Gibbs, 2 Donovan Court, Drayton Gardens, West Brompton, London W10.
Restoration and new work in 'period' style (to commission). Lacquerwork and gilding; specializes in large screens with Japanese motifs.

John Harwood, 11 Osiers Road, London SW18.
Craftsman/designer creating new pieces to commission, but also experiments with traditional lacquer formulae and with improving decorative finishes.

Carole Kidd, Homeworks, Dove Walk, Pimlico Road, London SW1.
New work to commission – uses cellulose lacquers on modern furniture.

Christopher Lawrence, 283 Lillie Road, London SW6.
New work, using spray-on polyester lacquer. Furniture.

John Minshaw, c/o Osborne & Little, 304 King's Road, London SW3.
New work using cellulose and polyester lacquers, to commission. Furniture only.

Miracles, 436 King's Road, London SW10.
New work using cellulose and polyester lacquers, to commission. Furniture – specialists in Art Deco.

Albert Cummings, Stenhouse Conservation Centre, 3 Stenhouse Mill Lane, Edinburgh 11.
Restoration.

Walter Goldsmith, Ochiltree Castle, Linlithgow, West Lothian.
Restoration.

Antique Restorations, 45 Windmill Road, Brentford, Middlesex.
Oriental lacquer and japanning on furniture; painted decoration on furniture; gilding. Mainly restoration work.

Arundel Workshops, 2 River Road, Arundel, West Sussex.
Mainly decoration of reproduction furniture, including lacquering, japanning and gilding. Also restoration work.

Edmund Czajkowski and Son, 96 Tor-o-Moor Road, Woodhall Spa, Lincolnshire.
Restoration and new work (to commission), usually using reproduction styles. Lacquer and decoration.

David C.E. Lewry, Wychelms, 66 Gorran Avenue, Rowner, Gosport, Hampshire.
Restoration of antique furniture, including lacquering, japanning, inlay and gilding.

Mac & Me (Antiques) Ltd, The Old Exchange, 19 Mill Lane, Welwyn, Hertfordshire.
Cleaning and restoration of European *chinoiserie* lacquer.

The Crafts Council has an up-to-date list of craftsmen working in England and Wales, and it is useful to consult this in addition to the list of workshops given above. The address is:

Crafts Council, 12 Waterloo Place, London SW1Y 4AU.
Tel. 01-930 4811

If writing, state what kind of craft work interests you and you will be sent details of all the craftsmen who may be able to help.

The United States

Lacquer and Linen, 670 Madison Avenue, New York, NY.
Restoration.

Michaelangelo Moderna, 875 Broome Street, New York, NY.
Restoration.

Tarrytown Restorations and **Sleepy Hollow Restorations**, Tarrytown, NY.
Restoration.

Kembal & Sons, 1335 Tremont Avenue, Newton Corner, Boston, Massachusetts.
Restoration.

As with specialist suppliers, it is not possible to list all the workshops and studios throughout the country. Contact your local museum or craft society for further information.

The following museums have outstanding examples of restoration work, and will also provide information about professional lacquer-workers:

Henry Ford Museum, Oakwood Boulevard, Dearborn, Michigan.

Henry Francis du Pont Winterthur Museum, Winterthur, Delaware.

Canada

For information about restoring lacquer, contact:

Association for Preservation Technology, APT Box 2487, Station D, Ottawa, Ontario.

Bibliography

Europe and the United States

Fairbanks, J., and Bates, E. B., *American Furniture 1620 to the Present*, Orbis, London, 1981.

Fales, D. A., *American Painted Furniture 1660–1880*, E. P. Dutton, New York, 1972.

Honour, H., *Chinoiserie; the Vision of Cathay*, John Murray, London, 1961.

Huth, H., *Lacquer of the West; the History of a Craft and an Industry 1550–1950*, University of Chicago Press, Chicago and London, 1971.

Impey, O., *Chinoiserie; the Impact of Oriental Styles on Western Art and Decoration*, Oxford University Press, London, 1977.

Ketchum, W., *Catalogue of American Antiques*, Routledge, 1981.

O'Neil, I., *The Art of the Painted Finish*, William Morrow, American Antiques Dealer Association, New York.

Osborn, B., and Osborn, B. N., *Measured Drawings of Early American Furniture*, Dover Publications, New York, 1975.

Tuttle, C. E., *Antique Tin and Toleware, Its History and Romance*, Rutland, Vermont, 1957.

Wall, W., *Graining, Ancient and Modern*, Drake Publications, New York, 1972.

Waring, J., *Early American Stencils on Walls and Furniture*, Dover Publications, New York, 1968.

Watson, F. J. B., *Wallace Collection Catalogues: Furniture*, Trustees of the Wallace Collection, London, 1956.

The Near and Middle East and India

Adle, C., *Ecriture de l'Union Reflets du Temps des Troubles. Oeuvre Picturale (1083–1124/1673–1712) de Hâji Mohammad*, Soustielle, Paris, 1980.

Aslanapa, O., 'The art of bookbinding', *The Arts of the Book in Central Asia, 14th–16th centuries*, Part 3, pp. 59–91, Serindia Publications, London, 1979.

Cig, K., 'Turkish lacquer painters and their works', *Sanat Tarihi Yilligi*, vol 3, 1969–70, pp. 243–57.

Cig, K., 'The Iranian lacquer technique works in the Topkapi Saray Museum', *The Memorial Volume of the Vth International Congress of Iranian Art and Archaeology, 1968*, vol 2, pp. 24–33, Tehran, 1972.

Cig, K., 'The decoration on the ceiling of the throne which belongs to Mehmet III in the Topkapi Palace', *IV Congress Internationale d'Art Turc*, Éditions de l'Université de Provence, pp. 47–8, 1976.

Dimand, M. S., 'Lacquer: Iran and the Islamic world', *Encyclopaedia of World Art*, vol 8, col 1061, plate 421, McGraw Hill, New York, 1963.

Duda, D., *Innenarchitektur Syrischer Stadthäuser des 16, bis 18. Jahrhunderts. Die Sammlung Henri Pharaon in Beirut, Beiruter Texte und Studien, Band 12*, Franz Steiner Verlag, Wiesbaden, 1971.

Falk, S. J., *Qājār Paintings*, Faber & Faber, London, 1972.

Fehérvári, G., 'A seventeenth-century Persian lacquer door and some problems of Safavid lacquer-painted doors', *Bulletin of the School of Oriental and African Studies*, vol 32/2, 1969, pp. 268–80.

Grube, E. J., 'A lacquered panel painting from the collection of Lester Wolfe in the Museum of the University of Nôtre Dame', *Orientalia Hispanica*, vol 1, 1974, pp. 376–97.

Ivanov, A., 'The life of Muhammad Zamān: a reconsideration,' *Iran*, vol 17, 1979, pp. 65–70.

Kühnel, E., 'Die Lachstube Schah ᶜAbbas I in der islamischen Abteilung der Staatlichen Museen', *Jahrbuch der preussische Kunstsammlungen*, vol 58, 1937, pp. 47–58.

Riefstahl, R. M., 'A Scljuk Koran stand with lacquer-painted decoration', *Parnassus*, vol 4/4, 1932, p. 25; *The Art Bulletin*, vol 15, 1933, pp. 361–73.

Robinson, B. W., 'The court painters of Fath ᶜAlī Shāh', *L. A. Mayer Memorial Volume, Eretz-Israel*, University of Jerusalem, vol 7, 1964, pp. 94–105.

Robinson, B. W., 'A lacquer mirror-case of 1854', *Iran*, vol 5, 1967, pp. 1–7.

Robinson, B. W., 'Persian lacquer in the Bern Historical Museum', *Iran*, vol 8, 1970, pp. 47–50.

Robinson, B. W., 'Book covers and lacquer', *Islamic Painting and the Arts of the Book*, Part 8, pp. 301–8, Faber & Faber, London, 1976.

Sarre, F., 'Bemalte Wandbekleidung aus Aleppo', *Berliner Museen*, April–May, 1920, cols 143–58, Berlin.

Ünver, A. S., 'Du Style Edirne adopté par les travaux sur laque et de ses artistes dans l'histoire des arts turcs', *L. A. Mayer Memorial Volume, Eretz-Israel*, University of Jerusalem, vol 7, 1964, pp. 118–126.

Twair, K., 'Die Malereien des Aleppo-Zimmers im Islamischen Museen zu Berlin', *Kunst des Orients*, vol 6/1, 1969, pp. 1–42, Berlin.

Watson, W. (editor), 'Lacquer work in Asia & beyond', *Colloquies on Art & Archaeology in Asia*, No. 11, Percival David Foundation of Chinese Art, London, 1982.

Zebrowski, M., 'Decorative arts of the Mughal period', *The Arts of India*, edited by Basil Gray, pp. 180–81, Phaidon, Oxford, 1981.

The Orient

Arakawa, H., and Togugawa, Y., *Craft Treasures of Okinawa*, Nihon Keizai Shimbun-sha, 1977.

Becková, D., 'Barmské laky' *Novy Orient*, 4/80, Prague.

Bowie, T. (editor), *The Arts of Thailand*, Bloomington, Indiana, 1960.

Boyer, M., *Catalogue of Japanese Lacquers*, Walters Art Gallery, Baltimore, 1970.

Boyer, M., *Japanese Export Lacquers from the Seventeenth Century in the National Museum of Denmark*, The National Museum, Copenhagen, 1959.

Bushell, R., *The Inrō Handbook*, Weatherhill, New York and Tokyo, 1979.

Casal, U. A., 'Japanese art lacquers', *Monumenta Nipponica Monographs*, no.18, Sophia University, Tokyo, 1961.

Casal, U. A., 'The Inrō', *Transactions of the Proceedings of the Japan Society*, no. 37, 1939–41.

Coedès, G., 'L'art de la lacque dorée au Siam', *Revue des Arts Asiatiques*, 1925.

Döhring, C., *Art and Industry in Siam*, Bangkok.

Eckhart, A., *History of Korean Art*, Edward Goldston, 1929, Karl W. Hiersemann, Leipzig, 1929.

Figgess, J., 'A group of decorated lacquer caskets of the Yuan dynasty', *Transactions of the Oriental Ceramic Society*, vol 36, 1964–66, London.

Figgess, J., 'A Letter from the Court of Yung-Lo', *Transactions of the Oriental Ceramic Society*, vol 34, 1962–3, London.

Garner, H. M., *Chinese and Associated Lacquer from the Garner Collection*, The British Museum, 1973.

Garner, H. M. 'Diaper backgrounds on Chinese carved lacquer', *Ars Orientalis*, vol 6, 1966.

Garner, H. M., 'Technical studies of oriental lacquer', *Studies in Conservation*, vol 8, no. 3, 1963.

Garner, Sir H., *Chinese lacquer*, Faber & Faber, London, 1979.

Garner, Sir H., *Ryukyu Lacquer*, Percival David Foundation Monograph no. 1, 1972.

Gyllensvärd, B., 'Lo-tien and Laque Burgautée', *Bulletin of the Museum of Far Eastern Antiquities*, Stockholm, no. 44, 1972.

Gyllensvärd, B., 'Old Japanese lacquers and japanning in Sweden', *Opuscula in Honorem C. Hernmarck*, National Museum, Stockholm, 1966.

Hejzlar, J., *The Art of Vietnam*, Hamlyn, London, 1973.

Herbert, K., *Oriental Lacquer: Art and Technique*, Thames & Hudson, London, 1962.

Hornby, J., 'Japan', *Ethnographic Objects in the Royal Danish Kunstkammer 1650–1800*, National Museum, Copenhagen, 1980.

Huard, P., and Durand, M., *Connaissance du Viêt-nam*, EFEO, Paris, 1954.

Hutt, J., 'Inrō decoration: its individual character', *Colloquies on Art and Archaeology in Asia*, no. 6, Percival David Foundation, London, 1977.

Hutt, J., 'Japanese lacquer painting', *Colloquies on Art and Archaeology in Asia*, no. 11, Percival David Foundation, London, 1982.

Impey, O., *Chinoiserie*, Oxford University Press, London, 1978.

Impey, O., 'Japanese export lacquer of the seventeenth century', *Colloquies on Art and Archaeology in Asia*, no. 11, Percival David Foundation, London, 1982.

Irwin, J., 'A Jacobean vogue for oriental lacquer-ware', *Burlington Magazine*, vol 95, London, 1953.

Jahss, M., and Jahss, B., *Inrō and Other Forms of Japanese Lacquer Art*, Kegan Paul, London.

Jorg, C. J. A., 'Japanese lacquerwork decorated after European prints', *Collection of Essays in Commemoration of the 30th Anniversary of the Institute of Oriental and Occidental Studies*, Kansai University, Osaka, 1981.

Kim, C., and Kim, W., *The Arts of Korea*, Thames & Hudson, London, 1966.

Lacquerwork in Asia and Beyond, Colloquies on Art and Archaeology in Asia, no. 11, Percival David Foundation, London, 1982.

Lacquer Art of Modern Japan, Tokyo National Museum of Modern Art, Tokyo, 1979.

Lee, Y., *Oriental Lacquer Art*, Weatherhill, New York, 1972.

Link, H. A., *The Art of Shibata Zeshin*, Honolulu Academy of Arts, 1979.

Lovell, H., 'Sung and Yuan monochrome lacquers in the Freer Gallery', *Ars Orientalis*, vol 9, 1973.

Lunsingh Scheurleer, T. H., 'Aanbesteding en Verspreiding van Japansch Lakwerk door de Nederlands in de Zeventiende Eeuw', *Jaarverslag van het Koninklijk Oudheidkundig Genootschap*, Amsterdam, 1941.

Morris, A. P., 'Lacquerware industry of Burma', *Journal of the Burma Research Society*, vol 9, 1919.

Pekarik, A. J., *Japanese Lacquer 1600–1900*, Metropolitan Museum of Art, New York, 1980.

Prunner, G., *Meisterwerke Burmanischer Lackkunst*, Museum für Volkerkunde, Hamburg, 1966.

von Rague, B., *A History of Japanese Lacquerwork*, translated by Anne Wassermann, University of Toronto Press, 1976.

Report by Her Majesty's Acting Consul at Hakodate on the lacquer industry of Japan, *Foreign and Consular Reports for Japan and Siam, 1879–83*, no. 2, Japan, 1882.

Scott, R., 'The Earliest Chinese Lacquer', *Colloquies on Art and Archaeology in Asia*, vol 11, Percival David Foundation, London, 1982.

da Silva, J., 'A small group of eighteenth century Chinese court lacquers', *Transactions of the Oriental Ceramic Society*, vol 44, 1979–80, London.

Special Exhibition of Cultural Relics Found off the Sinan Coast, National Museum of Korea, 1977.

Strange, E. F., *Catalogue of Chinese Lacquer in the Victoria & Albert Museum*, H.M.S.O., London, 1925.

Strange, E. F., *Catalogue of Japanese lacquer in the Victoria & Albert Museum*, H.M.S.O., London, 1924–5.

Sun-U, C., and Yang-Mo, C., *Art of Korea*, vol 13, Dong-Wha publishing Company, Seoul, 1974.

Tomio, Y., *Japanese Lacquer Ware*, Japan Travel Bureau, Tokyo.

Tsao, C., *Chinese Connoisseurship*, edited and translated by Sir Percival David, Praeger, New York, 1971.

Volker, T., 'Japanese export lacquer', *Oriental Art*, vol 3, no. 2, 1957.

Watson, F., 'Beckford, Mme. de Pompadour, the Duc de Bouillon and the taste for Japanese lacquer in eighteenth century France', *Gazette des Beaux Arts*, France, 1963.

Watson, W. (editor), *The Great Japan Exhibition of the Edo Period 1600–1868*, Royal Academy of Arts, London, 1981.

Wirgin, J., 'Some Chinese carved lacquers of the Yuan and Ming periods', *Bulletin of the Museum of Far Eastern Antiquities*, no. 44, Stockholm, 1972.

Yoe, S. (George Scott), *The Burman*, Norton, New York, 1963.

Yonemura, A., *Japanese Lacquer*, Freer Gallery of Art, Washington, 1977.

Oriental languages

Since the majority of readers will not be able to read oriental languages, only a very abbreviated oriental language bibliography is included.

Arakawa, H., and Togugawa, Y., *Ryūkyū Shitsu Kōgei*, Tokyo Kodansha, Serindia, London, 1979.

Changsha Mawangdui yihao Han mu, Wen Wu Press, Peking, 1973.

Gegu yaolun, Cao Zhao, 1388.

Ji Jiangsu Wujin xin chutu de Nan Song zhen qi qi, *Wenwu*, no. 3, 1979.

Okada, J., et al, *Nihon no shitsugei*, Chuokoronsha, Tokyo, 1978.

Qishu, Zhu Qiqian, 1957.

Ryūkyū Shikki No Biten, Urasoe City, Okinawa, 1983.

Suixian cenghou yi mu, Wen Wu Press, Peking, 1980.

Suzhoushi Ruiguang sita faxian yi pi Wu Dai, Bei Song wenwu, *Wenwu*, no. 3, 1979.

Restoration

Harral, A., 'How others got in on the secrets and skills of the traditional Chinese craft of lacquering', *House and Garden*, London, July, 1982.

Innes, J., *Paint Magic*, Frances Lincoln Publishers, 1981.

Johnson, L., *How to Restore and Repair Practically Anything*, Michael Joseph, London, 1977.

The Twentieth Century

Garner, P., *The Contemporary Decorative Arts*, Phaidon, Oxford, 1980.

Hillier, B., *The World of Art Deco*, Studio Vista, London, 1971.

Johnson, S., *Eileen Gray, Designer, 1879–1976*, Debrett, London, 1979.

Museums

Australia
Melbourne★ National Gallery of Victoria
Sydney ★Museum of Applied Arts & Sciences

Austria
Innsbruck Castle Museum, Schloss Ambras

Belgium
Brussels★ Royal Museum of Art & History
Liège Museum of Walloon Life
Spa District Museum

Burma
Pagan Lacquerware Museum
Rangoon ★National Museum

Canada
Montreal ★Montreal Museum of Fine Art;★ Montreal Museum of Primitive Art
Quebec Quebec Museum of the Applied Arts
Toronto Royal Ontario Museum

China, The People's Republic of
Peking ★Imperial Palace
Shanghai Art & History Museum

China, Republic of (Taiwan)
Taipei National Palace Museum & National Central Museum

Denmark
Copenhagen National Museum of Denmark; David's Collection

Egypt
Cairo ★Museum of Islamic Art

France
Paris Guimet Museum; Museum of Decorative Arts; Museums of the Louvre

Germany, Democratic Republic of
Berlin Berlin State Museum
Potsdam Sans Souci Palace: New Palace

Germany, Federal Republic of
Bayreuth Hermitage
Berlin Charlottenburg Palace; Museum of Islamic Art
Bonn Rhineland Museum
Braunschweig Municipal Museum
Cologne Herbig Haarhaus Museum of Lacquerware; Museum of Oriental Art; Museum of the City of Cologne
Frankfurt ★Museum of Applied Art
Hamburg Museum of Arts & Crafts
Munich State Museum of Ethnography

Great Britain
Birmingham City Museum
Bournemouth Russell-Cotes Art Gallery & Museum
Brighton Royal Pavilion
Bristol Bristol City Museum
Broadway Snowshill Manor
Cambridge Fitzwilliam Museum
Cardiff National Museum of Wales
Edinburgh National Museum of Antiquities of Scotland; Royal Scottish Museum
Glasgow Burrell Collection
Liverpool Walker Art Gallery
London British Museum; Geffrye Museum; Victoria & Albert Museum; Wallace Collection
Oxford Ashmolean Museum
Port Sunlight Lady Lever Art Gallery

Wolverhampton Bantock House Museum

Greece
Athens ★Benaki Museum

Hawaii
Honolulu Honolulu Academy of Art

India
Calcutta Indian Museum
Hyderabad Salarjung Museum

Iran
Teheran Museum of Decorative Arts

Israel
Haifa Tikotin Museum of Japanese Art

Italy
Genoa Museum of Oriental Art
Milan ★Museum of Ancient Art
Rome ★National Museum of Eastern Art
Turin Stupinigi Palace, Stupinigi
Venice Eastern Museum; Museum of 18th century Venice

Japan
Kyoto Kyoto National Museum
Nagoya Tokugawa Art Museum
Osaka Fujita Art Museum
Sendai Sendai Municipal Museum
Tokyo Japanese Sword Museum; Nezu Art Museum; Suntory Museum of Art; Tokyo National Museum

Korea
Seoul Kansong Museum of Fine Arts; National Museum of Korea

Netherlands
Amsterdam National Museum:

Department of Asiatic Art; Rijksmuseum
Rotterdam Museum of Geography & Ethnology
The Hague Huis ten Bosch; Municipal Museum
Utrecht Central Museum

Norway
Drammen Drammens Museum
Oslo Museum of Applied Arts; Norwegian Folk Museum

Portugal
Lisbon Calouste Gulbenkian Foundation

Spain
Madrid ★National Museum of Decorative Art

Sri Lanka
Kandy National Museum

Sweden
Stockholm Museum of Far Eastern Antiquities; Nordic Museum; Royal Palace

Switzerland
Bern Bern Historical Museum

Thailand
Bangkok National Museum

Turkey
Istanbul Museum of Turkish & Islamic Art; Topkapi Palace Museum

USA
Boston Boston Museum of Fine Arts
Chicago Art Institute of Chicago
Cleveland Cleveland Museum of Art
Dearbourn, Michigan Henry Ford Museum

Deerfield, Mass. Historic Deerfield
Houston Museum of Fine Arts
Kansas City William Rockhill Nelson Gallery
Los Angeles Los Angeles County Museum of Art
Malibu J. Paul Getty Museum
New York Metropolitan Museum of Art; Museum of the City of New York; New York Historical Society; Sleepy Hollow Restorations, Tarrytown
Philadelphia Philadelphia Museum of Art
Salem, Mass. Essex Institute
San Francisco Asian Art Museum of San Francisco
Seattle Seattle Art Museum
Washington Freer Gallery of Art
Winterthur, Delaware Henry Francis du Pont Winterthur Museum

USSR
Leningrad Peter the Great's Summer Palace Museum
Moscow ★Museum of Folk Art

Vietnam
Hue Archaeological Museum
Saigon ★National Museum

★The art of lacquer covers such a wide field that an enquiry at museums with collections of Eastern art and applied arts, such as those marked with an asterisk, will often provide further sources.

Index

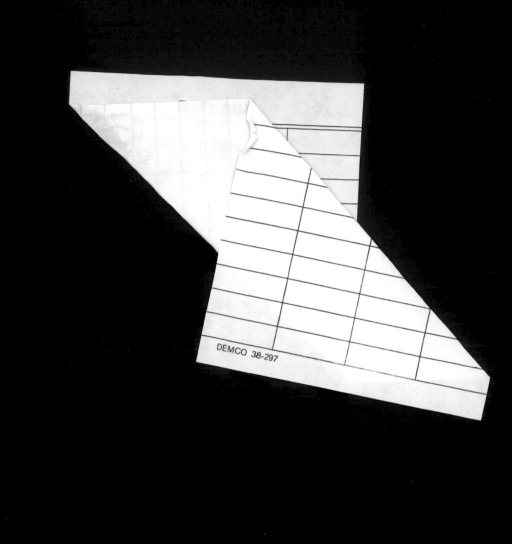